THE
WHOLE
BACKPACKER'S
CATALOG

THE
WHOLE
BACKPACKER'S
CATALOG

Tools and Resources for the Foot Traveler

ED SOBEY

Camden, Maine • New York • San Francisco • Washington D.C. •
Auckland • Bogotá • Caracas • Lisbon • London • Madrid • Mexico City • Milan
Montréal • New Delhi • San Juan • Singapore • Sydney • Tokyo • Toronto

Ragged Mountain Press

A Division of The McGraw-Hill Companies

10 9 8 7 6 5 4 3 2 1

Library of Congress Cataloging-in-Publication Data
Sobey, Edwin J. C., 1948–
    The whole backpacker's catalog : tools and
    resources for the foot traveler / Ed Sobey.
        p.   cm.
    Includes bibliographical references (p.   ) and index.
    ISBN 0-07-059599-2
    1. Backpacking—United States—Equipment and
supplies. 2. Hiking—United States—Equipment and
supplies. I. Title.
    GV199.62.S63   1998
    796.51'028'4—dc21   98-37378
                                         CIP

Questions regarding the content of this book should be
addressed to:
Ragged Mountain Press
P.O. Box 220
Camden, ME 04843

Questions regarding the ordering of this book should
be addressed to:
The McGraw-Hill Companies
Customer Service Department
P.O. Box 547
Blacklick, OH 43004
Retail customers: 1-800-262-4729
Bookstores: 1-800-722-4726

Printed by Quebecor Printing, Fairfield, PA
Design by Carol Gillette
Production by Deborah Krampf and Dan Kirchoff
Edited by John Vigor

Quote from *The Backpacker's Handbook* © Chris
Townsend. Used by permission.

Quotes from *John Muir In His Own Words* © Great
West Books, Lafayette, California. Used by permission.

Quote from *The Pacific Crest Trail Hiker's Handbook* by
Ray Jardine © AdventureLore Press, LaPine, Oregon.
Used by permission.

Quote from Aldo Leopold in *A Sand County Almanac*
published by Oxford University Press, 1987. Permission
requested.

Quote from Colin Fletcher in *The Complete Walker III*
published by Alfred Knopf, New York City, 1984.
Permission requested.

Quote from Harvey Manning in *Backpacking One Step
at a Time* published by Vintage Book / Random House,
Inc., in 1986. Copyright © held by Recreational
Equipment, Inc., Seattle, Washington. Permission
requested.

Quote from Roald Amundsen in *My Life as an Explorer*
published by Doubleday, Page & Company, 1927.

Quote from Edward Abbey in *Desert Solitaire* published
by Simon & Schuster, 1990.

Quote from Richard Halliburton in *The Glorious
Adventure* published by Garden City Publishing
Company, 1927.

To my backpacking and hiking friends:
Bill and Molly Davis,
and the members of Troop 301,
and the Irascible Order of Soararsis.

Contents

Acknowledgments.......... ix

1 Starting Out 1
Buy Just Enough 2
Start by Renting 2
Ask Questions 3
Retail Stores 3
Helpful Organizations 6
From Rails to Trails 8
Magazines 8
Backpackers Online 9
Keeping Fit......................... 10
Hiking with Kids 11
Leave No Trace 14
Private Affairs..................... 15
Critters on the Trail 16
Human Predators 24
The Weather 24
Tales of Great Adventures 26

2 Planning Ahead 28
Rules of Thumb 28
Know When to Stop............. 29
Graphing Your Route 30
Planning with the Internet 31
Seeing It in Advance............ 34
Watch from a Tower 34
Using Guides....................... 35
Using Pack Animals 36
Tour Organizers 37
Tours for Senior Hikers 39
Clubs and Groups that
    Sponsor Outings 39

**3 Long-Distance
American Trails........ 40**
The National Trails System 40
American Discovery Trail....... 41
Appalachian National
    Scenic Trail 42
The Arizona Trail 43
Buckeye Trail 43
Continental Divide
    National Scenic Trail 44
Florida Trail 44
Great Western Trail 44
Ice Age National
    Scenic Trail 45
Iditarod National
    Historic Trail 45
Natchez Trace National
    Scenic Trail 46
North Country National
    Scenic Trail 47
Ouachita National
    Recreation Trail 47
Pacific Crest National
    Scenic Trail 47
Pacific Northwest Trail 48
Potomac Heritage National
    Scenic Trail 48
The Sierra High Route........... 49

4 Hiking Abroad 50
Avoiding Problems 51
Mexico 51
Costa Rica 51
Guatemala 52
South America 52
Europe 52
South Africa 53
Kenya.................................. 53
Australia.............................. 53
New Zealand 53
The Himalayas 53

**5 The Pacific Coast
and Hawaii 54**
British Columbia................... 54
California 55
Hawaii................................. 59
Oregon 60
Washington 62

6 Staying Found 65
Are We Lost Yet? 65
Selecting a Compass 66
    Sources of Compasses 68
GPS Satellite Navigation 68
    Sources of GPS 69
Maps................................... 69
    USGS Maps...................... 70
    Map Sources.................... 70
    Degree-of-Difficulty Maps .. 71
    Mountain Images.............. 71
    Maps of Europe 71
    Protecting Your Maps 71
Altimeters 71

7 The Far North 72
Alaska 72
Yukon Territories.................. 75
Northwest Territories............ 75

8 Outfitting Yourself.... 76
The Essentials 77
Getting Help 80
Light Packs and Heavy 81
Online Information 84
Your Checklist...................... 85

9 The Rockies 86
Alberta................................ 86
Colorado............................. 87
Idaho 88
Montana 90
Utah.................................... 92
Wyoming 94

10 Good for Your Soles.. 96
The Importance of Boots 96
Boots are Your Passport 96
Learn to Love Leather......... 97
Boot Manufacturers 99
Caring for Your Boots 100
Waterproofing Products ... 101
Boot Repairers.................. 101
Get the Right Socks 102
Caring for Socks............... 102
Your Other Footwear.......... 103
Gaiters 103

**11 The U.S. Midwest and
Central Canada 104**
Illinois................................ 104
Indiana 105
Iowa................................... 106
Kansas................................ 106
Manitoba 106
Michigan 106
Minnesota 107
Missouri 108
Nebraska 109
North Dakota 109
Ohio 109
Ontario............................... 111
Québec 111
Saskatchewan 112
South Dakota 112
Wisconsin........................... 112

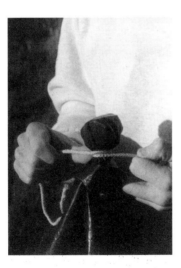

12 Portable Castles 114
Choosing Your Tent 114
Tent Stakes........................ 116
Pitching Your Tent............. 117
Caring for Your Tent 119
Tent Repairs 120
Tarpaulins......................... 120

13 The Southwest 122
Arizona 122
Nevada.............................. 124
New Mexico 124

14 Z-Z-Z-Time 126
Sleeping Bags 126
Cleaning Your Bag 129
Extra Warmth.................. 129
Sleeping Bag Liners 130
Sleeping Bag Repairs 130
Insulating Pads 130
Bivouac Bags 132
Pillows............................... 133
Insect Screens.................... 133

**15 Southern and
Southeastern U.S.A. 134**
Alabama............................. 134
Arkansas 135
Florida 137
Georgia 139
Kentucky 139
Louisiana 141
Mississippi 141
Oklahoma 142
Tennessee 142
Texas.................................. 144

16 Choosing a Backpack 145
What Size? 145
What Type? 146
  Internal-Frame Packs 146
  External-Frame Packs 146
Hipbelts 146
  Suspender Packs 147
Checking Packs on Aircraft . 149
Tumpline Technology 150
  In Praise of Head Straps 150

17 The Mid-Atlantic States 152
Delaware 152
District of Columbia 153
Maryland 153
New Jersey 154
New York 155
North Carolina 157
Pennsylvania 158
South Carolina 160
Virginia 161
West Virginia 162

18 Not-So-Sweet Water 163
Water Contaminants 164
  Methods of Treatment 164
Filtration and Membranes ... 165
  Filter and Purifier
    Manufacturers 165
Purifying with Iodine 166
Water Containers 167
Water Buckets 167

19 New England and the Maritime Provinces . 168
Connecticut 169
Maine 169
Massachusetts 170
New Brunswick 171
Newfoundland and
  Labrador 172
New Hampshire 172
Nova Scotia 172
Prince Edward Island 172
Rhode Island 173
Vermont 173

20 Feeding the Weary .. 174
Backpacking Stoves 174
  An Alternative 176
  Stove Repair 177
Trail Food 178
  Freeze-Dried Food 178
  Greater Variety 179
  Deciding What to Take 179
  Dry It Yourself 179
  Low-Cost Glops 180
  Repackage Your Food 180
  Squeeze Tubes 180
  Backcountry Baking 181
Backpacking Cookware 181
Voice of Experience 182
  Practical Cookware 182
  Washing Up 184
  Cookbooks 185

21 First Aid 187
Your First-Aid Kit 188
  Medications
    Non-Prescription 188
  Medications:
    Prescription 189
  For Trained Personnel 189
Sources of Kits 190
Reference Material 190
Blister Treatment 190
Personal Hygiene 190

22 Dressing for Comfort 192
Layering 192
  Layer One: Underwear 192
  Layer Two: Insulation 193
  Layer Three: Weather
    Protection 193
Rainwear 194
Heads Up! 195
The All-Purpose Bandanna .. 196
Waterproofing 196
  Sunglasses 196

23 All the Other Stuff .. 198
Pocket Knives 198
Hand Saws 200
Hiking Staffs 201
Fire Starters 202
Survival Kits 203
Trail Binoculars 203
Photography in the Wild 204
Lights 205
Repair Kits 205
Rope and Knots 206
Choosing a Towel 209
Keeping a Journal 209

Index 211

Acknowledgments

Shane Krogen is co-owner, and Mike Beers is manager, of California Outfitters, the backpacking, climbing, and Nordic skiing store in Fresno, California. They answered hundreds of questions and contributed their time and expertise to get the best information available. Some stores radiate good feelings; California Outfitters is one.

In Redmond, Washington, Wilderness Sports is the brother of California Outfitters. Independently owned and operated by an enthusiastic and proud staff, Wilderness Sports is that special store providing individual attention. Owner Herb Nesbitt encouraged me to poke through his inventory and ask questions. Herb and his staff answered many questions.

Not to be outdone by their smaller competitors, REI staff at the Bellevue, Washington, "approach" store helped on several occasions.

John Weigant made many helpful suggestions while reviewing the manuscript, as well as writing two articles. Gene Rose, a gifted writer and fellow member of the Irascible Order of Soararsis, contributed two articles. Bill Reese wrote a definitive article on water pathogens and how to get rid of them. Bill, a former neighbor of mine, is a water treatment engineer and an active hiker. The absolute authority on backpacking first aid and medicine has to be an emergency-room physician who is also an outdoorsman. Dr. Scott Ford fit that prescription perfectly. To all I give my thanks.

The vast majority of people I talked to were delighted to help. They made assembling this catalog so much fun.

—Ed Sobey

CHAPTER 1

Starting Out

It's the great, big, broad land 'way up yonder,

It's the forests where silence has lease;

It's the beauty that thrills me with wonder,

It's the stillness that fills me with peace.

—Robert Service, The Spell of the Yukon

Humans evolved in the wilderness, and only comparatively recently—say, during the last 6,000 years—forsook the wilderness for civilization. Ever since, when we've wanted to return to wild areas we've needed specialized equipment.

Today, the need for that special equipment is even greater than it was just a few generations ago. In many parts of the United States, active hikers can remember a time when they could drink pure water directly from flowing streams. No longer.

Many of us grew up with saws and axes and blazing fires to cook every meal. That has changed, too.

Finding your way meant using a map and a compass, or navigating with natural features. Now orbiting satellites do the work for us.

Outdoor clothing was made only of cotton or wool; now we have a bewildering choice of high-tech materials.

Like everything else in our lives, equipment for hiking and backpacking has changed and is continuing to change. The message is simple: if you want to enjoy hiking and backpacking, you need accurate information about what equipment is currently available, and where to get it.

That's the goal of this book. We want to give you the information to help you make intelligent decisions.

Two themes override all others in this book. First, know your capabilities and your desires. Decide what kind of hiking or backpacking you want to do. Second, buy your supplies and equipment from companies dedicated to outdoor sports, companies with experts who will help you now and in the future.

Buy Just Enough

Mike Beers manages California Outfitters in Fresno, California. He says his hardest job is to find out what a customer really needs.

Beers breaks down those needs into true needs and psychological needs. True needs, he says, are based on the type of outdoor activity the customer actually indulges in. For example, day hikes in Yosemite Valley don't require equipment designed to support week-long treks across ice-covered passes in the Sierra Nevada. But some day hikers, ignoring their true needs, want to possess the more expensive, more macho equipment and won't be satisfied with anything less.

Beers tries to steer a customer toward satisfying the true needs, not the psychological ones. But sometimes, he admits, it's a losing battle.

The lesson here is to beware of over-buying. Don't over-equip yourself. Spending money pointlessly does not necessarily mean greater safety or even comfort.

There's no sense in buying a Global Position System (GPS) for navigating the well-marked nature trails at state parks.

If you're just starting out and don't know what type of hiking

you will gravitate toward, why not put off buying equipment? Rent it instead. Although renting is not cheap, it's less expensive than buying expensive gear you simply won't need in the future.

Start by Renting

Renting allows you to try a variety of equipment and see if it suits your needs. If you need equipment for growing kids, renting saves you from buying new stuff after every growth spurt.

Renting also gives you an opportunity to develop a rapport with the store staff. Are they knowledgeable and helpful? Do they backpack, and can they suggest favorite routes or routes to avoid? When you're ready to plunk down your dollars for a major purchase, are these the people you want to do business with? Stores are like shoes: they should feel comfortable before you buy.

You can rent gear from backpacking stores. Typically they will rent stoves, sleeping bags, sleeping pads, packs, tents, and bivouac (bivy) bags. Here are some typical daily hire costs:

- Backpacking stove: $5 to $6

- Pack:
  internal frame: $11 to $14
  external frame: $9 to $11
  children's: $6 to $8

- Sleeping bag: $12 to $15

- Tent: $14 to $20

Check the store's terms and conditions. How clean must the

The Cascade Mountains, Oregon. Photo by Ed Sobey

equipment be when you return it? Is there insurance against damage or loss?

If you like the gear you rent, ask whether it will be part of a year-end sale. Many stores sell rental equipment at greatly reduced prices.

Admittedly, renting equipment demands a bit more planning on your part, as you can't wake up Saturday morning and decide to hit the trails. Yet, aside from this inconvenience, renting offers lots of benefits.

Ask Questions

The caliber of the store you buy from is important, especially if you're a beginner. Are they happy to talk to you and help you, even when you're not buying anything? Here are a few questions to ask the sales force:

• Do they backpack, climb, or hike? (Why would you accept advice from someone who doesn't?)

• Do they do the same type of hiking you do? Weekend packers have different needs and budgets from those of through-hikers on the Appalachian Trail.

• Which stove, water filter, or pack do *they* use? Why did they choose that one?

• Do they repair the equipment they sell? If not, can they steer you to someone who does?

• Do they conduct equipment clinics that might be helpful to you?

• Do they offer other training, or organize trips?

Ask yourself if, when they offer you advice, they truly keep your needs in mind. Or are they following some other agenda? It's not always safe to forecast the future from the past, but a company that has a long track record has a better chance of being in business in the future than does a start-up. That generalization applies to retail stores and equipment manufacturers.

If there are hundreds of customers with credit cards or cash in hand, the staff obviously can't devote all their attention to you. So, if you have lots more questions, visit the store during off-peak hours when the sales force has more time to spend with you.

The staff should be asking you questions, too. This shows you they are trying to meet your needs; they are providing a service to you. Showing you equipment without knowing what you need indicates a sell-sell mentality.

No store carries all brands of all equipment, so you might choose a store based on the brands of equipment you want. If you don't know where to find retail outlets for your favorite brands, call the manufacturers (the numbers are listed in the Equipment Section).

BARGAINS
 TIP

If you already know what equipment you like from renting it, check out end-of-season sales for new equipment and newspaper ads for used equipment. You may find some bargains.

Retail Stores

If you've never been to a dedicated outdoor retail store, you might be wondering what to expect. Here are three examples.

First, let's say you're in Fresno, California, and it's 104°F outside. One hour (and 5,000 vertical feet)

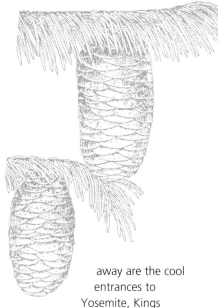

away are the cool entrances to Yosemite, Kings Canyon, and Sequoia National Parks. But before you start up the foothills of the Sierra Nevada, you need to pick up some supplies. You're in the right place: California Outfitters.

California Outfitters

Much smaller than its giant cousin, Recreational Equipment Inc. (REI), California Outfitters is still big enough to carry 4,000 products. It's cool and slightly dark inside. Sleeping bags and clothing hang off to the right, tents dominate the middle of the store, climbing gear fills the left side, next to stoves.

Food, boots, books, and maps are in the left rear.

Shane Krogen started California Outfitters in 1983. He disagrees with the notion that he sells equipment. It doesn't tell the whole story. "We're a service store," he says sincerely, "we sell knowledge."

Large general sports stores don't have the experience or time to dispense knowledge; rather, they depend for sales on cheap prices. Shane's staff are all avid outdoors people who gladly answer questions about where to go, as well as what to buy. They recognize customers and learn their names. Shopping there is like being among helpful friends. Which is good for business, of course.

Wilderness Sports

About 1,000 miles to the north, in Bellevue, Washington, is another store like California Outfitters: Wilderness Sports. Unlike California Outfitters, they live almost in the shadow of the Seattle headquarters of REI, the world's top outdoor retail chain. Tough competition, but Wilderness Sports not only survives, it thrives. How do they do it?

Herb Nesbitt, owner of Wilderness Sports, is almost cocky in his response: "We sell only stuff that you use and need in the backcountry. We don't carry cotton clothing and other stuff that you wouldn't use when backpacking, hiking, or climbing."

Herb profits from the loyalty of his customers. "People come in here unhappy with other stores because they got equipment that

wasn't right for them, or worse yet, that wasn't safe. Once they find us, they stick with us."

Like California Outfitters, Wilderness Sports employees are true believers. They run the store, they know their gear, and they take pride in offering advice and help.

REI

Also in Bellevue, Washington, down the street from Wilderness Sports, is REI. REI was founded in 1938 by a group of mountaineers who wanted quality climbing equipment. It has grown into a chain of 48 retail operations, a multi-million dollar mail-order business, a travel company, and three manufacturing subsidiaries. The subsidiaries are MSR (stoves, helmets, and carabiners), THAW (outdoor clothing and sleeping bags), and Walrus, Inc. (tents).

Compared to California Outfitters and Wilderness Sports, even this smaller REI "approach" store is large. The flagship REI store in Seattle is absolutely huge, and if you arrive early enough on a slow day, you can get in line to climb their indoor wall, the largest, they claim, in the world. It's like an outdoor experience indoors.

REI is a cooperative: You join as a member and share the profit at the end of the year. The more you buy, the bigger your refund.

Despite the organization's giant size, the staff at REI is friendly and helpful. You can buy equipment

from REI by visiting one of the chain's 48 stores, call toll-free (800-426-4840), or order on the Internet: http://www.rei.com.

IT JUST GREW AND GREW

In his book *REI: 50 Years of Climbing Together* (REI, 1988), Harvey Manning tells how mountaineer Lloyd Anderson bought an ice ax by mail in 1938, but found, when it arrived, that the price was twice that advertised and the quality far less.

Lloyd set out to find a quality ice ax for a reasonable price. When he succeeded, his climbing friends wanted one, too. Lloyd and Mary Anderson started a table-top enterprise that just grew and grew, eventually becoming a major co-op business with 48 stores.

Members receive gear catalogs throughout the year, enjoy annual refunds on their purchase prices, and get discounts on travel and gear repair. REI also donates more than $500,000 each year to environmental and outdoor recreational causes.

Special Advantages

The less experienced you are, the more you need the services specialty stores provide. With new fabrics and equipment entering the market every year, it takes a professional to keep track of it all. Specialty stores provide special advantages.

Outside the kind of specialty stores we've discussed, you're on your own, because few of the very

MAIL-ORDER CATALOGS

If you don't have a dedicated backpacking and hiking store near you, get the catalogs of several mail-order companies. In Chapter 8 you'll find phone numbers and web addresses, so you can request a catalog (see page 84).

It's easy to order by phone or fax, but remember that returns and service are tougher, and asking questions is nearly impossible, so be quite sure you know exactly what you want.

large sports retailers train sales staff specifically to sell backpacking equipment. Another advantage of the specialty store is that its staff can suggest local hikes that fit your tastes and abilities, as well as the equipment you'll need for them. And backpacking stores will help you with minor repairs and rental equipment.

Helpful Organizations

Training in Outdoor Skills

Many retail stores offer classes on backpacking, as do some colleges. Nonprofit organizations also provide training, the best-known being the National Outdoor Leadership School (NOLS) and Outward Bound.

The Audubon Expedition Institute offers degrees in Environmental Studies and Education. Contact: (207) 338-5859; www.audubon.org/educate/aei/index.html

Boulder Outdoor Survival School teaches basic survival skills. Contact: (800) 335-7404

The Grand Canyon Association offers learning programs through its Field School and has a bookstore. Contact: (520) 638-2481; www.thecanyon.com/gca

The National Outdoor Leadership School (NOLS) began more than 30 years ago when mountaineer Paul Petzoldt wanted to train outdoor leaders. His method was to take people into the outdoors for extended periods, let them experience wilderness conditions, and teach them outdoor and leadership skills. Today, NOLS has

more than 40,000 graduates. They offer courses in a wide variety of environments throughout the world. Contact: (307) 332-6973; www.nols.edu

Outward Bound is a group of independent schools in 26 countries. In the United States there are five wilderness schools and several urban centers. Outward Bound alumni number 400,000. Outward Bound began in Britain during World War II when its founder noted a high fatality rate among raw young mariners cast away at sea after their ships had been sunk by German U-boats. Curiously, old salts survived at a much higher rate. The difference seemed to be life experience: The old salts knew they could hang on through adversity. After a training program of progressively challenging experiences, survival rates climbed dramatically. Contact: (800) 243-8520; www.outwardbound.org

Prescott College offers undergraduate degrees in Adventure Education, Environmental Wilderness, Wilderness Leadership, and more traditional fields. Contact: (800) 628-6364; www.prescott.edu

Sterling College in Vermont offers programs in outdoor leadership and environmental resource management. Contact: (800) 648-3591

The Wilderness Education Association promotes outdoor safety and leadership for professionals. Located in Nashville, Tennessee, it offers courses and conferences. Contact: (615) 331-5739; www.ebl.org/wea/profile.htm

National Hiking Clubs

There are hundreds of local clubs that organize trips and programs and provide information; they are listed in the chapters headed Hiking Information by Region. National organizations perform the same functions. To find out about them and their programs in your area, contact their national offices. Here are three of the most prominent:

The American Hiking Society, (301) 565-6704; ahs.simplenet.com/index.html or www.orca.org/ahs

The Appalachian Mountain Club, (617) 523-0636; www.outdoors.org

The Sierra Club, (800) 477-2627; www.sierraclub.org

Hiking Advocacy Groups

The American Hiking Society promotes hiking and the creation of foot trails in America. It has 100 member trail clubs, and represents half a million outdoors people. It strives to "strengthen grassroots organizations and to engage trail advocates as active participants in planning, funding, and developing trails in their communities." It sponsors National Trails Day (the first Saturday in June) and is building The National Trail Endowment. Contact: (301) 565-6704; www.orca.org/ahs

American Trails is a nonprofit organization established to "lead the nation in the creation of trail systems for all Americans, by fostering communication and complementary action." It organizes symposiums on trails, publishes the trails newspaper *Trail Tracks,* and supports local and national efforts to build and protect trails. Contact: (520) 632-1140; www.outdoorlink.com/amtrails

The Appalachian Mountain Club (AMC) is America's oldest conservation and recreation organization and has 72,000 members. It offers outdoor activities, skills training, and support for conservation. It has a number of local chapters on the East Coast, a list of which you can find through the AMC's website, www.outdoors.org.

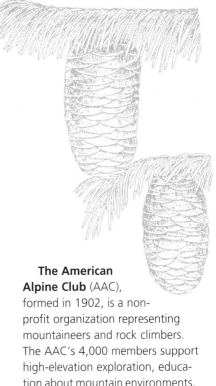

The American Alpine Club (AAC), formed in 1902, is a nonprofit organization representing mountaineers and rock climbers. The AAC's 4,000 members support high-elevation exploration, education about mountain environments,

AMERICAN CONSERVATIONISTS

Among the leaders of the conservation movement in this country, the names of Henry David Thoreau, John Wesley Powell, Gifford Pinchot, John Muir, and Aldo Leopold loom large.

Their stories and others are chronicled in *Dreamers & Defenders: American Conservationists*, by Douglas H. Strong (University of Nebraska Press, 1988). Strong details the personal background and the accomplishments of the people who started the U.S. Park Service, the U.S. Forest Service, and the Sierra Club in a very readable style.

and conservation.
Contact: (303) 384-0110;
www.AmericanAlpineClub.org

The National Parks & Conservation Association (NPCA) is dedicated to protecting, preserving, and enhancing the National Park System. Founded in 1919, the NPCA today has more than 500,000 members. Contact: (800) 628-7275; www.npca.org

The Sierra Club, founded by John Muir and friends, now accommodates more than half a million members. Muir was a pioneer of grassroots eco-activism. The club is now dedicated to preserving what remains of our unspoiled wilderness, protecting endangered species, cleaning the air we breathe and the water we drink, and ensuring a safer, healthier planet for future generations. Contact: (800) 477-2627; www.sierraclub.org

The Wilderness Society was formed by Aldo Leopold, Bob Marshall, and six others in 1935 to preserve and protect wilderness. Leopold defined the "land ethic" in *A Sand County Almanac* as having respect for land and acting as a citizen of the earth rather than as a conqueror of it. This ethic became the foundation of the Wilderness Society. Contact: (800) THE-WILD; www.wilderness.org

From Rails to Trails

Transforming abandoned railroad rights-of-way into hiking trails is an idea that

has caught on. Railroads originally obtained the rights-of-way with government and public support: something that would be nearly impossible today. Once a right-of-way is lost, it is nearly impossible to regain it, and so fast action is required when the railroad company decides to quit a rail line. There are more than 800 rail-trails nationally, totaling more than 7,000 miles.

You can find out about existing and proposed projects by contacting The Rail-Trail Resource Center: www.halcyon.com/fredwert

The Rails-to-Trails Conservancy (www.railtrails.org) is a 10-year-old nonprofit organization dedicated to creating a nationwide network of public trails from former rail lines and connecting corridors. Their website has information about existing rail-trails and the resources to support travel on them. Their mailing address is 1100 Seventeenth Street NW, 10th Floor, Washington, D.C. 20036.

Magazines

For issue upon issue of good information on equipment, where to go, and everything else remotely related to hiking and backpacking, check out
Backpacker magazine**.** It provides the latest information in a colorful and engaging style, with descriptions, reviews, and ads. You can buy issues at the newsstand or call (800) 666-3434 to subscribe. *Backpacker* also offers information online at www.bpbasecamp.com

Adventure Journal, formerly *Adventure West,* covers the outdoor waterfront from skiing to scuba diving. They have articles and advertisements of interest to backpackers. Contact: (800) 846-8575.

Outside is a monthly glossy filled with articles on a variety of subjects from rock-climbing contests to tourism. It offers some ideas on where to go and lots of ads for what to take along. Contact: (800) 678-1131; //outside.starwave.com

Explore is Canada's outdoor adventure magazine.
Contact: (800) 567-1372.

Incidentally, you can find an Internet listing of other outdoors magazines at www.yahoo.com/Recreation/Outdoors/Magazines

Backpackers Online

The Internet is a rich source of information about backpacking. You can join an online listserv by logging on to the Backpackers Forum at www.switchback.com/backpack. The home page also allows you to review dialog sorted by month or subject.

Here are a few suggestions to get you started. Then you'll be in a position to discover a host of other sources for yourself:

Get Lost Adventure Magazine is online at: www.itsnet.com/home/getlost/mag.html. It offers links to pages on equipment and places.
Yahoo connects to a large source of information.
Start at: www.yahoo.com/Recreation/Travel/Backpacking
Backers.com is a great place to find and share travel information. There is no charge for membership

and e-mail accounts.
REI offers an online course on backpacking. It includes tips on navigation, where to go and what gear to buy: //merc.rei.com/OLC/courses/bkpacking101/cbk101top.html
About Hiking is an online information source with stories and information on equipment, destinations, and books: www.abouthiking.com
GreatOutdoors.com provides weather reports at national parks and information on equipment: www.greatoutdoors.com
Princeton University offers an outdoor action guide

with information on hypothermia and cold weather injuries at: www.princeton.edu/~oa/hypocold.html. You can find information on other outdoor subjects at: www.princeton.edu/~oa/oa.html
The Hiking and Walking Home Page offers links to walking events, places to hike, and tours: www.teleport.com:80/~walking/hiking.html
L.L. Bean offers a Park Search feature to get information on hundreds of state and national parks, national wildlife refuges and forests, and land under the control of the Bureau of Land Management: www.llbean.com/parksearch

Peak to Peak Trail and Wilderness Links claims to have the most links to trail and wilderness websites: //home.earthlink.net/ ~swfry/pk2pk/peak_to_peak. html

What's Wild's website includes pictures and information on wildlife and experiences while hiking: //members.tripod.com/ ~pscragg/index.html

What's Wild also supports a walking and hiking page with many links: www.teleport.com ~walking/places.shtml

The Mining Company, an equipment retailer, offers a guide to backpacking: //backpacking. miningco.com/

Keeping Fit

You'll enjoy your hikes much more if you're in good physical shape. You'll be safer on the trail and less likely to have an accident. What's the best way to get in shape?

Train year-round; make it a part of your life.

For hiking and backpacking you need flexibility, strength, and cardiovascular endurance. That means you need to train in all three areas—stretch, do strength training, and do cardiovascular training. Of course, the best training for hiking is hiking, but when you can't take the time to hit the trails, hit the gym, the road, or whatever, and hit it on a regular basis.

INTERNET ACCESS

If you aren't connected to the Internet, you can get online to take advantage of these free sources of information by going to a library, many of which offer free access. You might also try an "Internet Cafe"— these surfing-and-sipping hotspots are springing up all over, offering free or cheap access to the Web.

TRAINING GUIDE

The Outdoor Athlete by Steve Ilg (Cordillera Press, 1992) contains a comprehensive training schedule for climbing, skiing, kayaking, and hiking/backpacking. He explains what exercises to do and integrates strength, stretching, and cardiovascular training into workout schedules.

My own **Strength Training Book** and **Aerobic Weight Training Book** by Ed Sobey (Runner's World Books) are out of print but available in many libraries. Both set out training programs for backpacking.

The best resource for stretching remains the aptly named **Stretching**, by Bob Anderson (Shelter Publications, 1987).

To hell with you, ignoble paunch, abhorrent in my sight!

I gaze at your rotundity, and savage is my frown.

I'll rub you and I'll scrub you and I'll drub you day and night,

But by the gods of symmetry I swear I'll get you down.

Your smooth and smug convexity, by heck! I will subdue,

And when you tucker in again with joy will I refulge;

No longer of my toes will you obstruct my downward view . . .

With might and main I'll fight to gain the Battle of the Bulge.

—Robert Service, The Battle of the Bulge

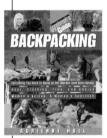

Hiking with Kids

Let children walk with Nature, let them see the beautiful blendings and communions of death and life, their joyous inseparable unity, as taught in woods and meadows, plains and mountains and streams of our blessed star, and they will learn that death is stingless indeed, and as beautiful as life.

—John Muir, A Thousand-Mile Walk to the Gulf

Photo by Ed Sobey

Sharing the wilderness with children can be pleasure or misery, depending, in part, on how you plan it. Kids go at kid speed. They need to look under rocks, check out that lizard or butterfly, and chuck a pebble into the stream. All that activity makes pounding the trail a slow endeavor. If you make the mistake of biting off too many miles, you will end up teaching kids to hate hiking. But if you allow plenty of time to explore, you'll instill a love of the outdoors that they will pass on to their children. Here are some books to consult for expert advice:

Illustration by Daisy dePuthod

Adventuring with Children: An Inspirational Guide to World Travel and the Outdoors by Nan Jeffrey (Avalon House Publishing, 1995) empowers families to take off with kids. This is as much a book on parenting as on hiking and backpacking but could be very helpful on the trail.

Backpacking with Babies and Small Children by Goldie Silverman (Wilderness Press,

1986) is another useful reference. **Kid Camping from Aaaaii! to Zip** by Patrick F. McManus (Avon Books, 1979) is a book the little nippers will love. McManus has the heart and mind of your average 13-year-old kid. He covers such topics as the "Crouch Hop," the result of pounding your fingers between a flat rock and a tent stake. In a section on getting lost, he notes, "Usually a lot of fun." Sprinkled here and there are useful bits of wisdom for kids to digest. Not so many as to spoil the book, though.

Camping & Backpacking with Children by Steven Boga (Stack-

pole Books, 1995) is another guide to taking the kids along.

The Outdoor Family Fun Guide: A Complete Camping, Hiking, Canoeing, Nature Watching, Mountain Biking, Skiing, Climbing, and General Fun Book for Parents and Kids by Michael Hodgson (Ragged Mountain Press, 1998) is just what the subtitle claims—a guide to helping parents introduce kids to outdoor sports, teach basic skills, and share with them a love of the outdoors.

Take a Hike: The Sierra Club Kid's Guide to Hiking and Backpacking by Lynne Foster (Sierra Club Books, 1991) was written for kids.

Kids Outdoors by Victoria and Frank Logue and Mark Carroll (Ragged Mountain Press, 1996) is a "totally nonboring" guide to backcountry skills for kids from 11 to 15.

The Mountaineers' Series of Best Hikes with Children includes destination guides for several states.

Staying Found: The Complete Map and Compass Handbook by June Fleming (The Mountaineers, 1994) has a chapter on teaching kids to stay found, and what to do if they get lost.

Nature with Children of All Ages by Edith A. Sisson (Spectrum Books, 1982) is crammed with activities you can do at home or on the trail to share nature with kids.

KID CARRIERS

If you're planning to take infants backpacking, you'll need a child carrier. Try these manufacturers: Kelty Kids: (800) 423-2320; Tough Traveler: (800) 468-6844.

A thing is right when it tends to preserve the integrity, stability, and beauty of the biotic community. It is wrong when it tends otherwise.

—Aldo Leopold,

A Sand County Almanac

Leave No Trace

If you want the wilderness to remain untrampled, unlittered, and wild, you have to commit yourself to minimal-impact camping and leave no trace of your presence. This means using your head and understanding the environment and your effect on it. Following are general guidelines adapted from the Leave No Trace (LNT) program spearheaded by the National Outdoor Leadership School. The school publishes booklets, posters, wallet cards, and pamphlets describing the LNT principles, which are available at outdoor equipment stores.

The materials include recommendations for all of North America, and for specific regions. Information is also available on the Leave No Trace website at www.lnt.org or by calling (800) 332-4100.

1. Make preparations in advance so you don't have to make bad choices in the backcountry. Choose a route appropriate to your goals and the level of your outdoor skills. Make sure that you are self-sufficient and your equipment is adequate to keep you safe without having to use the area's natural resources.

2. Hike and camp with care and consideration for your surroundings. Where there are established trails, walk on them. Where there aren't trails, walk where you will do the least damage, and have your group spread out rather than beat down a new path. Pick camp sites on durable ground such as sand, rock, or dry grassy meadows.

3. Don't disturb the wildlife. It's tough enough for them without having to flee from human intruders. Don't approach animals when they are aware of your presence or trying to avoid you. Keep food safe and out of reach of animals, and don't leave food scraps lying around.

4. Leave what you find. Take pictures, but leave every-

thing else as you found it. Let others discover what you have found.

5. Pack out everything you take in. This will test your resolve but why should the next person find your residue? Cut down on the amount of packaging for your trail food, so you don't have to haul excess packaging out again.

INFORMATIVE READING

Soft Paths by Bruce Hampton and David Cole (Stackpole Books, 1995) was written for the National Outdoor Leadership School (NOLS) to persuade back-country users to tread softly and create minimum impact. NOLS also sells video copies of Soft Paths through its Leave No Trace program. They are available on 15-minute and 30-minute tapes.

Walking Softly in the Wilderness by John Hart (Sierra Club Books, 1984) touches on the same topic. This comprehensive, serious book offers ideas on how to enjoy backpacking without disturbing your surroundings.

Backwoods Ethics: Environmental Issues for Hikers and Campers by Laura and Guy Waterman (Countryman Press, 1993) looks at values and ethics of wilderness travel.

6. If you aren't going to haul out human waste, make sure you dispose of it properly. The general rule is to bury human waste in the top few inches of the soil, and cover it well. And remember that a campsite that is littered with someone else's toilet-paper residue is disgusting. Don't do that to someone else.

7. Use fire responsibly. Don't light fires where they are prohibited or when fire danger is high. Don't cut wood—use what's on the ground or go without a fire. Keep fires small, and don't leave smoke-blackened rocks for the next group. If you try to burn garbage or trash in the fire, you are responsible for pulling out everything that doesn't burn; pack it out. Make sure the fire is out before you leave; if you can't run your hands through the remains of the fire, it's not out.

Private Affairs

Going to the bathroom in the wilderness requires a lot of care. Pick a site at least 200 feet from any stream, river, or lake to prevent bacteria from washing into the water. Naturally, the site should also be off the trail and out of sight of hikers.

A downed log makes a perch to lean against. Otherwise, use a simple squat. You can dig a "cathole" first, or you can dig a hole afterward and move the waste into it. A deep hole is neither necessary nor preferable because all the microbes needed to rapidly decompose the waste live in the top few inches of the soil.

Carry out your toilet paper. A few resealable plastic bags will do the trick. If you don't want to carry out toilet paper, don't use any. An alternative is to use leaf litter, but be careful not to grab poison ivy or its relatives!

HOW TO DO IT IN THE WOODS

A book devoted to defecation in forested areas wouldn't seem to be best-seller material, but *How to Shit in the Woods*, by Kathleen Meyer (Ten Speed Press, 1989), has sold hundreds of thousands of copies. Meyer takes an in-depth look at the subject, tackling such subjects as

what to do when you can't dig a cat hole and what to do when diarrhea strikes. Fret not that she might have overlooked the delicate subject of urinating: She didn't.

To summarize, the procedure is stop, plop, and roll it into the cat hole. Make sure you take away anything that won't degrade immediately, and leave the area without a trace.

READY TO HAND

Pack these items ready for easy access:

- Sunscreen
- Sunglasses
- Map and compass
- Water
- Toilet kit

Critters on the Trail

Various people react differently to outdoor experiences:

"Ah, to walk through the wilderness and share a day with nature's bounty!"

"Darn mosquitoes!"

"Hey, some animal ate through my tent and got into our food!"

The irony is that we desperately want to see wildlife, but only on our terms. We want them close, but not in our faces. We want to make them look or move; but we don't want them to make us move or to experience fear or pain.

There is always the chance that when we escape civilization we'll become a part of the food chain. Fortunately, the things that attack us are usually a tiny fraction of our size. Unfortunately, there are lots more of them. The bigger animals usually have the good sense to keep away.

GIVE THEM SPACE

Here's a general rule for observing wildlife: If your presence causes animals to change their behavior, you're too close.

Repelling Bugs

DEET has been providing protection against bugs for 40 years. The U.S. Department of Agriculture created diethyl-toluamide, now known as DEET, and it still probably provides the best protection.

When you use DEET you might notice that it removes the printing from its plastic bottle. You have to be careful about letting it contact plastics, leather, and paint. And as far as human beings are concerned, it is a potentially dangerous chemical that has been linked to skin irritation, headaches, insomnia, and toxic encephalophy, or swelling of the brain.

With these possible side-effects, the general recommendation is: Don't use DEET carelessly on kids; use it sparingly and in low concentrations—10 percent solutions or less. Adults shouldn't use any more than is needed, either.

A marmot glances at visitors to its Rocky Mountain home.

Photo by Ed Sobey

DEET works by filling the air with large molecules that desensitize the insect's ability to home in on a victim, so it works well if it's applied lightly to hair, clothes, shoes, and backpacks. You might not need to apply it to your skin at all. It might attack some synthetic fabrics, though. Wool, cotton, nylon, and rubberized fabrics are usually immune, but if you're not sure, spray a little DEET on a hidden surface and wait a few minutes to see what happens.

By the way, don't lather up at the first sign of bugs; try swishing them away until they become truly annoying. The worst times for mosquitoes are at dawn and dusk, when you can put on long sleeves, tuck your pants into your socks, and add a hat, bandanna, and

gloves to give the thirsty beasties a smaller target. A smoky fire keeps them at bay, and a breeze grounds them, so pick a campsite in the open. Keep DEET away from your eyes and any cuts. If you notice a reaction to DEET, switch to another repellent.

DEET is effective in keeping away mosquitoes, ticks, and some biting flies. But its protection isn't perfect. You can watch a mosquito land on a DEET-covered arm and bury its proboscis for a drink, because the insect has blundered into you by accident. Black flies will annoy you through a layer of DEET, and other repellents might work better.

The common DEET-based repellents include Apica, Ben's 100, Cutters, Jungle Juice, Muskol, and Repel. Choose your brand based on the percentage of DEET (higher percentages are more effective but could cause health problems), scents that manufacturers add, and cost.

The holy grail of bug repellent is a safe and effective replacement for DEET. Alternatives to DEET include cit-

ronella, which smells better, and isn't harmful, but doesn't work especially well. Buzz Away has a concentration of 5 percent citronella.

Many people credit Avon's Skin-So-Soft with repellent powers much greater than experience or studies support. Common experience is that bugs avoid it for a few minutes after you apply it.

Bite Blocker might be the best alternative to DEET. Made of soybean oil, it repels black flies and mosquitoes. It is waterproof and lasts for hours. The smell is only slightly repugnant.

These insect repellents contain no DEET:

• Bite Blocker, Consep, 213 SW Columbia St., Bend, OR 97702

• Buzz Away, (800) 449-9694

Soothing That Sting

Once the bee stings or the mosquito bites, what can you do? There are at least two lotions that reduce the pain: After Bite, made by the Tender Corporation in Littleton, New Hampshire; and StingEze, made by Wisconsin Pharmacals in Jackson, Wisconsin. You'll find these at drug stores and outdoor

Photos of Buzz Away and After Bite courtesy of Tender Corporation

Photo of Sting Eze courtesy of Wisconsin Pharmacal

MOSQUITOES

Mosquitoes have survived successfully for 50 million years. Unfortunately, part of their success involves you.

Female mosquitoes need the protein in animal blood, including human blood, to nourish their eggs. They gulp down a lot—about two and a half times their body weight.

What turns on the feeding frenzy of a female mosquito? The gas you exhale: carbon dioxide. A whiff of the gas alerts mosquitoes that it's meal time. Then she uses her sensors to follow warm, moist air currents—all the way to you.

Most repellents don't actually repel insects. They merely interfere with the insect's ability to home in on you. DEET and some other repellents jam the mosquitoes' sensors, which causes them to lose the trail to your arm.

Tonkass National Forest, Alaska. Photo by Ed Sobey

stores. Anyone who is sensitive to bug bites should carry one.

All About Bears

In an article in the November 1898 issue of the *Atlantic Monthly,* John Muir noted: "In my first interview with a Sierra bear we were frightened and embarrassed, both of us, but the bear's behavior was better than mine." This recollection is contained in *John Muir in His Own Words, A Book of Quotations,* compiled and

JOHN MUIR
IN HIS OWN WORDS
A Book of Quotations

Compiled and Edited by
Peter Browning

edited by Peter Browning (Great West Books, 1988).

Scuba divers talk about sharks. Florida canoeists think about alligators. Backpackers and hikers dream of mountain lions. And bears. Undying respect for predators is a healthy habit.

How can you prepare for an unplanned encounter? For a start,

find out about the particular dangers of the area you're going to visit. Local information, based on local experience, is the best.

Then, too, learn how to avoid bad encounters. Keep food away from your sleeping area. And don't act as if you were the prey by running at the sight of a predator.

Most encounters with predators will be brief and distant, but you should prepare yourself, as far as possible, for close encounters.

There is still lots we don't understand about bears but we have learned a great deal over the years. Here are some books on the subject of encounters with bears:

Crossing Paths: Uncommon Encounters with Animals in the Wild, by Craig Childs (Sasquatch Books, 1997), chronicles the author's meetings with animals, from bears and mosquitoes to porcupines and hawks. Childs is a river guide, adventurer, and writer. His collection of stories is well-written and engaging.

Bear Encounter Survival Guide, by Gary Shelton (Heritage House, 1997), tells how you can minimize your danger in bear country. Call Heritage House at (800) 665-3302.

Grizzly Years: Encounters with the Wilderness, by Doug Peacock (Holt and Company, 1990), describes 20 years of watching bears.

Safe Travel in Bear Country, by Gary Brown (Lyons Press, 1996), examines the causes of bear attack and what

you should do to avoid it.

Bear Attacks: Their Causes and Avoidance, by Stephen Herrero (Lyons Press, 1985), recounts encounters with black and brown bears, with suggestions for lessening the danger.

Pepper Spray

Bear spray deters most bears. Take it with you if you travel in bear country. It's made from capsaicin, the chemical that gives peppers their zip.

There are three things to know about pepper spray. First, it doesn't do any good buried in the bottom of your pack. Carry it on your belt, ready to use. Second, it doesn't do any good unless you know how to use it. Read the directions carefully and try a quick squirt or two, but not indoors or at any living creature. In most cases the spray will incapacitate a human, causing pain in the chest, the eyes, and even on the skin. The effects diminish after 45 minutes and can be washed away with water but it's reported to be a very unpleasant experience. Third, be careful where you carry the spray. In a convenience store at 10 P.M. the spray is a weapon. And, you can't carry it or pack it aboard a plane.

Check the label for the percentage of active ingredient. It should be about 10 or 15 percent.

Here are two products that will do the trick:

Counter Assault, (800) 695-3394; www.counterassault.com
Pepper Power, (800) 232-7941

Encounters with Bears

You might be wondering what an encounter with bears is really like. Here are two confrontations from our personal experience:

Carl was shaking me.

"Bears," he whispered.

"Yes, I know," I told him, "there's one walking around just outside camp. I heard it before."

"No," Carl said. "They're after our food."

So what? I thought. We had bear-bagged our remaining provisions. On this night in Glen Aulen, on the last night of a 50-mile crossing of the Sierra Nevada, we didn't have much food left but we had protected it well.

Photo courtesy of Universal Defense Alternative Products

and emptied of granola bars and other sweets.

The food in that last bag sustained us for our six-mile hike out. Had we encountered this band of desperado bears on our first day or two, we would have faced a more serious problem. The next time we camp in Glen Aulen, we'll use bear-proof canisters.

Protecting Your Food

Where bears are a problem, one solution to food storage is a bear-proof container. These heavy-duty plastic cylinders keep bears and other animals from stealing your food. The canisters add weight and take up room in your pack, but they offer the greatest security. At some sites, such as the huts along the Appalachian Trail, you'll find these canisters provided for hikers.

But the traditional approach to protecting food from bears is to set up a bear bag. In some national parks, like the Olympics in Washington, rangers have installed wire rope between trees, high enough for packers to hang food bags on. These rigs typically are proof against even the most precocious bears.

Where bear lines haven't been installed, you need to make your own. But, keeping in mind that an adult bear can have the equivalent of a master's degree in engineering, the strength and agility of a heavy-weight wrestler, and a primordial motivation to satiate hunger, you'd better do a good job of hanging your food.

"The bear's in the tree," Carl insisted.

I could tell I wasn't going to get any sleep until I had gone to look. We padded softly toward the sound of crunching branches. Carl flashed the beam of his light up our bear-bag tree where, sure enough, it fell upon a bear.

Dumb bear, I thought, *he can't reach the rope from the trunk, and the branch isn't big enough to support his weight.* "He'll never get it," I whispered.

Then a loud "crunch" changed my mind. The bear was eating through the branch. With each bite he took, the branch sagged lower, weighed down by our bags of food. "Crunch" again, and the tip of the branch was pointing toward the ground. Once more, and it was only a few feet off the ground. A last crunch, and the branch fell.

"Run and grab the food," Carl urged.

With economy of words I assured him I wasn't going to do that. We watched the bear clamber down the tree, grab the food bags and head for the dark hillside behind our camp.

So ended that encounter. But another was to come.

Our second "perfectly protected" bear bag was swiped by a mother bear and two cubs about an hour later. Mom sat on the ground and directed her offspring on the finer arts of chewing through the rope. She couldn't get up the tree herself, but Cub 1 and Cub 2 were able to. A loud "Bam!" as the food bag hit the ground was our first notice of this attack.

We arrived just in time to see Momma grab the food bags and take off, leaving us standing at the base of the tree looking up at the two cubs.

At that point we realized we couldn't outsmart the bears, so we lowered our lone remaining food bag and placed it by the fire, which we tended for the last few hours of the night. At dawn we recovered the pilfered food bags, each surgically opened by a claw

The basic approach to bear bagging is to toss a rope over a solitary limb at least 12 feet off the ground. Attach food bags to one end and hoist away. If the food is more than a paw's grasp away from the trunk, and if the limb is too small to support the bear, your food will be safe. That's the theory, but don't believe a word of it. Every bear is taught how to get at food protected this way in *Being a Bear*, Chapter 1. They will simply chew through the line supporting the food or chew through the branch.

The more advanced approach, (no doubt covered in Chapter 2 of *Being a Bear*,) involves two lines, each one strung over a branch of a different tree. The food bags are tied to one end of each line and positioned midway between the two trees. By pulling on the other ends of the lines you raise the bags into the air. Then tie off each line to the trunk of the tree. This approach removes reliance on the branch and makes the ropes less obvious and harder for the bear to find.

An even better approach is to tie a food bag to one end of a line and pull it to a very high branch. Then tie a second bag of food to the other end. Using a hiking staff or long branch, push the second bag as high as you can, the two bags balancing each other. Ideally both bags will be suspended too

Bear-bagging—a hiker hoists a food pack clear of the ground and out of reach of bears and other animals.

Photo by Ed Sobey

high off the ground and too far from the trunk for a bear to reach them. And, the bear won't be able to chew through the line, provided it can't climb out on the branch. Of course, better-read bears will know to eat through the branch. "Will that be take out?" You do need to have a plan to recover the food, though, such as fixing a

strap to one bag so that you can hook your hiking staff into it and pull it down.

What's Best For You?

Which method of bear-proofing food is the right one for you? First, you must realize that hanging a bear bag is one of the evening's primary entertainments. When the first person fails to lob the rope over the limb, it arouses the competitive juices of every male, and soon there is a line of people wanting to try. While watchers might suffer more injuries (from the flying rock tied to the end of the rope), the show is at least on a par with network television.

Second, be rational about the bear hazard. Although they can be formidable foes, they aren't lurking behind every tree. You might never see one. You can usually find out in advance how serious the bear problem is likely to be in any particular area. If it's minimal, use one of the basic bear-bag approaches. Hanging your food will help avoid problems with bears. It will also protect your provisions from smaller critters who are equally hungry and wary.

If the bear problem is reportedly severe, use more caution. Pack-slinger is a product that enables you to hang food easily. It provides a 40-foot rope, a handle for the

Photos courtesy of Backpackers' Cache™

you should learn how to avoid them in the first place. In brushy areas in snake country, stamp or shuffle your feet to let snakes know you're coming. They prefer to get out of your way and usually strike only when they're surprised or backed into a corner. Watch for sunny, sandy spots where they like to bask. Step onto downed logs, rather than over them, to avoid startling a snake underneath. Watch where you put your hands while climbing rocks, when navigating near the ground in heavy brush, and when you're searching for firewood under logs or ledges. Need we say it?—Don't pick up snakes, live or dead. Incidentally, the higher your boots, the more protection they offer your legs against snakes. Although snakebites rarely occur above the

rope, a quick connector to attach your food bags to, and a carrying bag that you can fill with dirt or pebbles and use as a throwing weight. Bear canisters work well, of course, but they're a pain to carry. Unfortunately, if you use canisters you won't have the fun of watching guys toss rocks over tree limbs in the evening. But that might be a small price to pay for knowing your food is safe, and that you won't be encouraging bears to be more aggressive by providing them with free meals.

Get bear-proof gear from these sources:

Garcia/Backpacker's Cache, (209) 732-3785
Packslinger, (800) 724-3529

Snakebites

Although snakes bite a few thousand people each year in the United States, fewer than a dozen people die. In this country, more people die from dog bites, bee stings, and lightning strikes than from snakebites.

In North America's major wilderness areas there are four kinds of poisonous snakes—the coral snake, the rattlesnake, the copperhead, and the water moccasin (also called a cottonmouth). But you won't find them in all areas, and their venom usually doesn't kill fit, healthy adults.

Although your chances of dying from a snake bite are very remote,

---

PAINFUL EXTRACTION

 TIP

An adult porcupine has about 30 thousand quills. Each is equipped with barbs, making it difficult to extract. Before you yank out a quill, check to see if it would be less painful to poke it through the flesh and out the other side.

HORSES AND PACK ANIMALS

TIP

When encountering horses and pack animals, give them the right of way. Step off the trail to let them pass. Be mindful that loud noises could spook the horses, which could run over you.

WATCH THOSE MICE

 TIP

Mice will chew through packs and sacks in a few minutes to get to food. So keep food bags out of reach of rodents as well as bears.

---

ankle, most snakes can rear up to knee height to strike.

Dogs on the Trail

If you want to take dogs on the trail with you, make sure before you go that they're allowed. National Parks do not allow dogs in the backcountry, and in wilderness areas, dogs are required to be on a leash when they're allowed at all.

Even if there are no prohibitions against taking dogs, consider other hikers, the environment, and your dog. No matter how cute your dog is, other hikers won't care to have it slobber over them in camp, bark at them on the trail, or leave its droppings everywhere.

Dogs might love chasing the wildlife, but it's probably not so much fun for the wildlife. Restrain your dog if it doesn't have the sense not to chase. Some creatures might defend themselves vigorously. Consider the effect on your dog, and on you, of a few well-place porcupine needles or the

---

DOG DROPPINGS

 **TIP**

How do you dispose of dog droppings on the trail? Here's advice from Cheryl S. Smith, in her book *On the Trail with Your Canine Companion* (Howell Book House, 1996):

"So whatever your dog deposits, you need to pick up. If you are hiking in a relatively developed area where trash cans are available, all it takes is a plastic bag. Pick up your dog's pile, and carry it along to the nearest trash can. But most trails do not have trash receptacles conveniently placed along them. So what do you do?

"You can still use a plastic bag to pick up the offending material. Then you can drop bag and all into a zipper-locked plastic bag and seal it up. With the mess and odor locked safely away, you can slip it into your dog's pack, your own pack, or a jacket pocket, and pack it out, as you should all garbage.

"For people who just can't deal with carrying excrement, no matter how many bags contain it, there is the cat-hole option. Backcountry campers will be familiar with this waste-disposal strategy. Dig a narrow hole about six inches deep. Place the feces in it and cover with dirt and leaves."

---

spray of a skunk. Are you ready to administer first aid to the pooch?

Dogs used to the easy life at home might not be good trail companions. If your pal's pads aren't toughened by miles of running, they'll be torn up on the trail. Letting your dog carry its own food in a doggie-backpack might seem like a good idea to you, but not to your dog. Some dogs are afraid of the wilderness—yours might insist on sleeping in your tent.

If you really want to take your dog, you'll have to train it. Start with small hikes and a leash, and see how well you fare together. Then decide.

HAPPY DOGGY TRAILS

Hiking with Your Dog: Happy Trails, by Gary Hoffman (ICS Books, 1998), tells how to train a dog for backpacking. It also covers first aid and poisons that Fido might find along the trail.

WHO WAS THAT MASKED ANIMAL?

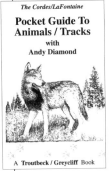

The Cordes/LaFontaine
Pocket Guide To Animals / Tracks
with
Andy Diamond

A Troutbeck / Greycliff Book

Photo by Ed Sobey

To assuage your morning curiosity about nocturnal visitors, tote along a copy of the *Pocket Guide to Animals/Tracks* by Ron Cordes and Andy Diamond (Greycliff Publishing Company, 1997).

Here are a few more resources to help you identify animal tracks: *Animal Tracks: An Introduction to the Tracks and Signs of Familiar North American Species* (Waterford Press, 1977). In the Pocket Naturalist series. *Animal Tracks and Signs of North America* by Richard P. Smith (Stackpole Books, 1991). *Familiar Animal Tracks* by John Farrand (Knopf, 1993). In the Audubon Society's Pocket Guides series.

Secrets of a Wildlife Watcher, A Beginner's Field Guide by Jim Arnosky (Beech Tree Books, 1991), is an attractive, well-illustrated introductory book. It guides readers through observing and stalking, and shows common tracks.

Tom Brown's Field Guide to Nature Observation and Tracking, by Tom Brown, Jr. and Brandt Morgan (Berkeley Books, 1983), is an extensive resource.

ANIMAL TRACKS and SIGNS Of North America
RECOGNIZE & INTERPRET WILDLIFE CLUES
Richard P. Smith

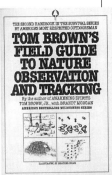

SECRETS OF A WILDLIFE WATCHER
A BEGINNER'S FIELD GUIDE
BY JIM ARNOSKY

THE SECOND HANDBOOK IN THE SURVIVAL SERIES BY AMERICA'S MOST RESPECTED OUTDOORSMAN
TOM BROWN'S FIELD GUIDE TO NATURE OBSERVATION AND TRACKING
By the author of AWAKENING SPIRITS
TOM BROWN, JR. with BRANDT MORGAN
AMERICA'S BESTSELLING WILDERNESS SERIES

ILLUSTRATED BY HEATHER BOLYN

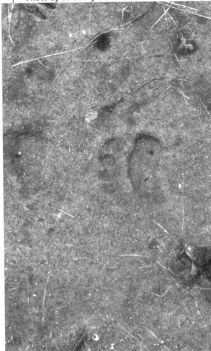

Bear tracks in the Tongass National Forest.

Human Predators

Most of the people you encounter on trails will be ordinary law-abiding human beings like you, out for a few days of recreation. In some areas, however, predators might emerge. Talking to rangers and the staff of local backpacking stores will help you discover the areas to avoid.

A common problem is car break-ins at trailheads. Again, get local advice. Certainly, don't leave anything of value visible in your car. If you know that cars parked in one area get vandalized, make arrangements to park in a driveway or garage miles away and get a ride to the trailhead.

If your car is empty, consider leaving it unlocked. On one trip we took, every car but ours had the driver's window smashed with a rock. We had left our car unlocked and returned to find no damage— just a five-pound rock sitting in the driver's seat.

If your car is damaged or things are stolen, take the time to report it. Only when criminal patterns emerge can law officers take action.

During the hunting season, be cautious about where you hike. Overzealous hunters might not distinguish between you and other prey. It's best to avoid hunting areas during the season. If you do venture forth, wear bright clothing.

The Weather

The weather is a central topic of every hiking trip, and predicting it is an art best learned from those with years of experience. But you can get a good idea of what might be about to happen by observing clouds and the wind's speed and direction. A pocket barometer is the piece of equipment most helpful in weather forecasting.

A pocket anemometer will give you an accurate reading of the wind speed, but you can also get a pretty good idea from the following table:

CONDITIONS	WINDSPEED (MPH)
Camp fire smoke drifts	1 - 3
Feel wind on your face, leaves rustle	4 - 7
Leaves and small twigs on trees move; time to stake the tent	8 - 12
Small branches sway, in dry areas, dust blows about	13 - 18
Small trees sway, waves break on lakes	19 - 24
Large branches move	25 - 31
Whole trees sway	32 - 38
Branches break off, hard to walk against	39 - 46

Now that you know the wind speed, a small thermometer will enable you to figure out the wind-chill factor. Use the thermometer-based temperature and look down the appropriate column to match the wind speed in the left hand column. Read the wind chill, or effective skin temperature, at the intersection of the column and row.

Knowing the wind-chill factor won't make you feel warmer, but it could give you bragging rights at the office.

WIND Speed (MPH)	TEMPERATURE (° F)							
	50	40	30	20	10	0	-10	-20
10	40	28	16	4	-9	-21	-33	-46
20	32	18	4	-10	-25	-39	-53	-69
30	28	13	-2	-18	-33	-48	-63	-79
40	26	10	-6	-21	-37	-53	-69	-85

BASIC METEOROLOGY

National Audubon Society Field Guide to North American Weather, by David M. Ludlum (Knopf, 1991), is a basic guide to meteorology.

Northwest Mountain Weather: Understanding and Forecasting for the Backcountry User, by Jeff Renner (The Mountaineers, 1992), covers backpacking in the Northwest.

The Sierra Club Book of Weatherwisdom, by Vicki McVey (The Sierra Club, 1991), is more basic and meant for kids, although much of the information is useful for adults, too. It's now out of print but might be available from libraries or used book stores.

DEALING WITH BAD WEATHER

And we mean really bad weather! In *Harsh Weather Camping in the 90s* (Mensha Ridge Press, 1997), Sam Curtis suggests ways to cope in conditions we hope you never encounter. He covers staying warm and dry, staying cool, and building a fire.

Farthest North by Fridtjof Nansen (Harper & Brothers, 1897)

First Footsteps in East Africa, or, an Exploration of Harar by Richard Francis Burton (Dover Publications, 1987)

From Pittsburgh to the Rocky Mountains: Major Stephen Long's Expedition, 1819–1820 edited by Maxine Benson (Fulcrum Publications, 1988)

NORTH TO THE NIGHT
A Year in the Arctic Ice

ALVAH SIMON

North to the Night by Alvah Simon (International Marine, 1999)

North to the Pole by Will Steger and Paul Schurke (Ivy Books, 1988)

Personal Narrative of Travels to the Equinoctial Regions of the New Continent During the Years 1799–1824 by Alexander Von

Tales of Great Adventures

Feeling in need of some inspiration? People have walked the globe in the harshest of conditions to explore and learn. Here are the accounts of some of the more notable foot-slogging explorers. Some of these are recent reprints; others are the original editions which you can find in out-of-print bookstores and libraries.

Burton: Snow upon the Desert by Frank McLynn (John Murray, 1991)

Douglas of the Forests: The North American Journals of David Douglas by David Douglas (University of Washington Press, 1980)

of Jedediah S. Smith: His Personal Account of the Journey to California, 1826-1827** by Jedediah Strong Smith, edited by George R. Brooks (University of Nebraska, 1989)

The Expeditions of Zebulon Montgomery Pike by Zebulon Montgomery Pike, edited by Elliott Coues (Dover Publications, 1987)

The Home of the Blizzard: The Story of the Australian Antarctic Expedition, 1911–1914 by Douglas Mawson (Wakefield Press, 1968)

The Journals of Lewis and Clark by Meriwether Lewis and William Clark, edited by Bernard DeVoto (Houghton Mifflin, 1997)

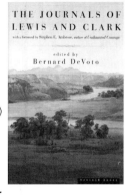

The South Pole: An Account of the Norwegian Antarctic Expedition in the Fram, 1910–1912 by Roald Amundsen (John Murray, 1912). Reprinted recently and published by Barnes & Noble.

The Worst Journey in the World by Apsley Cherry-Garrard (Carroll & Graf, 1997)

Through the Brazilian Wilderness by Theodore Roosevelt (Stackpole Books, 1994)

Through the Dark Continent by Henry M. Stanley (Dover Publications, 1988)

Women of the Four Winds: The Adventures of Four of America's First Women Explorers by Elizabeth Fagg Olds (Houghton Mifflin, 1985)

Humboldt, translated by Jason Wilson (Penguin USA, 1996)

Lewis and Clark: Partners in Discovery by John Bakeless (Dover Publications, 1996)

My First Summer in the Sierra by John Muir (Penguin USA, 1997)

On Top of the World: Five Women

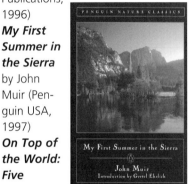

Explorers in Tibet by Luree Miller (The Mountaineers, 1985)

Scott's Last Expedition: The Journals by Robert Falcon Scott (Carroll & Graf, 1996)

Southwest Expedition

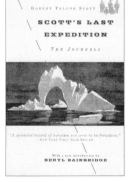

CHAPTER 2

Planning Ahead

> The tendency nowadays to wander in wilderness is delightful to see.
> Thousands of tired, nerve-shaken, over-civilized people are beginning
> to find out that going to the mountains is going home; that wildness
> is a necessity; and that mountain parks and reservations are useful
> not only as fountains of timber and irrigating rivers,
> but as fountains of life.
>
> —John Muir, *John Muir In His Own Words*, compiled by Peter Browning

Muir was right. It's a delight to see so many people heading to the hills. But it means that you might require reservations for campsites, and it also means that you will have to plan the trip well. To plan properly, you need to know the physical ability of the people in your group, and how able they are to deal with the difficulties of the trail. In both cases, experience provides the best guide, but if you have not yet gained that experience, the hints and tips in this chapter will help you with your planning.

Rules of Thumb

Here are some well-established rules of thumb to work from:

• **Flat ground.** Hikers can cover about three miles an hour on flat and easy ground. You might get four miles, but unless you're in great shape, you won't be able to keep up that pace all day.

Photo by Ed Sobey

• **Ascending trails.** Going uphill slows your pace. For every 1,000 feet of elevation gain, plan on taking an additional 30 minutes. So a three-mile hike that puts you on top of a ridge 1,000 feet above the trail head would take an hour and a half. If the trail is especially steep in places, it might take longer.

• **Descending trails.** Unfortunately, you don't gain time going downhill. In steep terrain or on trails with poor footing, descending can take nearly as long as ascending.

Adjust the Formula

To develop a feel for your hiking speed, use the formula above to estimate how long a particular hike should take. When you do the hike, compare actual progress with planned progress, and see how the terrain changes your speed. On your next hike, you can adjust the formula based on your experience.

How far you travel each day depends on your pace and how many hours a day you hike. Once again, experience is the best guide. Some groups like to rise at dawn, eat a fast breakfast, and get going. But sometimes that level of enthusiasm doesn't last. Ask yourself if they'll continue to jump out of their tents after three or four days on the trail? Does everyone have the energy to keep going until late in the afternoon? Dragging people along, beyond their comfort zones, is a quick way to destroy their zest for hiking.

Know When to Stop

When should you stop on the trail? For a start you should rest for at least five minutes every hour. Take off your pack, sit down, get a drink, and enjoy the scenery.

Another time to stop is after you've been going a little while on a chilly morning. You probably put on too many clothes. Stop when

you feel yourself about to sweat; you want to keep your clothes dry and your precious body fluids where they belong.

Stop when you're feeling tired. If you or your partner start to stumble or make missteps, it's time to take a break.

When you notice a hot spot developing on your foot (warning of a blister-to-be), take a break and cover the hot spot with tape or moleskin.

Catching Blisters

If you're leading less experienced hikers, stop after the initial 10 minutes of a hike and ask everyone to check how their feet are doing. Catching blisters early can save pain and time later.

If your group is starting to get spread out, stop, wait for the slower members catch up, and let them have a few minutes' rest before starting again. During the break, readjust packs by shifting weight from the slower hikers to the faster ones. Then have

It's hard to make yourself stop to look at a sore spot on your foot, but if you wait, you'll probably end up with a fat blister.

There are many cures for blisters, but the first and most important step is to cover it with a plaster, moleskin, or micropore tape to prevent infection. Opinions differ about lancing the blister before you cover it. If you don't and you keep on walking, you'll usually experience pain from the build-up of fluid. Then you'll have to lance it anyhow.

Part of the secret of having a good rest stop is not to stop for too long. You want to be up and on your feet again before your muscles cool and stiffen, which they will do after 15 or 20 minutes, making it even harder to get going again.

Your hiking pace and the length of your rest stops are directly related. If people are exhausted by the pace, they will want to rest longer. Try a slower pace with shorter rest breaks. For steep sections, use the "rest step." Place one foot uphill, take a breath, transfer weight to the uphill foot and pull the other leg forward. Hikers using this slow and steady pace will out-distance others of equal fitness who race ahead and then find they to have to sit and rest.

Photo by Burt Kornegay, Slickrock Expeditions.

the slower ones lead the way so they set the pace. This might frustrate the faster hikers and they might charge off to pass those ahead; if so, break into two groups and agree on places up the trail where you'll rejoin.

Graphing Your Route

Before setting out, collect all the information you can about your route. This will help you estimate where you can camp each night and how many days you need to hike the trail. Highlight your route on topographic maps with a colored marking pen. See how many streams your trail crosses and how much climbing is required; both will reduce your speed.

Can you locate good camping spots? On some hikes, you can camp anywhere along the route. On others, you might have only a few choices and therefore need to plan where you will spend each night. The spacing of campsites might dictate days of long walks or short walks.

Create a Profile

To get a better understanding of the terrain, make a slope profile of the route. Write the elevations of the trail every quarter mile. Prick off the distance with dividers, or mark a piece of paper with quarter-mile marks from the map scale. At each quarter mile, read the elevation and write it down in a column. Then, make a chart on a piece of graph

MAPS AND BROCHURES

T I P

Most states and many countries provide free travel information, including road maps, on request. Many
states have brochures specifically for
hiking or backpacking. See the listings under each state for phone numbers to call for travel information.

paper or lined paper. Show the distance along the trail in quarter-mile
increments along the bottom of the
paper, and mark elevation along
the left edge. Plot the data points
and connect them.

This illustration shows the slope
profile for a four-day hike in the
High Sierra, starting and ending at
Lake Thomas Edison. An inexperi-
enced hiker might not be impressed
by tracing this route on an ordinary
topographic map, but looking at
the rugged slope profile should
bring it alive. The profile helps you
plan for emergencies. It also shows
you where you can camp and how
much time you need for the hike.

Build Endurance

You can cover more distance on
a one-day trip or a weekend trip,
than you can sustain daily over
longer periods. For trips longer
than a few days, you will want to
include either rest days or less
strenuous days. If you are planning
a long trip, build your endurance
with several shorter hikes earlier in
the season. See the section on
Keeping Fit, page 10.

Planning with the Internet

If you have access to the Internet
you can find free information on
many of the major parks, national
forests, and other backpacking
locations. Try these sources:

GORP stands for the Great Outdoor Recreation Pages. Among
other information, it lists parks and
how to get additional information:
www.gorp.com

The Forest Service's home page
provides information on publications, maps, and a state-by-state
listing of national forests:
www.fs.fed.us

The U.S. Geological Survey gives
information on ordering maps, and
aerial and satellite photographs:
www.usgs.gov

The National Park Service's page
is rich with information on reservations, national park fees and more.
Many of the parks have their own
web pages, which you can access
through the NPS's home page:
www.nps.gov

**The U.S. Fish and Wildlife Ser-
vice:** www.fws.gov

Bureau of Land Management:
www.blm.com

AdventureZine has links and
information on places to go to and
equipment to use:
www.4x44u.com/pub/k2/
adventurezine/adventur.htm

Peak to Peak features travel
and wilderness resources:
home.earthlink.net/%7Eswfry/
pk2pk/p2p.html

**Peakware World Mountain
Encyclopedia** profiles nearly 400
peaks and 150 mountain ranges
worldwide: www.peakware.com

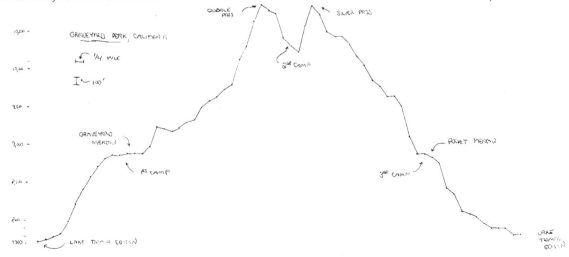

This is the slope profile for a four-day hike in the High Sierra, starting and ending at Lake Thomas Edison.

Canada's provincial governments (see Chapters 5, 7, 9, 11, 13, 15, 17, 19, and 21 for contact information) and Parks Canada (819-997-0055; parkscanada.pch.gc.ca) are great sources of free information about backpacking.

A Backpackers' Page gives general information: www.dreamscape.com/ matkoski/backpacker
Escaping to Nature: A Cyberspace Guide to Hiking. The name says it all: //outdoorphoto.com/ hiking/

Bookstores Online

We like local bookstores. Especially high on our list are bookstores with a strong inventory of outdoor or regional titles; even better are regional outdoor titles. The first place to consult for a hiking or backpacking book is your local bookstore or local outfitter.

Internet bookstores are convenient—not as much fun, but convenient. Here are some virtual bookstores you might find useful:

Adventurous Traveler Bookstore publishes a catalog and is a good place to look for guide books and books by explorers. Contact: (800) 282-3963; www. AdventurousTraveler.com
Amazon.com is the granddaddy of the Internet bookstores. They claim to have over two million titles. Using their advanced search engine, you can quickly find the book you want. Once your account is established, buying a book is a breeze. Contact: www.amazon.com
Pete & Ed Books has a great collection of hiking guide books for many parts of the country. You can easily find the book for the region you're interested in. They also have books on national parks, and on hikes with kids. Contact: www.a1.com/pebooks/books.htm
Other online bookstores to check out include **Barnes and Noble** (www.barnesandnoble.com), which has an "Outdoor Exploration—Hiking" section to scan, and **Mountain Zone** (800-644-5232; www.mountainzone.com/ toc.html), which sells a variety of equipment and books for outdoor sports.

Publishers

You can also order books directly from publishers. Here are the major publishers of books relating to backpacking and hiking:

Adirondack Mountain Club:
(800) 395-8080; www.adk.org
Burford Books: (800) 462-6420
Chessler Books: (800) 654-8502;
e-mail: chesslerbk@aol.com
Countryman Press:
(800) 233-4830; e-mail: Country manPress@wwnorton.com
Falcon: (800) 582-2665;
www.falconguide.com
Foghorn: (800) FOGHORN;
www.foghorn.com
Fulcrum Publishing:
(800) 992-2908;
www.fulcrum-books.com
Gibbs Smith Publisher:
(800) 748-5439;
www.Gibbs-Smith.com
ICS Books: (800) 541-7323;
www.icsbooks.com
Lyons Press: (212) 620-9580; www.justgoodbooks.com/lyons.html

Menasha Ridge Press:
(800) 247-9437;
www.menasharidge.com
Pruett Publishing:
(800) 247-8224
Ragged Mountain Press:
(800) 262-4729;
www.raggedmountainpress.com
Sasquatch Books:
(800) 775-0817;
www.sasquatchbooks.com

Sierra Club Books: (800) 935-1056;
www.sierraclub.org/books
Stackpole Books: (800) 732-3669;
www.stackpole.com

FREE CATALOGS

Most publishers print catalogs of their books. By calling their toll-free number you can request a copy of their current catalog.

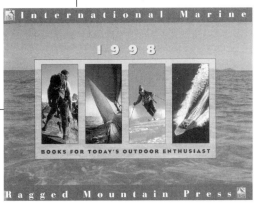

International Marine

1998

BOOKS FOR TODAY'S OUTDOOR ENTHUSIAST

Ragged Mountain Press

OUT-OF-PRINT BOOKS

When you need to find books that are out of print, follow these suggestions:

First, your local library might be able to locate a copy. If it's not in their stock, they might be able to get it through an inter-library loan.

Second, some bookstores might be able to find a copy for you. On the web, Amazon.com will conduct a search. Here are others to try:

- **Adventurous Traveler Bookstore:** (800) 282-3963; www.AdventurousTraveler.com
- **Northern Books:** (416) 531-8873
- **Wilderness Collection:** (616) 624-4410

The Mountaineers: (206) 223-6303; www.mountaineers.org
Wasatch Books: (801) 278-5826
Wilderness Press: (800) 443-7227; www.wildernesspress.com

Seeing It in Advance

If you'd like to see what a particular hiking area looks like before you get there, check out the **Trailside** series of videotapes. Produced for broadcast by Capital Cities/ABC, these tapes show many of the most popular hiking regions in the country. While the *Trailside* videos don't provide the details you need to plan a trip, they give you a feel for the type of hiking you're likely to encounter. Check your TV listings to see if the series is broadcast in your area, or check your local library for the tapes.

Check out the PBS series **Anyplace Wild**, produced in conjunction with *Backpacker* magazine. You can get information on shows by logging on to the *Backpacker* website at www.bpbasecamp.com or the PBS website at www.pbs.org

Adventurous Traveler Bookstore carries a large collection of hiking guide videotapes made by several different producers. Call (800) 282-3963 or order online at www.AdventurousTraveler.com

CD-ROMs

Another way to get a look at the trail you're considering is on CD-ROM.

The Cordillera Group produces CDs with photographs, video shots, topographic maps, plant life, animal life, and other travel information. To get a list of their products, call (303) 670-3848, or go online at www.corgroup.com

Cambrix Publishing, (800) 992-8781, produces *National Parks 3.0,* which includes driving directions, hikes to take, and information on permits.

For hiking in New England, check **TrailMaster.** This interactive software program was created through partnerships with the Appalachian Mountain Club, the Green Mountain Club, and the Connecticut Forest and Park Association. The program has hiking information and maps from six hiking guides published by New England's best-known hiking clubs, covering 1,000 trails and 1,000 peaks. You can search it for hikes appropriate to your interests and abilities. To order a copy, call (800 262-4455), or visit www.gtrek.com

Photos courtesy of The Cordillera Group

Watch from a Tower

Enjoy a unique experience by spending a night or two in a Forest Service fire watchtower. Over the years, the Forest Service has torn down more than 1,200 lookouts in the Pacific Northwest, and hundreds more throughout the rest of the country. There are some 200 left standing, however, which you can reserve for $20 to $40 per night. Most are 12 feet square or 14 feet square, perched between 20 and 60 feet off the ground.

For more information, see **How to Rent a Fire Lookout in the Pacific Northwest** by Tom Foley and Tish Sheinfeld (Wilderness Press, 1996). The book provides information on how to reserve fire lookouts, what to bring, and how to get there. The authors provide information on the setting and history of the area you're in, and show pictures of each tower.

Rex Kamstra runs a website dedicated to fire lookouts: www.triax.com/ab7iz/lookout.htm. It includes information on lookouts in New York, Tennessee, Kentucky, Idaho, Oregon, California, New Zealand, and Australia.

Using Guides

Glenn Kilgore, owner of Backcountry Odyssey outfitter and guide, suggests you ask four questions if you're planning to hire a guide or outfitter:

1. Ask if the guide is a member of the state guides' and outfitters' association. With two exceptions, every state has an association, and most guide services should belong to it and subscribe to its ethics.

2. If a service isn't a member, find out why (they might have a good reason). Other indicators of a trustworthy organization are the length of time they've been in business,

Photo by Stanlynn Daugherty

and references from past customers. A service established over the years is not likely to have a trail

CHECK IN ADVANCE

TIP

If you're leading a group, check with everyone in advance to make sure they have the gear you think is essential. Don't wait until you arrive at the trailhead to discover someone doesn't have matches or a pocket knife.

of dissatisfied customers; it's expensive to have to run a business with new customers every season. When customers come back several times to the same outfitter, you know that the guide is meeting their expectations and needs. What the customers say about the business is probably the best indicator of quality.

3. Ask a prospective guide for a list of five customers and call at least three of them. But before you call, decide on your most important measures of quality. Do you care

about gourmet cooking, five-star hotels, seeing big game, or easy hiking? Make sure you ask the customers about whatever would make the trip a success or disaster for you. The final questions should be: "Will you use this service again?" And, if not: "Why not?"

4. Find out what's included in the price. Will all meals, ground transportation, and lodging be provided? Will someone on the trip be qualified in first aid? Are there additional charges such as local or airport taxes?

Finding Guides

To find a guide service, contact the trade association **America Outdoors,** whose mission is to maintain access to recreation spots and enhance outdoor adventures. America Outdoors will send you the current listing of their member outfitters. Most are oriented toward hunting and fishing, but many will take care of backpackers. Contact: (423) 558-3595; e-mail:infoacct@americaoutdoors .org; www.americaoutdoors.org

Backcountry Odysseys connects customers with guide services in 11 western states. Contact: (800) 309-5008; www.cruising-america.com/backcountry. You can also find guides through the state offices of tourism (see Chapters 5, 7, 9, 11, 13, 15, 17, 19, and 21 for contact information) or through the tour-guide associations listed on page 37.

Using Pack Animals

Nowhere is it written that a healthy backpacker can't employ pack animals. In fact, pack animals provide the only means to get into the real wilderness, unless you have days and days to walk there. You can hire a string of mules and horses along with a wrangler or two to carry your supplies in and leave you at a base camp. They can return days later to pick you up, or you can do the return trip yourself.

Pack Horses

These two books contain all you need to know about packing with horses:

Packin' In, by Smoke Elser and Bill Brown (Mountain Press, 1980), points out that packing should have died out years ago, but instead seems to be growing. The book covers how to

choose pack horses and mules, how to pack them, and how to care for them. It is well illustrated with black-and-white photographs. It is a bit dated, however.

Vacationing with Saddle & Packhorse, by Bill Merrill (Arco Publishing, 1976), is even older. It lists national forests where pack animals are used, and gives prices for animals and wranglers.

BACKCOUNTRY LLAMA

June • 98

The Bear

Hal Johnson

Looking back, I should have realized that something was terribly wrong.

Rhonda and I had decided to buy two more llamas to add to the four geldings we'd owned for three years. When I first brought them home, there was a fair amount of jousting for space between the "new" and "old" llamas, but nothing particularly worrisome.

After we'd had them for three weeks, I had to leave home on a work-related trip. By this time, it seemed that the space issues between them were largely ironed out.

However, when I got home, it was clear that something unusual had happened in the llama enclosure. The top wire along the fencing had loosened in several places, and several t-posts were bent outward. Curiously though, three or four posts were bent *inward*, and I felt utterly dumbfounded about how the llamas could have pulled the posts inward rather than pushing them out. (Did they have hidden thumbs or something?) After spending many hours with the llamas without once seeing them run up against the fence, I

Continued on page 2

In this issue

Editorial 3
Conditioning 6
Cud for Chewing 13
Llama Trekking video 17
Book Review 19
Little Llama That Could 21

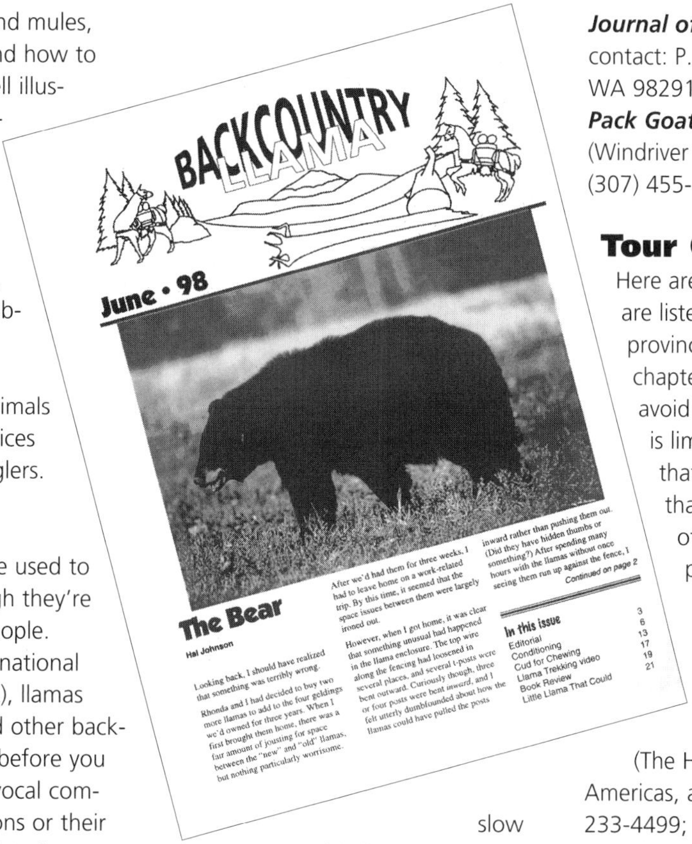

Pack Llamas

Increasingly, llamas are used to carry supplies, although they're never used to carry people. According to the International Llama Association (ILA), llamas often spot wildlife and other backcountry travelers well before you do. "They often give vocal comments on trail conditions or their opinions about when it's time to take a break," says the association, "and the way they negotiate obstacles with aplomb is a never-ending marvel." The ILA publishes a brochure entitled ***Packing with Llamas.*** You can order it by phone at (800) WHY-LAMA or by e-mailing intlllama@aol.com

There is even a bimonthly magazine called ***The Backcountry Llama.*** Contact the publishers at www.kalama.com/~llamapacker, or write them at 2857 Rose Valley Loop, Kelso, WA 98626.

Tom Landis, owner of Oregon Llamas, points out that llamas, like humans, have to get into shape. "You cannot simply take them out of the field after standing around all winter and expect them to perform," he says. "My llamas are slow and balky at the beginning of the summer, but after working several weeks they are in great shape and able to do prodigious amounts of work."

Tom quotes typical charges of $30 a day to rent a llama, plus $150 for transporting it to the trailhead and providing instruction on how to care for it. He recommends the book ***Packing with Llamas*** by Stanlynn Daugherty (Juniper Ridge Press).

Pack Goats

Pack goats are easier to use than llamas but harder to find. They are surefooted and able to carry 50 to 90 pounds. There are, however, only a few outfitters offering this service. For information about goat packers, subscribe to ***Goat Tracks: Journal of the Working Goat;*** contact: P.O. Box 447, Snohomish, WA 98291. Or order the book ***The Pack Goat*** by John Mionczynski (Windriver Pack Goats); contact: (307) 455-2410.

Tour Organizers

Here are the guide services that are listed separately by state, province, or country in later chapters of this book. To avoid duplication, this list is limited to organizations that offer services in more than one area. Their areas of operation are given in parentheses, followed by a telephone number and/or an internet and e-mail address.

Above the Clouds (The Himalayas, Europe, the Americas, and Madagascar): (800) 233-4499; www.gorp.com/abv-clds.htm

Adventures Unlimited (worldwide): (800) 567-6286; e-mail: advuntd@pathcom.com

American Wilderness Experience (Western U.S., Canada, Mexico, and South America): (800) 444-0099; e-mail: AWEDave@aol.com

Alaska Wilderness Journeys (worldwide): (800) 349-0064; www.alaska.net~akwildj/

Backcountry (worldwide): (800) 575-1540; www.webcom.com/bckcntry

Backroads (Europe, the Americas, Africa, New Zealand, and the Middle East): (800) GO-ACTIVE; www.backroads.com

Bahia Tours (Central America): (800) 443-0717; www.aventuras.com/bahia-tours

Photo by Stanlynn Daugherty

Llama packing.

Big Wild Adventures
(Western U.S.): (406) 821-3747
Butterfield & Robinson (Europe,
Africa, Asia, the Pacific, and South
America): (800) 678-1147;
www.butterfield.com
Camp 5 Expeditions
(the Himalayas and the Andes):
(800) 914-3834; www.camp5.com
Classic Adventures (North
America and Europe):
(800) 777-8090; e-mail:
classadv@frontiernet.net
Earthwatch (worldwide):
(800) 776-0188;
www.earthwatch.org
Ecosummer Expeditions (Canada
and Baja California):

(800) 465-8884
ExperiencePlus (Europe, Costa
Rica, and the U.S.):
(800) 685-4565; www.xplus.com
Getaway Adventures (California
and Hawaii): (800) 499-BIKE;
www.getawayadventures.com
Geographic Expeditions
(worldwide): (800) 777-8183;
e-mail: info@geoex.com
Himalayan Travel (the Himalayas,
Africa, Asia, Middle East, and
Central and South America):
(800) 225-2380
Journeys (Africa, Asia, South and
Central America, and the Pacific):
(800) 255-8735;
www.journeys-intl.com

KE Adventure Travel
(the Himalayas, Central
Asia, and South America):
(800) 497-9675;
 www.keadventure.com
Mountain Travel-Sobek (worldwide): (800) 227-2384;
www.mtsobek.com
Northstar (Alaska and Baja
California): (800) 258-8434; e-mail:
Northstar@AdventureTrip.com
Outer Edge Adventures (Australia, New Zealand, Borneo,
and Patagonia): (800) 322-5235;
www.outer-edge.com
Progressive Travels (Europe):
(800) 245-2229;
www.ProgressiveTravels.com

Illustration by Daisy dePuthod

Shott's Walks in the West
(Western U.S.): (719) 531-9577;
e-mail: Shottwitw@aol.com
Timberline Adventures (Western
U.S. and Canada): (800) 417-2453;
//timbertours.com/tours
Wilderness Travel (the Himalayas,
Asia, Africa, Europe, Latin America,
and the Pacific): (800) 368-2794;
www.wildernesstravel.com
Wild Horizons (Southwest U.S.):
(406) 821-3747
Willaard's Adventure Club
(Canada, U.S., South America,
and Antarctica): (705) 737-1881

Tours for Senior Hikers

Hiking is not just for young people.
For those over 50 who want to go
on guided treks with others their
own age, there is **Walking the
World.** This group offers a wide
assortment of hikes in the United
States and throughout the world.
Contact: (970) 225-0500; e-mail:
walktworld@aol.com

Another company catering to
senior hikers is **Senior World
Tours.** Contact: (888) 355-1686;
e-mail: zimhico@nwohio.com.

Clubs and Groups that Sponsor Outings

Most clubs that sponsor hikes are
local or state-wide, but here are
three national organizations that
organize hikes:

• **American Hiking Society:**
(703) 255-9304; www.orca.org

• **Appalachian Mountain Club:**
(617) 523-0655;
www.outdoors.com

• **Sierra Club:** (800) 477-2627;
www.sierraclub.org

3

Long-Distance American Trails

> The clearest way into the universe
>
> is through a forest wilderness.
>
> —John Muir,
>
> John Muir In His Own Words,
>
> compiled by Peter Browning

Many backpackers dream of taking months off to hike one of the major trail systems in the United States. The handful who make the trek come away with a lifetime experience to share with others.

The National Trails System

Some national trails are remnants of the routes taken by early settlers who traveled overland on foot, on horseback, or by wagon. The Oregon Trail, the Santa Fe Trail, and the Trail of Tears, among others, remind us of our exciting and sometimes tragic national heritage.

In 1921, the first interstate recreational trail, the Appalachian Trail, was conceived as a national preserve running parallel to the east coast. In 1968 Congress passed legislation to provide federal funding for the trail and to help establish a national system of trails.

Today the National Trails System consists of National Scenic Trails and National Historic Trails. Whereas the scenic trails are continuous, the historic trails comprise stand-alone segments.

Seventeen scenic and historic trails have been established so far, twelve of which are run by the National Park Service, four by the Forest Service, and one by the Bureau of Land Management.

The other category of trails, National Recreation Trails, are recognized by the federal government as part of the National Trails System but are managed by public and private agencies at all levels of government. They include nature trails, river routes, and historic tours.

The National Park Service's task is twofold: to administrate and coordinate existing national trails and to build new ones. To this end, the Park Service lends technical assistance to local, state, and private organizations working on river and trail corridor projects, including those involving abandoned railroad rights-of-way.

For more information on the National Trails System, contact the National Trails System Branch, National Park Service (782), P.O. Box 37127, Washington, DC 20013-7127; (202) 343-3780; www.nps.gov/htdocs1/pub_aff/naltrail.htm

The Park Service also has a Trails Office in Salt Lake City, Utah. Contact: (801) 539-4094.

More Factual Information

For free information on the National Trails System, log on to www.nps.gov/htdocs1/pub_aff/naltrail.htm.

For a first-class guide, read ***Trails Across America: Traveler's Guide to our National Scenic and Historic Trails*** by Arthur P.

Miller Jr. and Marjorie L. Miller (Fulcrum Publishing, 1996). It covers the history, location, and condition of the trails.

American Discovery Trail

This incomplete route is destined to become America's first coast-to-coast hiking, biking, and equestrian trail, but much work still

---

MILES PER DAY

On long trips, the typical hiker walks at an average speed of about 1.5 miles per hour and covers a distance of a little more than 13 miles.

---

needs to be done. It will be 6,356 miles long, winding through 14 national parks, 16 national forests, and thousands of historical and cultural sites. To get the latest information from the American Discovery Trail Society, contact (800) 663-2387; www.discoverytrail.org

Check out ***American Discovery Trail Explorer's Guide*** by Reese Lukei (Falcon Press, 1995).

JOHN MUIR

Probably no person has influenced our ideas on wilderness as much as John Muir. Born in Scotland in 1838, he emigrated to the United States with his family in 1849. Muir was raised under the stern guidance of his father and developed an unusually strict self-discipline of spirit and body. He thought nothing of taking off for an extended hike without any of the equipment or food that today we would consider absolutely necessary.

An eye injury changed his life. Upon recovery he turned his attention to the beauty of nature. His first quest was to walk from Indianapolis to the Gulf of Mexico, a distance of 1,000 miles. He followed that with a life of exploring and writing. Yosemite claimed Muir's spirit when he visited it in 1868, and he later spent six years there. His studies suggested to him that the valley was created by glaciation, a theory discredited at the time but later accepted. Later trips took him to Alaska, Europe, Asia, Africa, and the Arctic.

Muir published some 300 articles and 10 books and assumed leadership of the budding conservation movement. He is credited with convincing Congress to establish Yosemite and Sequoia National Parks and persuading President Theodore Roosevelt to conserve nearly 150 million acres of forest lands. In 1892 Muir and others formed the Sierra Club.

Appalachian National Scenic Trail

The Appalachian National Scenic Trail runs 2,159 miles along the crest of the Appalachian Mountains between Springer Mountain, Georgia, and Mount Katahdin, Maine. It is the brainchild of Benton MacKaye, who described his dream of a greenway in 1921.

Some 3 to 4 million people hike portions of the trail every year (a 94-percent increase in the 12 years between 1983 and 1995). More than 200 people walk the entire length each year, most starting early in the spring at the southern terminus and walking north as the weather warms up. The trail is administered by the National Park Service in Harpers Ferry, West Virginia, (304) 535-6278.

The **Appalachian Trail Conference,** a group of volunteer organizations, maintains the trail. Contact them at (304) 535-6331; e-mail: appalachiantrail@ charitiesusa.com

A series of a dozen books known as the **Appalachian Trail Conference Guidebooks** is published by Menasha Ridge Press. They give official descriptions of each section of the trail and include the locations of shelters, water, emergency contacts, directions, and maps.

More Factual Information

The Appalachian Trail Backpacker, by Victoria and Frank Logue (Appalachian Trail Conference, 1994), gives advice for planning the trip of your dreams. It covers what to take and what to expect along the way.

Edward Garvey's book **The New Appalachian Trail** (Menasha Ridge Press, 1997) relates his expe-

The Olympic Mountains. Photo by Ed Sobey

riences hiking the trail at age 75. Garvey also shares information on equipment and his own hiking philosophy.

For a naturalist's guide to the Appalachian Trail, try Leonard M. Adkins' *A Visitor's Companion to the Appalachian Trail* (Menasha Ridge Press, 1997).

For his book *Long-Distance Hiking: Lessons from the Appalachian Trail* (Ragged Mountain Press, 1998), Roland Mueser compiled information from interviews with AT through-hikers and combined it with his own experiences. He highlights hikers' favorites in such categories as boots, packs, clothing, places to stay along the way, and food on the trail.

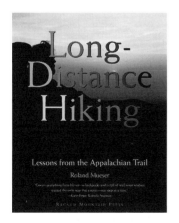

The Arizona Trail

This is another incomplete trail that exists today only in sections along its intended 750-mile total length. Dramatic changes in elevation mark this trail. Hikers can walk from the Sonoran Desert into alpine meadows in a surprisingly short distance. The trail is scheduled for completion in the year 2000, but you can already hike, bike, and ride horses on parts of it. For more information, call (602) 252-4794 or browse www.primenet.com/~aztrail

More Factual Information

On the Arizona Trail: A Guide for Hikers, Cyclists, and Equestrians, by Karen Tigbe

and Susan Moran (Pruett Publishing, 1997), leads readers through the completed sections of the trail and provides information on the history and ecology of the surrounding area.

Buckeye Trail

The Buckeye Trail, 1,200 miles long, is the longest continuous trail contained entirely in one state. Robert Folzenlogen states in his book *Hiking Ohio* (Willow Press, 1990):

"In northeastern Ohio [the trail] winds past glacial lakes, bogs and stands of hemlock. In southeastern Ohio it negotiates the forested hills, cool streams and rock-walled gorges of the Appalachian

Plateau. Heading west, the trail enters the fertile farmlands of Ohio's till plains and snakes past several of our larger reservoirs. Angling northward, the Buckeye Trail follows the abandoned towpath of the Miami-Erie Canal and then turns eastward, crossing through the Lake Plains of northern Ohio."

More Factual Information

Contact the **Buckeye Trail Association,** Box 254, Worthington, Ohio 43085, (419) 447-5464, for information and maps.

Continental Divide National Scenic Trail

On paper, the projected Continental Divide Trail is magnificent, stretching 3,200 miles from Canada to Mexico. The first 800-mile stretch is already in use, from Canada to Yellowstone National Park.

Despite its incomplete state, this national trail is acknowledged to be the most rugged of all the long-distance trails.

More Factual Information

Contact the **Continental Divide Trail Society** at (410) 235-9610; e-mail: cdtsociety@aol.com
Contact the **Continental Divide Trail Alliance** at (303) 838-3760; www.CDTrail.org
Colorado's Continental Divide Trail: The Official Guide, by Tom Lorang Jones (Westcliffe, 1997), is

rich with color photographs, trail information, and maps.

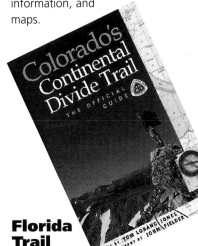

Florida Trail

If you haven't considered Florida a state for hiking, investigate the Florida Trail. It's 950 miles long already and will grow to 1,300 miles when it's completed. It will connect the Big Cypress National Preserve on the western side of South Florida to the Gulf Islands National Seashore in the western panhandle.

BE BREEZY

TIP

During insect season, look for campsites that have a steady breeze. Don't camp in sheltered areas where the bugs will be most fierce.

Although anyone can use sections of the trail that cross public land, some private sections are open only to members of the Florida Trail Association. But membership is open to anyone who pays dues, which are $25 for individuals and $30 for families. Send checks, payable to the Florida Trail

Association, to FTA, P.O. Box 13708, Gainesville, Florida 32604.

Great-grandmother Joan Hobson (66) finished the trail early in 1997. "The trip was long, 93 days, and covered about 1,100 miles," she said. "I realized when I finished that if I had been walking the Appalachian Trail I would have been halfway to Maine." Her trek was totally inside the borders of Florida, however.

More Factual Information

Contact the **Florida Trail Association** at (904) 378-8823. The U.S. Forest Service administers sections of the trail; contact (904) 942-9305.

Great Western Trail

Still in the early stages, this trail is not yet accepting hikers. Organizers envision the Great Western Trail running through Arizona, New Mexico, Utah, Montana, and Idaho. To get the most recent information, contact the Great Western Trail Association, P.O. Box 1428, Provo, Utah 84602.

Ice Age National Scenic Trail

In Wisconsin, a band of moraine hills left by retreating glaciers zig-zags across the state for 1,000 miles from Lake Michigan to the Saint Croix River. A trail along these hills was conceived by Ray Zillmer in the 1950s and publicized by Representative Henry Reuss in his book *On the Trail of the Ice Age* (Ice Age Park and Trail Foundation, 1990).

Today, with help from the state of Wisconsin and the Ice Age Park and Trail Foundation, almost half the trail is open to the public, forming part of the National Park Service's National Scenic and Historic Trail System. Sections of the Ice Age Trail are popular for marathons, ski races, and ultra-running.

More Factual Information

You can contact the **Ice Age Park & Trail Foundation** at (800) 227-0046 or www.execpc.com/~iat/ Call the **National Park Service** office in Madison, Wisconsin, at (608) 264-5610.

Iditarod National Historic Trail

Most North American trails are hiked in summer, after snow and

The Ice Age National Scenic Trail. Photo by Tom Bean

ice have retreated. But in Alaska, things are different. To hike the Iditarod Trail, you need to go in winter, after the rivers have frozen. Warmer seasons make rivers and tundra impassable for walkers.

"The Iditarod is a series of trails starting in Seward and stretching 2,300 miles officially ending in Nome. The historic trails were used by gold prospectors during the gold rush. Hiking is only possible during the winter when the tundra is passable and rivers frozen. The trail is the site for the annual 1,150-mile Iditarod Sled-Dog Race from Anchorage to Nome, which commemorates the struggle to get diphtheria serum to Nome during an epidemic."

More Factual Information

For more information on the Trail, contact the **Bureau of Land Management,** (907) 287-1248; or the Iditarod Trail Committee in Wasilla, Alaska, (907) 376-5155.

Natchez Trace National Scenic Trail

The Natchez Trace was the return route traders used after floating their goods on flat boats from Nashville, Tennessee, to Natchez, Mississippi. The route was designated a National Parkway in 1938 and today includes the Natchez Trace National Scenic Trail. Only a portion of the designated 450 miles of trails has been completed.

More Factual Information

The trail is administered by the **National Park Service** in

Olympic National Park. Photo by Ed Sobey

Tupelo, Mississippi. Call (601) 842-1572. Contact the **Natchez Trace Trail Conference** at (601) 680-4016.

North Country National Scenic Trail

This enormous trail could eventually extend as far as 4,000 miles from the Adirondack Mountains in New York to the Missouri River in North Dakota. About half of it is open already, and the National Park Service is working with several citizens' groups and local governments to develop it.

More Factual Information

Contact the **North Country Trail Association** at (616) 454-5506, or the **National Park Service** office in Madison, Wisconsin, at (608) 264-5610.

Ouachita National Recreation Trail

Stretching 225 miles from Talimena State Park in Oklahoma to Pinnacle Mountain State Park in Arkansas, this trail is managed by the U.S. Forest Service, (501) 321-5202. The trail ranges in elevation from 600 feet to 2,600 feet and has many access points.

Ernst Wilderness publishes **The Ouachita Trail Guide** by Tim Ernst, available at bookstores and camping stores or by calling (800) 838-HIKE.

Pacific Crest National Scenic Trail

The Pacific Crest Trail is the West Coast version of the Appalachian Trail, resplendent with snow-capped ridges and mountain passes as high as 13,200 feet. It follows the Sierra Nevada and the Cascades from Canada to Mexico.

After Clinton C. Clarke proposed the trail in 1932, both the Forest Service and the National Park Service embraced the idea. Their support was essential, since

80 percent of the trail crosses public lands. The Civilian Conservation Corps began work on the trail, and in 1942 Clarke proclaimed the trail complete. In fact, however, years of finishing work lay ahead.

The trail is tough on hikers and equipment; some through-hikers wear out four pairs of boots on the trip. In its 2,638 miles it takes backpackers through 25 national forests and seven national parks including Yosemite, Rainier, and Crater Lake. For more information or to help support the trail, contact the Pacific Crest Trail Association at (888) 728-7245; www.gorp.com/pcta

More Factual Information

The Pacific Crest Trail, by Jeffrey P. Schaffer and Andy Setters (Wilderness Press), is a two-volume guide to the Pacific Crest Trail with topographic maps and trail information. Wilderness Press periodically updates the book. *Volume 1* covers California; *Volume 2* covers Oregon and Washington.

Ray Jardine wrote the companion book **The Pacific Crest Trail Hiker's Handbook** (Wilderness Press, 1996), which prepares hikers for the trek. His book guides readers not along the trail but through the outfitter's store to purchase the right equipment. Here's lots of advice from someone who has hiked the trail twice.

WHERE WERE YOU?

Do you remember where you were on May 18, 1980? If you were living anywhere in the Northwest you probably remember that day. For the first time in nearly 60 years, a volcano in the lower 48 states erupted, killing 57 people and blowing the top 1,000 feet off Mount St. Helens.

Now you can hike through the new Mount St. Helens National Volcanic Monument. For a guide to the area, see **Mount St. Helens: Pathways to Discovery** by David Sheesholtz (A Plus Images, 1993).

Mount St. Helens: A Changing Landscape by Chuck Williams (Graphic Arts Center Publishing Company, 1980) is a coffee table book showing historic and modern photographs of the mountain and surrounding areas. An awesome series of photos shows the initial eruption blowing half a cubic mile of mountain into the sky.

Pacific Northwest Trail

The plan for the Pacific Northwest Trail is to connect the Continental Divide to the Pacific Ocean, thereby tying together other major trail systems. The trail will cross Montana, Idaho, and Washington. To check on its progress, visit the website at www.pnt.org or call (360) 424-0407.

BY ANY OTHER NAME

What do you call a mountain? Here are some of the alternative names we've found:

Mount, hill, peak, knob, bald, mesa, butte, point, azimuth, mound, brae, fell, knoll, hummock, picacho, hump, pike, and *summit.*

Potomac Heritage National Scenic Trail

Sections of the history-rich, 700-mile-long Potomac Heritage Trail are already open, including 184 miles of towpath along the Chesapeake and Ohio Canal. The National Park Service is coordinating efforts to build the trail. Contact: (202) 819-7027.

The Sierra High Route

This trail has 195 miles of high-elevation, sub-alpine backpacking through Kings Canyon and Yosemite National Parks with long ascents and spectacular views. Contact the parks for more information (see page 57) See also Steve Roper's book *Sierra High Route* (The Mountaineers, 1997).

BOB MARSHALL

One million acres of wilderness were named in honor of one of this country's most effective conservationists, Bob Marshall.

In his book *A Wilderness Original: The Life of Bob Marshall* (The Mountaineers, 1986) author James M. Grove tells how Marshall came from a family of conservationists. "His father helped create the Adirondack Park. Bob was educated at the best schools in the East, and received a Ph.D. in plant physiology. He conducted research for three years on tree growth in Montana. He was a prodigious hiker, thinking nothing of hiking 35 miles a day, sometimes in tennis shoes.

"He accepted appointments from the Secretary of the Interior, Harold Ickes, and became a point man for preserving wilderness areas. In 1935, Marshall and several others created the Wilderness Society. He would have liked to accept the position of President of the Society, but passed it up when Ickes thought it would be a conflict of interest with his government job.

"Nonetheless, he was the power and energy behind the society and was its first big contributor. He died well before his time, and, in 1940, the Secretary of Agriculture designated a wilderness area in the Flathead and Lewis and Clark National Forests in Montana as the Bob Marshall Wilderness Area.

"In 1935, Marshall wrote to Secretary Ickes: '. . . the danger to primitive outdoor conditions has never been so great as at the present moment.' Marshall fought to make conditions better."

High Onions, Olympic National Park. Photo by Ed Sobey

CHAPTER 4

Hiking Abroad

I only wanted my senses to be passionately alive,

and my imagination fearlessly far-reaching. And instead,

I felt I was sinking into a slough of banality. Adventure! Adventure!

That was the escape; that was the remedy.

—Richard Halliburton, The Glorious Adventure

If you're considering backpacking in countries where you're not sure of the political climate or the health risks, you can get up-to-date information from the U.S. federal government. For health questions, contact the **Centers for Disease Control's International Travelers' Hotline** at (404) 332-4559, or consult their website at www.cdc.gov/travel/travel.html

You should also check with your physician on what medicines to take and what medical dangers lurk in the countries you're going to visit. And check out Ellen Dudley's *The Savvy Adventure Traveler: What to Know Before You Go* (Ragged Mountain Press, 1999); the author includes her own hard-won tips about preparing for travel abroad.

Avoiding Problems

Water is often the biggest problem when traveling in developing countries. Locals might drink the stuff and develop a tolerance, but strangers can become violently ill. The general rules are: Don't drink the water unless you're sure it's safe, and don't eat fruit or vegetables without peeling them.

The best knowledge of a region comes from people who have visited it recently. Check with local outfitters to see if they know of someone who has traveled where you intend to go. Also ask them about local customs you should observe.

Make sure you have medical insurance that specifically covers travel in a foreign country; several companies provide medical insurance and assistance for travelers. Your travel agent can help you find one.

You can inquire about a country's political climate by contacting the U.S. State Department's **Citizens' Emergency Center** at (202) 647-5225. The official U.S. State Department **Travel Warnings and Consular Information Sheets** provide information on the Internet at
//travel.state.gov/travel_warnings.html

Note that in the following regional information, a telephone number beginning with 011 is an overseas long-distance call.

Mexico
Government Resources
Mexican Ministry of Tourism:
//mexico-travel.com

Guides and Outfitters

Baja Expeditions:
(800) 843-6967; e-mail:
travel@bajaex.com
Expediciones Mexico Verde:
(011) 52-36411005
OM Sundance (Copper Canyon):
(907) 479-8203; e-mail:
wildakmx@polarnet.com
Remarkable Journeys (Copper Canyon): (800) 856-1993;
www.remjourneys.com
TrekAmerica: (800) 221-0596;
www.trekamerica.com

THREE FOR HELP

An international distress signal is three fires. Three of anything attracts attention in the wilderness.

Costa Rica
Government Resources
Costa Rica Tourist Board:
(800) 343-6332,
www.tourism-costarica.com

Guides and Outfitters

Adventuras Naturales:
(800) 514-0411;
www.toenjoynature.com
Coast to Coast: (800) 747-2833;
www.ctocadventures.com

Costa Rica Experts: (800) 827-9046; www.gorp.com/crexpert
Rios Tropicales: (011) 506-233-6455; www.riostro.com

Guatemala
Government Resources
Guatemala Tourism Commission: (800) 742-4529; www.infovia.com.gt/inguat

Guides and Outfitters

Guatemala Maya Expeditions: (011) 502-363-4965; www.nortropic.com/areaverde

South America
The South American Explorers' Club (SAEC) provides advice and information for travel in South America. The stated mission of the non-profit club is "to collect and make available information about South and Central America's peoples, cultures, geography, flora and fauna."

Supported almost entirely through the contributions of its members, the SAEC aids educational and scientific projects, sponsors expeditions, promotes community service organizations, and stimulates greater interest in, and appreciation of, Latin America. They have clubhouses in Lima, Peru; Quito, Ecuador; and Ithaca, New York (607) 277-0488. Their website, www.samexplo.org, includes information on each country, including exchange rates, travel advisories, and weather. You can join the club for a modest fee.

Hiking in Costa Rica.

Photo by Ed Sobey

Guides and Tour Operators

Condor Expeditions: (800) 729-1262
Explore Bolivia: (914) 782-0080
International Expeditions: (800) 633-4734; www.ietravel.com/intexp
Southwind Adventures: (800) 377-9463

Europe
Government Resources
Austrian Tourist Office: www.anto.com
British Tourist Authority: www.visitbritain.com

Karwendel, Austria's largest nature reserve: www.xs4all.nl/~rvlaam
Northern Ireland Tourist Board hiking pages: www.interknowledge.com/northern-ireland/ukiwalk1.htm
Switzerland Tourist Office: www.schweizferien.ch/shadwelcome.html

Guides and Outfitters

Butterfield & Robinson: (800) 678-1147; www.butterfield.com
CBT Tours: (800) 736-BIKE
Ciclismo Classico: (800) 866-7314
European Walking Tours: (800) 231-8448; e-mail: EWTWALK@aol.com

Europeds: (800) 321-9552;
www.eurobike.com
Eurotrip: www.eurotrip.com
Spanish Specialists:
(800) 938-9311
World Adventures:
(800) 225-2380

EUROPE'S TRAILS

If you hike in Europe, you'll find a well-established and well-maintained network of trails with plenty of mountain lodges that provide meals and beds.

This makes long-distance walking possible with very light loads in the Alps, the Pyrenees and the mountains of Scandinavia.

Other information
European Ramblers Association:
www.gorp.com/gorp/activity/
Europe/ERA.htm; e-mail:
dt.wanderverband@t-online.de
Hiking information about Sweden's Lapland:
www.utsidan.se/areas/lappland
Slarti's web server for Ireland:
//slarti.ucd.ie/maps/ireland.html

South Africa
Government Resources
National Hiking Way Board:
27 (012) 299-2632

Guides and Outfitters

Africa Dot Com
lists links to trail sites:
www.ecoafrica.com/hike&cyc/
hikebike.htm
African Adventure:
(800) WARTHOGG; e-mail:
warthogs@charleston.net

Other Information
Hiking in South Africa:
www.cs.uct.ac.za/~iwebb/
hikelinks.html
Trail descriptions:
www.ecoafrica.com/trailwkr/
trailwca.htm

Kenya
Guides and Outfitters

Kenyan Association of Tour Operators: www.gorp.com/kato

Australia
Guides and Outfitters

Pacific Exploration:
(805) 687-7282
Southglen Llamas
(llama outfitters):
(619) 298-8617

New Zealand
Government Resources
New Zealand Tourism Board:
(800) 888-5494

Guides and Outfitters

New Zealand Action-Adventure:
(800) 411-5724
New Zealand Nature Safaris:
e-mail: nzns@globe.co.nz
New Zealand Travelers:
(800) 362-2718
Outland Adventures:
(800) 411-5724; e-mail:
outland@bga.com
Trek New Zealand:
(800) 688-9709

Worldwise Travel Services:
(310) 829-5334

The Himalayas
Guides and Outfitters

Camp 5 Expeditions:
(800) 914-3834;
e-mail: camp5@softsolutions.com
Himalayan High Treks:
(800) 455-8735
Himalayan Travel:
(800) 225-2380
Himalayan Travel & Treasures:
(800) 223-1813;
www.instantweb.com/p/peterowens
Snow Lion Expeditions:
(800) 525-TREK

HIKING WITH PORTERS

If you ever reach the hiker's dream destination, the Himalayas, you'll find porters usually accompany treks there, as they do in parts of Africa.

Himalayan porters usually number two for small groups, but armies of 40 porters often carry gear for large, organized groups.

Photo by Ed Sobey

Hiking Information by Region:

(BRITISH COLUMBIA, CALIFORNIA, HAWAII, OREGON, AND WASHINGTON)

Mount Jefferson, Oregon. Photo by Ed Sobey

For the purposes of this catalog, American states and Canadian provinces are listed together under broad geographical regions. More information about Canada in general is, however, available from two national clubs:

• **Canada Adventure Guide:** (800) 577-2266

• **The Alpine Club of Canada:** (403) 678-3200

Details regarding Canada's national parks are published on the **Parks Canada** website: //parkscanada.pch.gc.ca/parks/alphape.htm

British Columbia
Highest point: Fairweather Mountain, 15,300 feet.

West Coast Trail—Vancouver Island
Stunning color photographs by David Nunuk showcase

Hiking on the Edge: Canada's West Coast Trail by Ian Gill (Raincoast Books, 1995). How can a 47-mile, maintained trail with an elevation gain of only 100 feet above sea level be described as "grueling?" We're not sure, but the photographs beckon us to find out. Only 8,000 others will give it a try this year. To book a trail reservation, call (800) 663-6000, but check out the book to learn how to plan your transportation.

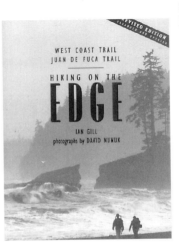

The Pacific Coast and Hawaii

Have ever you stood where the silences brood,

And vast the horizons begin,

At the dawn of the day to behold far away

The goal you would strive for and win?

Yet ah! in the night when you gain to the height,

With the vast pool of heaven star-spawned,

Afar and agleam, like a valley of dream

Still mocks you a Land of Beyond.

—Robert Service, The Land of Beyond

Kumsheen Raft Adventures:
(800) 663-6667

California
Highest point:
Mount Whitney, 14,491 feet.

Reference Material
Sources of maps in California and the

West include:

• **Earthwalk Press** in Eureka,
(701) 442-0503

• **Tom Harrison Cartography** in
San Rafael, (415) 456-7940

• **Wilderness Press in Berkeley,**
(510) 843-8080

Government Resources

British Columbia Provincial Tourism Office:
(800) 663-6000
British Columbia Tourism and Reservations:
(800) 663-6000; //travel.bc.ca
Glacier National Park: (250) 837-7500
Kootenay National Park: (250) 347-9615
Yoho National Park: (250) 343-6783
Pacific Rim National Park Reserve: (250) 726-7721

Guides and Outfitters

Confluence Tours: (888) 3-GO-TO-BC;
www.confluencetours.com

Mountain Images makes CD-ROM trail guides for the
Sierra. They include topographic maps, color photographs, and trail informa-
tion. Contact:
(800) 788-8958;
www.mtnimage.com/
~mtnimage

Mt. Shasta Area

Driving north from Sacra-
mento on a clear day, you
can see the mountain loom-
ing ahead of you hours

THE
MT. SHASTA
BOOK
A Guide to Hiking, Climbing, Skiing,
and Exploring the Mountain
and Surrounding Area

*Andy Selters
Michael Zanger*

before you get to it. Mt. Shasta dominates the landscape and invites exploration. Andy Selters and Michael Zanger wrote the hiking, climbing, and skiing guide to the area: *The Mt. Shasta Book* (Wilderness Press, 1989).

Also including hikes in the Mt. Shasta area is John R. Soares's book, *75 Hikes in California's Lassen Peak and Mt. Shasta Regions* (The Mountaineers, 1996). He describes 21 hikes in Lassen Volcanic National Park, 27 others just outside the park, two hikes in the Lava Beds National Monument, and 20 in or near Mt. Shasta Wilderness.

North Coast

John R. Soares's *100 Hikes in Northern California* (The Mountaineers, 1994) covers the Coast Range, the North Coast, the Bay Area, and the Klamath, Cascade, and Sierra Nevada Mountains. Also covering the North Coast is *Hiker's Hip Pocket Guide to the Humboldt Coast* by Bob Lorentzen (Bored Feet Publications, 1993). It details Prairie Creek Redwoods, Redwood National Park, King Range Conservation Area, and the Humboldt Redwoods.

Yosemite

When you think of California, Yosemite must poke its way into your mind. As wonderful as Yosemite is, there are hundreds of miles of spectacular hiking outside Yosemite National Park with fewer people on the trails. But if Yosemite itself is your goal, you can get hiking information from *High Sierra Hiking Guide to Yosemite* by Jeffrey P. Schaffer (Wilderness Press, 1985). This guide is published as part of a series, each book covering an area equal to or greater than a 15-minute quadrangle.

Wilderness Press publishes guides for *Tuolumne Meadows* (Jeffrey P. Schaffer, 1977); *Devil's Postpile* (Ron Felzer, 1990); *Hetch Hetchy* (Ron Felzer, 1991); *Mineral King* (Ron Felzer and Marian Mayeda, 1992); *Mt. Whitney* (Thomas Winnett, 1978), and other areas in the Sierra Nevada.

The Sierra

Other well-known guides to the Sierra include:

Sierra North: 100 Back-Country Trips in the High Sierra edited by Thomas Winnett, Jason Winnett, Lyn Haber, and Kathy Morey (Wilderness Press, 1997)
The Tahoe-Yosemite Trail by Thomas Winnett (Wilderness Press, 1997). This is a comprehensive guide to the 180 miles of trail between Meeks Bay at Lake Tahoe and Yosemite Park's Tuolumne Meadows.

Deserts

These books cover hikes in California's deserts:

50 Best Short Hikes in California Deserts by John Krist (Wilderness Press, 1995)
75 Great Hikes: In and Near Palm Springs and the Coachella Valley by Philip Ferranti, Bruce Hagerman, and Denice Hagerman (Kendall/Hunt, 1995)

State Parks

The Golden State has some beautifully majestic state parks. John McKinney's *Walking California's State Parks* (Harper Collins, 1994) is the comprehensive guide to them.

South Coast

Guide books for the southern coast of California include:

Hiking the Big Sur Country: The Ventana Wilderness by Jeffrey P. Schaffer (Wilderness Press, 1988)

Los Angeles Hikes: The Best Day-Hikes in the Los Angeles Foothills & Nearby Areas by Eugene Mezereny (Mountain n' Air Books, 1997)
San Bernardino Mountain Trails: 100 Wilderness Hikes in Southern California by John W. Robinson (Wilderness Press, 1986)

Olympic National Park. Photo by Ed Sobey

Federal and State Resources

Anza-Borrego Desert State Park: (619) 767-5311
Bureau of Land Management, California:
(916) 978-4400
Cabeza Prieta National Wildlife Refuge:
(520) 387-6483

California State Office of Tourism: (800) 862-2543
California State Parks and Recreation:
(800) 444-7275; **reservations:** (800) 444-7275;
website: //cal-parks.ca.gov
California State Road Conditions: (916) 445-7623
Channel Islands National Park: (805) 658-5700
Death Valley National Monument: (619) 786-2331
Devil's Postpile National Park: (619) 934-2289
Eldorado National Forest: (916) 622-5061
Inyo National Forest: (619) 873-2400
Inyo National Forest Wilderness: (619) 938-1136,
(888) 374-3773
Joshua Tree National Monument: (619) 367-7511
Kings Canyon National Park: (209) 565-3341
Klamath National Forest: (916) 842-6131
Lassen Volcanic National Park: (916) 595-4444,
(916) 257-2151
Lava Beds National Monument: (916) 667-2282
Los Padres National Forest: (805) 245-3731,
(805) 683-6711
Modoc National Forest: (916) 233-5811
Mono Lake Ranger Station: (619) 647-6565
Mojave National Preserve: (619) 733-4040
Muir Woods National Monument: (415) 388-2596
National Park Service, reservations: (800) 365-2267
National Park Service, Pacific West Region:
(415) 556-0560
Pinnacles National Monument: (408) 389-4485
Point Reyes National Seashore: (415) 663-8522
Redwood National Park: (707) 464-6101
**Santa Monica Mountains National Recreational
Area:** (818) 597-1036
Sequoia National Park: (209) 565-3341,
(209) 784-1500
Sequoia National Park Wilderness: (209) 565-3759
Shasta-Trinity National Forest: (916) 246-5222
Sinkyone Wilderness State Park: (707) 986-7711
Siskiyous Wilderness: (916) 493-2243
Smith River National Recreation Area:
(707) 457-3131
Tahoe Rim Trail: (702) 588-0686
U.S. Forest Service, California: (415) 705-2870
U.S. Forest Service, reservations: (800) 280-2267
Whiskeytown-Shasta-Trinity N. Recreational Area:
(916) 241-6584
Yosemite National Park, trail conditions:
(209) 372-0200;
permits: (209) 372-0740

Guides and Outfitters

Adventure Rents: (888) 881-4386
Baja AirVentures: (800) 691-WAVE;
www.bajaairventures.com
CBOC Whitewater: (800) 356-2262;
e-mail: rapids@pacbell.net
Mountain Sobek: (800) 282-8747;
www.mtsobek.com
High Sierra Goat Packing: (209) 536-9576;
www.mlode.com/~goatpack
High Sierra Packers, (horse packers): (619) 873-8405
Presidio of Monterey Outdoor Recreation:
(408) 242-6133
South Yosemite Mountain Guides: (800) 231-4575;
www.symg.com
The Adventure Company: (213) 848-8685;
4X4abc.com
White Magic Unlimited: (800) 869-9874

Llama Packers

BonneVenture West Llamas:
(916) 663-2184; e-mail: pnreitz@calweb.com
Llamas of Circle Home:
(209) 532-5411; e-mail: llama@sonnet.com
Sierra Llamas: (916) 269-2204
Sonshine Llamas: (916) 342-1230

Clubs and Organizations

Bay Area Women Adventurers is a women's organization that encourages women to hike and backpack. Contact: e-mail: bawa-l-request@netcom.com

What else would you call a group based at the University of California, Berkeley, but CHAOS? The **Cal Hiking and Outdoor Society** is organized on campus but is open to all. Contact: www.emf.net/~chaos

With 450 members, the **Canyon Explorers Club, Inc.,** organizes hiking, backpacking, skiing, kayaking,

Heart Lake, Olympic National Park. Photo by Ed Sobey

canyoneering, and world travel. They are based in Fullerton. Contact: e-mail: members.aol.com/explorx/ canyonhp.htm#cec

Hawaii

Highest point: Mauna Kea, 13,796 feet.

Reference Material

For maps of Hawaii and Samoa, contact the **University of Hawaii Press** at (808) 956-8255.

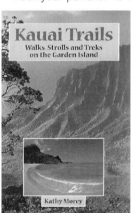

Pack your poncho. To visit the wettest spot on the planet, hike the trails of Kauai. Kathy Morey describes the hiking in her book **Kauai Trails: Walks, Strolls, and Treks on the Garden Isle** (Wilderness Press, 1997).

The Fernglen Press, (503) 635-4719, publishes a series of hiking guides to Hawaii. They offer three guides written by Craig Chisholm covering all the islands.

Bob Smith has written hiking guides to Maui, Kauai, Hawaii, and Oahu, published by **HOA Publications,** (808) 878-2664.

Federal and State Resources

Haleakala National Park: (808) 572-4400
Hawaii State Parks: (808) 587-0300
Hawaii Volcanoes National Park: (808) 985-6000; www.nps.gov/havo

East side of the Sierras. Photo by Ed Sobey

Kokee State Park: (808) 335-9975
State Office of Tourism: (808) 586-2550
State Online Environmental Directory:
//eelink.umich.edu/GAIN/HI.dir/html.dir/
toc.Organization.html

Guides and Outfitters

Eye of the Whale: (800) 659-3544;
www.aloha.net/~e-whale
Kayak Kauai Outbound: (800) 437-3507;
//kayakkauai.com or //planet-hawaii.com/outbound

Clubs and Organizations

The **Hawaiian Trail and Mountain Club** organizes
hikes, camping, and good fellowship. They operate a
clubhouse near the beach in Waimanalo:
www2.hawaii.edu/~turner/htmc/main.htm.

Oregon

Highest point: Mount Hood, 11,235 feet.

Reference Material

Oregon has lots of great hikes,
and easily overlooked are those
along 350 miles of sandy
beaches and rugged head-
lands with some of the most
famous marine views in the
country. Paul Williams cor-
rects that oversight in his
Oregon Coast Hikes
(The Mountaineers,
1985).

The **100 Hikes**
series of books pro-
vides in-depth information for
hiking in the Northwest, Central, Coast,
and Coastal Range areas of Oregon. *Northwest* covers
Mt. Hood, the area surrounding Portland, and the

Columbia Gorge. Three Sis-
ters and Mount Jefferson
areas are included in the
Central book. All are written by William L. Sullivan
and published by Navil-
lus Press, (541) 683-
6837.

**Hiking Central
Oregon and
Beyond,** by Vir-
ginia Meissner (Meissner
Books, 1987), gives short trail
descriptions, hand-drawn maps, and a
few photographs. Meissner covers a dozen or more
hikes in each of 16 areas. Contact Meissner Books at
P.O. Box 5296, Bend, Oregon, 97708.

If the rocks under your feet catch your attention,
you'll want to see **Hiking
Oregon's Geology** by Ellen
Morris Bishop and John
Eliot Allen (The Moun-
taineers, 1996). The 51
hikes described are in
search of the rocks
that tell the story of
Oregon.

For information
on hiking in the
Wallowas see **50
Hikes in Hells
Canyon and
Oregon's Wallowas,**
by Rhonda and George
Ostertag (The Moun-
taineers, 1997), part of
The Mountaineers' *100
Hikes in . . .* series. The
Ostertags also wrote **50
Hikes in Oregon's
Coast Range and
Siskiyous** (The
Mountaineers,
1989). Another
reference worth
consulting is
**Portland
Hikes: The Best Day-**

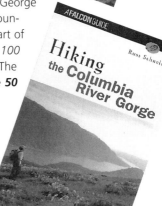

Hikes Within 100 Miles of Portland by Art Bernstein and Andrew Jackman (Mountain North Air Books, 1994).

One more area to explore is along the Columbia River. The guide is *Hiking the Columbia River Gorge* by Russ Schneider (Falcon Press, 1997). For information on the 35-mile-long Columbia Gorge Trail, call the **Columbia River Gorge National Scenic Area,** (541) 386-2333.

A new magazine, *Oregon Outside,* covers outdoor activities in the state. Contact: (800) 348-8401; www.ohwy.com/or/x/xoom.htm

Federal and State Resources

An unofficial website with information on Oregon State Parks is www.oregonlive.com/parks/index.html

Alvord Desert, Bureau of Land Management: (541) 573-4400
Bureau of Land Management, Oregon: (503) 952-6024
Columbia Gorge Trail (Forest Service): (503) 872-2750;
Columbia River Gorge National Scenic Area: (541) 386-2333
Crater Lake National Park: (503) 594-2211
Eagle Cap Wilderness: (541) 426-4978
John Day Fossil Beds National Monument: (503) 575-0721
Mt. Hood National Forest: (503) 666-0771, (503) 666-0700
Opal Creek Wilderness: (503) 854-3366
Oregon Caves National Monument: (503) 592-2100
Oregon Department of Fish and Wildlife: www.dfw.state.or.us
Oregon State Office of Tourism: (800) 547-7842
Oregon State Parks and Recreation: (800) 551-6949; **reservations:** (800) 452-5687; e-mail: res.nw@state.or.us
Rogue River National Forest: (541) 858-2200
Steens Mt., Bureau of Land Management: (503) 573-2071
U.S. Forest Service, Northwest: (503) 872-2750; **reservations:** (800) 280-2267
Wallowa-Whitman National Forest: (541) 523-6391
Willamette National Forest: (541) 782-2291, (541) 465-6521

Hoh Valley, Photo by Ed Sobey

Guides and Outfitters

Back Country Odysseys:
(800) 309-5008
Galice Resort: (888) 8-GALICE
Hells Canyon Adventures:
(800) 422-3568
High Desert Outfitters:
(541) 947-5526
**Rogue River Reservations &
Paradise Lodge:** (541) 247-6022
Rogue Wilderness, Inc.:
(800) 336-1647;
www.wildrogue.com
Wilderness River Outfitters:
(541) 726-9471

Llama Packers

Hurricane Creek Llamas:
(541) 432-4455; e-mail:
Stanlynn@oregontrail.net
Oregon Llamas: (888) PAC-Llama;
www.packllama.com

Olympic National Park. Photo by Ed Sobey

Clubs and Organizations

The Mazamas is one of the oldest outdoor clubs in America. Founded in 1894 on the summit of Mt. Hood, the club has 3,000 members. Contact: (503) 227-2345; www.mazamas.org

   The Chemekatans offer a variety of outdoor activities in the Salem area. Contact: P.O. Box 864, Salem, OR 97308.

   The Desert Trail Association, headquartered in Madras, Oregon, is dedicated to providing a contiguous trail from Canada to Mexico, primarily through desert terrain. Contact: www.madras.net/dta.htm

Washington

Highest point: Mount Rainier, 14,410 feet.

Reference Material

A book with a striking title is ***Don't Waste Your Time in the North Cascades*** by Kathy and Craig Copeland (Wilderness Press, 1996).

You know immediately that the authors have something to say. They rate more than 100 hikes and give the pertinent information, along with some attitude.

Mount Rainier looks down on Seattle and dominates the skyline—at least on days when the skies are clear. To find your way around the massive mountain, consult **Mount Rainier National Park: Tales, Trails, & Auto Tours** by Jerry and Gisela Rohde (Mountain Home Books, 1997). This is not a typical hiker's guidebook, as it appeals to a wider audience. It includes information on hiking trails and the history of the area, and includes maps. Contact the publisher: (707) 839-0078.

For years the premier guide to the area has been **50 Hikes in Mount Rainier National Park** by Ira Spring and Harvey Manning (The Mountaineers, 1988). The authors are two of the great veterans of Northwest hiking.

Other guidebooks include **Hiking Olympic National Park** by Erik Molvar (Falcon Press Publishing, 1996); **55 Hikes in Central Washington: Yakima, Pot Holes, Wenatchee,** **Grand Coulee, Columbia River, Snake River, and Umtanum** by Ira Spring and Harvey Manning (The Mountaineers, 1997); and **100 Hikes in Washington's Glacier Peak Region** by Harvey Manning and Ira Springer (The Mountaineers, 1996).

Walks and Hikes in the Foothills and Lowlands: Around Puget Sound, by Harvey and Penny Manning (The Mountaineers, 1995), starts with an explanation that the authors do not write books "purely or even primarily to serve recreation. Re-creation ranks higher. Highest of all," they say, "is preservation." Preservation, that is, of ideals.

Pack and Paddle is a magazine providing Washington hikers and kayakers with up-to-date information on trail conditions. To subscribe, write to P.O. Box 1063, Port Orchard, WA 98366.

Mt. Washington, OR. Photo by Ed Sobey

Federal and State Resources

Coulee Dam National Recreation Area:
(509) 633-9441
Gifford Pinchot National Forest: (360) 494-0600
Lake Chelan National Recreation Area:
(360) 856-5700
Mt. Baker-Snoqualmie National Forest:
(206) 470-4060
Mt. Rainier National Park: (206) 775-9702 or
(360) 569-2211
Mt. St. Helens National Volcanic Monument:
(360) 569-2211
National Park Service, Northwest Region:
(206) 220-7450
Nez Perce National Historic Park: (208) 843-2261
North Cascades National Park: (360) 856-5700
Olympic National Forest: (360) 956-2400
Olympic National Park: (360) 956-2300
Okanogan National Forest: (360) 452-4501,
(360) 452-0330
Ross Lake National Recreation Area:
(360) 856-5700
San Juan Island National Historic Park:
(360) 378-2240
Washington State Ferry System: (206) 464-6400
Washington State Parks: (800) 233-0321;
www.parks.wa.gov;
reservations: (800) 452-5687; e-mail:
res.nw@state.or.us
Washington State Tourism: (800) 544-1800
Wenatchee National Forest: (509) 662-4335
Willapa National Wildlife Refuge: (509) 997-2131

Guides and Outfitters

You can get the **Washington Outfitters' & Guides'
Association** list of members by calling (206) 392-6107
or visiting www.webstercorp.com/woga

Cascade Alpine Guides: (206) 688-8054
Cascade Corrals: (509) 682-4677
Cascade Wilderness Outfitters: (509) 997-0155
Deli Llama Wilderness Adventures: (360) 293-5523

Early Winters Outfitting: (800) 737-8750; e-mail:
horse@methow.com
Gray Wolf Outfitters: (360) 692-6455
Icicle Outfitters and Guides: (800) 497-3912
Indian Creek Corral: (509) 672-2400
National Outdoor Leadership School:
(360) 445-6657
North Cascades Outfitters: (509) 997-1015
Outdoor Recreation Information Center:
(206) 470-4060
Pacific Crest Outward Bound: (800) 547-3312
Reachout Expeditions, Washington:
(800) 697-3847; www.yd.org/rewa.htm
Three Queens Outfitting: (509) 674-5647
Whatcom Skagit Outfitters: (360) 595-1136

Llama Packers

Casa De Millama: (360) 985-2553
Deli Llama Wilderness Adventures: (360) 293-5523
Kitt's Llamas: (206) 857-5274
Pasayten Llama Packing: (509) 996-2326

Clubs and Organizations

The Mountaineers is a most venerable club. It was
formed in 1906 to "explore, study, preserve, and enjoy
the natural beauty of the Northwest." Today it is the third-
largest outdoor club in America, and its publishing arm,
The Mountaineers Books, has published over 300 titles.

One of the most active hiking clubs anywhere is the
Issaquah Alps Trails Club. Located east of Seattle,
it conducts at least five hikes each week.

The **Washington Trails Association** organizes trail
teams to help the Forest Service improve trails. Their
volunteer hotline is (800) 587-7032 or (206) 517-7032.
They also publish *Signpost for Northwest Trails,* a
monthly 40-page newsletter with information on hiking
in the Northwest.

Other clubs and associations include:

Issaquah Alps Trails Club: (206) 328-0480;
www.issaquah.org/comorg/ialps/mialps.htm
Ptarmigan Mountaineering Club: P.O. Box 1821,
Vancouver, WA 98668
Washington Trails Association: (206) 625-1367;
www.halcyon.com/wta

Staying Found

The golden rule is this: When you're confused and disoriented, trust your compass. Perversely, this seems just what we are least likely to do when lost, preferring to defer to that creature of fiction— our sense of direction. A not-uncommon phrase heard from those recently rescued is that when they consulted their compass, "There seemed to be something wrong with the damn thing." There hardly ever is.

—David Seidman,

The Essential Wilderness Navigator

Are We Lost Yet?

The key to never getting lost is always staying "found." In other words, always knowing where you are. It's simple in concept but more difficult in practice.

You start each hike at a known location, the trailhead. If you walk for 100 yards, you still know where you are. By studying the map and being aware of what you expect to find along the way, you will always know where you are. If, for example, you know from the map that a mountain peak should become visible when you turn out of a valley, you'll be looking for it. If it doesn't appear, you know you have to stop and check your map.

Similarly, if you expect to cross a major stream in an hour, crossing it confirms your position and gives you valuable information on your pace of progress, which helps you predict how long the next stretch of trail will take. If you don't cross it when you expect to, it's an alarm signal.

Your wristwatch is therefore an important piece of navigation equipment. If you maintain a fairly constant pace, then the time elapsed relates to the distance traveled. In other words, if you walk for 1½ hours at a pace of 2 mph, you know you have covered 3 miles, and you can mark your new position on the map.

It's a good idea to announce times upon reaching each landmark. At the trailhead announce: "We're getting under way at 9:15 a.m. Everyone please remember the time." Keep track of the time you spend resting and subtract it from the total time it takes to cover the distance. Some people keep written notes of the times and landmarks and then refer to them when repeating the trip or recommending it to others. With practice, you'll develop the skill to predict how long it will take to cover distances.

Knowing where you are obviously eliminates the possibility of getting lost, but it also puts you more in touch with your surroundings, and you learn more about your physical capabilities under different conditions.

STOP AND WAIT

TIP

If you're lost:

1. Stop.
2. Look around for familiar surroundings.
3. Wait for rescue. (Is your whistle handy?)

References

Staying Found: The Complete Map and Compass Handbook, by June Fleming (The Mountaineers, 1994), provides techniques to avoid getting lost, in addition to basic map and compass information. The author also has chapters on how to use nature's direction finders, and on how to train kids to stay found.

Selecting a Compass

Ready to purchase a compass? Consider first how you will use it. Will you be hiking along well-marked trails and need a compass only to identify distant points of interest? Or will you be hoofing it over hill and glen on virgin stretches where, if you miss your bearings, you might wander down the wrong side of a mountain?

Here's basic advice from veteran hikers John Long and Michael Hodgson in **The Dayhiker's Handbook** (Ragged Mountain Press, 1996) that applies to your choice of compass, no matter what kind of hiking you'll be doing: "As a minimum, your compass should feature a rotating bezel with a 360-degree dial in 2-degree graduations, a clear base-plate with inch and millimeter scales, a direction-of-travel arrow engraved into the base plate, and a rotating magnetic needle mounted in a clear capsule filled with liquid to reduce shake and movement. Orienting lines should also be engraved or printed onto the bottom of the rotating capsule. A basic compass costs around $10."

Beyond the basic requirements, you might want an adjustable declination scale, which allows you to compensate for magnetic declination in your area. Declination is the angle between true north, located at the North Pole, and magnetic north, located near Bathurst Island in northern Canada, about 1,000 miles from the North Pole. Declination is always shown on a map, but on a nautical chart it is shown as variation, because in nautical terms declination is the angle between compass north and magnetic north, which can differ because the compass needle is deflected by metal on a boat.

Since the magnetic pole slowly migrates, you will want to get an update if your map is more than a few years old. Many maps list the annual change in declination, so that you can calculate the present declination for yourself. Otherwise, contact the U.S.

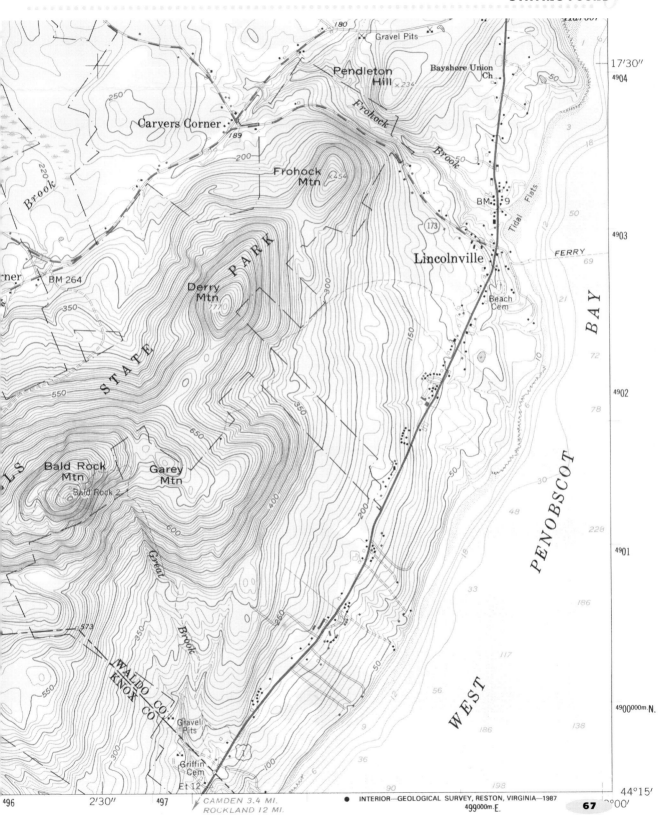

BREATHSAVER

TIP

The sound of a whistle can be heard three times as far as the sound of a human voice, and it takes less energy to blow a whistle. Carry one with you at all times.

Geological Survey (USGS) at (303) 273-8488.

Mirror-sighting compasses allow you to read the bearing of a geographic feature without moving the compass. This feature is helpful on cross-country routes. By transferring the bearing to your map and extending it through your present position, you can identify the features around you. Or, if identifiable features are marked on your map, the intersection of two or more bearings will give you your position. Taking a bearing with a flat-base compass is difficult for one person, but works well when one person sights and another reads the dial.

Unfortunately, when you're lost, it's often because you've wandered off alone. And usually you've left your compass behind. So carry your compass with you at all times, not in your pack.

PRACTICE FIRST

TIP

Practice with your new compass or GPS at home before using it on a trip. At home you can refer to the directions, or a reference book. Alternatively, you can call a store salesmen to help you figure it out. Once you're on the trail, you're on your own.

Carefully check any compass before you plunk down your cash. Don't buy it if there is a bubble in the liquid inside the compass housing. Make sure the compass points northward by comparing it with other compasses in the display case; but be aware that neither it nor the others will point to *true* north if there is deviation in your area, as there probably is. Know that a compass can lose its magnetic properties over time. Also, ask the sales staff to show you all its features. If you buy it, go home and read the instructions carefully.

Sources of Compasses

Brunton: (307) 856-6559; www.brunton.com

Nexus: (307) 856-6559
Silva: (800) 572-8822; www.jwa.com
Suunto: (800) 543-9124; www.suuntousa.com

References

Be Expert with Map and Compass by Bjorn Kjellstrom (Charles Scribner's Sons, 1976) covers land navigation from the basics up to competitive orienteering.

GPS Satellite Navigation

Not since the invention of the magnetic compass has navigation

---

EARLY COMPASSES

Although magnetic effects were observed in China as early as 1000 B.C. it wasn't until around the year 1040 A.D. that the Chinese began using compasses for navigation. Norsemen are believed to have used a narrow piece of magnetite, or magnetic iron ore, floated in cork in a bowl of water, as early as 900 A.D. The Chinese placed magnetized metal on straw floating in a bowl of water, a simple system you can use if you find yourself without a compass.

More as a science experiment than a way-finding procedure, you can make a crude compass by magnetizing a pin or needle. Stroke it on one end of a permanent magnet or rub it through a fold in wool clothing. For the needle to point poleward, it must be able to rotate freely. With lots of care, you may get the needle to float in a bowl of water (easier if you rest the needle atop a small piece of float-

ing bark), or suspend it from a thread. (Neither is necessarily easy to do in an emergency situation.) Once you've got the needle pointing steadily in one direction, figure out which end is north and which is south. Without the sun, stars, or other clues, you're pretty much where you started: lost.

A simple compass.

THE GREAT ADVANTAGE

"The advantage of using a GPS receiver for navigating is that you know your location with certainty.... It will show your position on a map with an error of between 15 and 100 meters."

—Lavern Littan, *GPS Made Easy* (The Mountaineers, 1995).

taken such a leap forward as it has with the Global Positioning System (GPS). This technology allows you to find your position with the aid of satellites orbiting 12,000 miles overhead.

Twenty-one high-altitude satellites provide worldwide coverage, with three other satellites orbiting as spares. Each satellite carries an atomic clock and a radio transmitter so it can broadcast its position and time. Hand-held receivers use the signals from three or more satellites to compute your position.

GPS is accurate to within 100 yards, on average. There are several variables, but assuming your receiver can get three or more signals, the position it shows could be within 25 or even 10 yards of your true position.

Sources of GPS

Adventure GPS Products: (805) 726-9474; www.gps4fun.com
Eagle: (503) 972-3524; www.eaglegps.com
Garmin: (913) 397-8200; www.garmin.com
Lowrance: (800) 324-5763; www.lowrance.com
Magellan: (800) 707-7840; www.magellangps.com
Trimble Navigation Ltd.: (800) 959-9567; www.trimble.com

Maps

To nurture the holiday spirit on a minor trip into unfamiliar country I often go without maps. [This stratagem] injects into each day a steady stream of that titillating element, the unexpected. But sometimes I find that traveling without a map becomes so inefficient that it diminishes my freedom rather than amplifies it.

—Colin Fletcher, The Complete Walker III

Joyce Kilmer-Slickrock Wilderness, Nantahala National Forest, North Carolina. Photo by Burt Kornegay, Slickrock Expeditions

Most experts would not recommend that you travel without maps. True enough, you can find your way on the well-worn trails of many national parks, but maps give you freedom to explore. Studying maps gives you an understanding of the lay of the land, why a stream runs here, or how the mountains were formed. They also let you make decisions about changing routes or going cross-country, and they show you what's coming. It certainly can be an adventure going without a map; possibly too much adventure for most.

MEET ME THERE

TIP

Before setting out for the day, check your maps to pick a meeting place in case the group becomes separated.

USGS Maps

Topographic maps show three-dimensional terrain on a two-dimensional surface by using contour lines. The maps most commonly used for backpacking are the 7.5-minute series published by the U.S. Geological Survey (USGS). The number 7.5 refers to the area covered by the map, 7.5 minutes of longitude and latitude. The map scale on a 7.5-minute map is 1:24,000. That is, one inch on the map equates to 24,000 inches (2,000 feet) on the ground.

More convenient to use for long trips are maps in the 15-minute series. Here the scale is 1:62,500; that is, one map inch equates to 62,500 inches on the ground, nearly a mile. Since it takes four

7.5-minute maps to cover the same area as one 15-minute map, you're often better off with fewer 15-minute maps. Maps with scales larger than 1:62,500 aren't much good for navigation on foot.

Check the contour intervals, printed below the distance scale along the lower edge of the map. Most 7.5-minute maps have contour intervals of 40 feet. That is, for each contour line you cross, you are either gaining or losing 40 feet of elevation. However, some 7.5-minute maps have contour intervals of 20 feet, while the 15-minute series typically has intervals of 80 feet.

NEARLY-FREE MAPS

FREE

Free maps? Well, almost. Check your library to see if they have topographic maps for the region you want to visit. Take a few dimes along to photocopy the ones you need. Store the pages in a sealable plastic bag to keep them visible, yet dry.

Map Sources

The first place to check for maps is a backpacking store in the region you're interested in. Stores that sell maps exclusively are listed in the yellow pages of telephone directories. If you don't find one, call the **Map Dealers' Association,** (815) 939-4627, and ask them for the closest map store.

To get a better idea of the three-dimensional geography of the area you're visiting, study the raised relief maps by **Hubbard Scientific.** You won't be able to roll these up or fold them to fit in your

pack, but hanging on your wall at home these maps give an impressive sense of topographic diversity. They have raised relief maps for much of the United States (although for few areas in the central part of the country). Contact: Hubbard Scientific, (800) 523-5485; www.amep.com

Map Link publishes an impressive catalog for $3, listing its offerings for each state and many of the countries of the world. The company has a toll-free fax number, but you need to have the catalog to place an order. Contact: Map Link, (805) 692-6777.

National Geographic is synonymous with high-quality maps, and although they don't publish maps suitable for way-finding on trails, their maps can get you to the trailhead or stimulate your interest in hiking to another part of the world. Contact: National Geographic, (888) 494-MAPS; www.geosys.com

Omni Resources makes and sells topographic and travel maps and map accessories. Their business is geared mostly to supplying the needs of scientists and science teachers, but they also provide maps for recreation. Contact: Omni Resources, (800) 742-2677; www.omnimap.com

Trails Illustrated offers waterproof and highly durable topographic maps of national parks and several Western states. They print their maps on durable plastic. The maps contain information on wildlife, history, geology, and archaeology. Contact: Trails Illustrated, (800) 962-1643; www.colorado.com/trails

USGS is making its collection of 54,000 topographic maps available.

Contact: U.S. Geological Survey, (800) USA-MAPS or (800) HELP-MAP; //mapping.usgs.gov/mac/maplists.html
USGS maps on CD-ROM, (605) 594-6151.

Here is contact information for a few other map sources:

Canadian Map Office:
(800) 465-6277
DeLorme Mapping Company:
(207) 865-4171;
www.delorme.com
Earthvisions: (800) 627-7236;
www.earthvisions.com
Europe Map Service:
(914) 221-0208
U.S. Forest Service:
(202) 205-1760; www.fs.fed.us

Degree-of-Difficulty Maps
A different approach to providing trail information is being taken by **Trail Tracks Hiking Maps.** The company publishes four-color aerial illustrations that depict a trail's degree of difficulty with a distinctive color.

According to the company, "The back side of each map provides a quick, easy reference for more information about each trail, so you can select the hikes that meet your needs based on elevation gain, distance, and what you'll

see (streams, lakes, tundra, and so on). Additional information is provided about wildlife, safety, weather, and permits. Both day hikers and avid backpackers find the maps a welcome resource for their outdoor experience."

The map series covers Zion, Rocky Mountain National Park, Indian Peaks Wilderness, Yosemite, and Grand Teton. See the company's website at www.gorp.com/trailtracks. You can order maps through The Adventurous Traveler Bookstore, (800-282-3963).

Mountain Images

Mountain Images produces CD-ROM trail guides that include topographic maps, color prints, and narrations of trips in the Sierra Nevada. There are two CD-ROMs, one covering the northern areas and the other covering southern. Contact: (800) 788-8958; www.mtnimage.com/~mtnimage

Maps of Europe
To order maps of European countries, contact **European Map Service** at (914) 221-0208.

Protecting Your Maps
Many commercially produced maps are waterproofed, but if yours aren't, you can protect them from the elements. The simplest way is to store them in sealable plastic bags. Fold the map so the section you need shows through.

You can also spray or paint on a protective coat. **Thompson's Water Seal,** sold in hardware stores, and **Stormproof,** sold by outfitters, work well. For spray-on

protection, visit an art supply and ask for clear lacquer spray. You need to coat both front and back and let the map dry thoroughly. Nikwax makes **MapProof.** One bottle contains enough waterproofing for six maps. (Contact Nikwax at (206) 303-1410; www.nikwax-usa.com) Another option is to purchase specially made plastic map covers. **Sun Dog** makes covers for maps and books. (Contact Sun Dog (206) 782-5404; www.sun-dog.com)

Altimeters
You might consider carrying an altimeter. Used with a topographic map, and calibrated for atmospheric pressure at the trailhead, an altimeter provides estimates of elevation changes. It's not as useful when the weather changes, though, unless you can re-calibrate the altimeter by listening to the atmospheric pressure reports in a weather forecast.

Casio makes three watches that have built-in altimeters. One, the Triple Sensor Pathfinder, gives date, time, altitude, barometric pressure, compass heading, and temperature. All on your wrist!

Cateye makes a stand-alone altimeter (not a watch) that incorporates other features. Purchase either brand from retail stores or stores on the Web.

Hiking Information by Region:

(ALASKA,

NORTHWEST TERRITORIES,

AND YUKON TERRITORIES)

Crossing the Sierras. Photo by Ed Sobey.

Alaska

Highest point: Mount McKinley,
20,320 feet.

Alaska may evoke images of white-out conditions in the far north, but the state is so large and its ecosystem so varied that it offers very diverse hiking opportunities. From hiking the Brooks Range to walking through the largest temperate rain forest in the world, you'll never run out of trails here.

Reference Material

Hiking Alaska, by Dean Littlepage (Falcon Press,

1997), is one of a series of guides to hiking in Western states. It lists 100 hikes including some in Denali National Park. Littlepage formerly managed the Iditarod National Historic trail.

The Hiker's Guide to Alaska, by Evan Swensen and Margaret Swensen (Falcon Press, 1992), covers 100 hikes and backpack trips throughout the state.

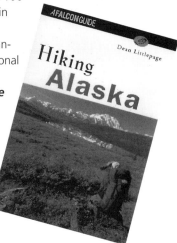

The Far North

with *Pack and Paddle,* by Margaret Piggott (The Mountaineers, 1990). Now in its second edition, this has long been the authoritative guide for hiking in this region.

For information on state parks, see *Alaska's Accessible Wilderness: A Traveler's Guide to Alaska's State Parks,* by Bill Sherwonit and Jeff Schultz (Alaska Northwest Books, 1996).

Natural Wonders of Alaska: A Guide to Parks, Preserves and Wild Places, by Kent Surgis (Country Roads, 1994), is another great guide to these wild places.

Backpacking in Alaska: Walking Guide, by Jim DuFesne (Lonely Planet, 1995), provides maps, directions, and information on the environment.

Alaska's Parklands: The Complete Guide, by Nancy Lange Simmerman (The Mountaineers, 1983), describes wilderness areas and state and national parks. This is a general reference on parks and not specific to hiking.

Walking the Yukon, by Chris Townsend (Ragged Mountain Press, 1993), recounts his adventures while walking from Skagway to the Arctic Circle. If you're ready to follow his footsteps, this book has the planning information you need.

To explore southeast Alaska, get a copy of **Discover Southeast Alaska**

Federal and State Resources

Alaska Public Land Information Center: (907) 271-2737

Alaska Maritime National Wildlife Refuge: (907) 235-6961

Alaska State Office of Tourism: (907) 465-2010; www.travelalaska.com

Alaska State Parks, public information: (907) 269-8400; **reservations:** (907) 762-2617

Arctic National Wildlife Refuge: U.S. Fish & Wildlife Service, P.O. Box 20, Fairbanks, AK 99701

Bureau of Land Management: (907) 271-5960
Chugach National Forest: (907) 276-1472
Denali National Park: (907) 683-2294
Gates of the Arctic: (907) 456-0281
Glacier Bay National Park: (907) 697-2232
Katmai: (907) 246-3305
Kenai Fjords: (907) 224-3175
Kigllusik Mountains, Bureau of Land Management: (907) 474-2330
Klondike Gold Rush National Park: (907) 983-2921
Kobuk Valley National Park: (907) 442-3890
Lake Clark National Park: (907) 271-3751
National Forest Service, Alaska: (907) 586-8863
National Park Service, Alaska: (907) 271-2737
Noatak Nature Preserve: (907) 442-3890
Tongass National Forest,
   information center: (907) 586-7928
   Craig: (907) 826-3271
   Hoonah: (907) 945-3631
   Juneau: (907) 586-8800
   Ketchikan: (907) 225-2148
   Petersburg: (907) 772-3871
   Sitka: (907) 747-6671
   Thorne Bay: (907) 828-3304
   Wrangell: (907) 874-2323
   Yakutat: (907) 784-3359
Wrangell-St. Elias: (907) 822-5234

Guides and Outfitters

Adventure Alaska: (800) 365-7057;
www.alaska.net/~advenak
Alaska-Denali Guiding: (907) 733-2649;
www.alaska.net/~adg/
Alaska Discovery: (800) 586-1911
Alaska Wildland Adventures: (800) 334-8730;
www.alaskawildland.com
Arctic Treks: (907) 455-6502; e-mail: arctreks@polar-net.com
CampAlaska Tours: (800) 376-9438
Kennicott-McCarthy Wild
(907) 554-4444
North Star: (800) 258-843‹
www.adventuretrip.com
NOVA: Alaska's Adventu
Company: (800) 746-5753

www.alaska.net/ ~nova/nova.htm
Sourdough Outfitters: (907) 692-5252; e-mail:
sour@nigu.sourdough.com
Wilderness Alaska: (907) 345-3567;
www.gorp.com/wildak

Clubs and Organizations

The Mountain Club of Alaska promotes "the exercise of skill and safety in the art and science of moun-

Beach camp fire, Tankass. Photo by Ed Sobey.

taineering." Members organize hikes, climbs, skiing trips, and mountain biking. Contact: www.alaska.net/~mca/MCAIntro.htm

Yukon Territories

Highest point: Mount Logan, 19,524 feet

Gold-rush prospectors climbed the Chilkoot Trail, starting in Skagway, Alaska, and crossing into the Yukon Territory of Canada, and the trail is still popular with modern backpackers, who travel with less than the ton of equipment the miners had to tote.

Government Resources

Chilkoot Trail National Historic Site: (800) 661-0486
Ivvavik National Park:
(867) 777-3248
Kluane National Park:
(867) 634-2251
Tourism Department:
(867) 667-5340;
www.touryukon.com

Guides and Outfitters

Big Bear Adventures:
(867) 633-5642; www.bear.yk.net
Canadian Wilderness Travel Ltd.:
(867) 863-5404
Cloudberry Adventures Ltd.:
(867) 668-7711;
www.cloudberry.ca
Due North Journeys:
(867) 668-4437; e-mail:
duenorth@yt.sympatico.ca

Nature Tours of Yukon:
(867) 667-2028; www.naturetoursyukon.com
Wanderlust Wilderness Adventures: (867) 668-2633
Yukon Wilderness Llama Adventures: (867) 634-2828

Northwest Territories

Highest point: Mount Sir James MacBrien, 9,062 feet

Government Resources

Aulavik National Park: (867) 690-3904
Auyuittuq National Park Reserve: (819) 473-8828
Nahanni National Park Reserve: (867) 695-2713
Travel Information: (800) 661-0788;
www.nwttravel.nt.ca
Tuktut Nogait National Park: (867) 777-3248

Outfitting Yourself

Overweight backpacks not only sap strength, they tax the feet and ankles. They increase the hiker's risk of injury, and they effectively steepen the hills and magnify the distance.

—Ray Jardine,

The Pacific Crest Trail Hiker's Handbook

Olympic National Park. Photo by Ed Sobey

How much should your backpack weigh? Veteran hiker Harvey Manning offers a rule of thumb in his book **Backpacking One Step at a Time** (Vintage Books, 1986).

A person of average strength can carry about one third of his or her body weight, says Manning. That amounts to 60 pounds for a 180-pound man, or 40 pounds for a 120-pound woman. Manning admits, however, that those figures are above the comfort range. The man would be happier with 40 pounds, the woman with 25.

But can you get away with as little as 25 pounds?

For several years we led high-adventure trips for Boy Scouts in the Sierra Nevada. We would start out each season with three or four three-day trips before logging a 50-miler. When we gathered for the first hike of the season, each boy and each father would weigh his pack. We repeated the process for each succeeding trip.

During the three-day trips we tried to call attention to all the stuff in the packs that never got used. For instance, people carried two or three pots and used only one. We asked them to pull everything out when they got home and ask themselves if they used it on the trip. Now, obviously there are some safety items you hope you never need, and always carry. But there was always lots of other stuff that didn't contribute to safety or comfort.

Packs, we noticed, weighed more at the first hike of the sea-

son, although it was only about 15 miles long, than they did at the start of the 50-mile trip. Yet no one on the long trip ever complained about having left something at home. The experience of the shorter trips paid great dividends in comfort on the longer trips.

Let's examine the contents of your pack in greater detail:

The Essentials

There are some things you just can't do without, no matter how determined you are to lighten your pack. And it doesn't matter whether you're going for a day's hike or a trek across the continent. You might want to keep them in a fanny pack or nylon stuffsack at home, so they're always ready to go when you are, and so you won't forget anything.

These are the essentials for every hike:

• **Pocket knife.** You can substitute a survival tool, but make sure it's on your body, not in your pack.

We recommend carrying a multi-purpose knife or tool. Carry it in a pocket or in a sheath on your belt. (For sources, see page 200.)

• **Water.** You can go days without food, but only hours without water. True, you can almost always find water to drink, but unless you treat it you stand a good chance of making your excursion more memorable than you planned. A good rule of thumb is to carry one quart of water per person in cool climates without packs. Take more along if you're carrying heavy loads and if temperatures are high. Better to err on the side of carrying more than you need.

• **Clothes.** You need clothes to shelter you from sun, wind, rain, and cold. A nylon shell takes up little room in a pack and gives protection from foul weather. Bring a hat, too, to protect you from the sun and help you regulate your body temperature. (For more on clothes for outdoors activities, see page 192.)

• **Bandana.** A multipurpose tool. A bandanna can be a hat, potholder, bandage, or a sponge to draw up cool water to wipe across your brow.

• **Matches.** Keep matches in a waterproof container, or use a cigarette lighter.

• **Fire starters.** Why fool around with just matches? If you need a fire, you need it now. Make some

fire starters at the beginning of each season and carry several. To make bombproof fire starters, collect lint from your drier and pack it in a cardboard egg carton. Pour in molten paraffin, filling up the egg cups. When cool, cut apart each cup. Another method is to roll three matches inside a strip of newspaper, tie with twine, and soak in molten paraffin. Or cut old T-shirts into 3-inch squares, drop into molten paraffin, and spread on newspaper to dry. Fold up and carry in your pocket. Light one fire starter under damp kindling to get a fire going quickly.

KEEP THEM CLOSE

Keep your knife, matches or fire starter, whistle, compass and bandanna in your pockets, not in your pack. If you get separated from your pack, you'll still have basic survival tools.

• **Whistle.** If your group tends to separate on the trail, you need whistles. Kids should always carry one, too. Yelling when you're lost not only drains energy, it tends to aggravate your anxieties. Use your whistles only for safety reasons, though. No one wants to listen to them blowing all day.

• **Map and compass.** Even if you plan to follow a well-established trail, a map and compass allow you to stray from your chosen path and enjoy your hike more, as you can identify features and understand the geography. (For more on use of maps and compasses, see pages 66-71.)

Illustration by Daisy dePuthod

These are the essentials for every hike.

- **Food.** Carry more than you think you'll need and leave all the wrappers at home so you have less to tote back. (For more on trail food, see page 178.)

- **Sun protection.** Protect your eyes and your skin. Sunglasses should block both UVA and UVB rays. If you're near water or snow, you'll want polarized sunglasses with side shields.

- **Bug repellent.** To DEET or not to DEET, that is the question. But carry *something*. (For more on repellents, see page 16.)

- **Toilet paper.** Leaves work well, but if you use toilet paper, carry it in a plastic (waterproof) bag along with a trowel to dig a cat hole. Carry the ensemble in a small bag.

- **First-aid kit.** You can be sure that someone will need aspirin or its substitute, and that someone will need a Band-Aid or protection for a blister. And you might end up needing more serious first-aid options, too. (See Chapter 21 for more on first-aid in the wild.)

- **Pack.** Don't forget your pack. You'll need it to carry all the stuff

above, and some more. (For more on backpacks, see page 145.)

For overnight treks, add the following equipment to the list above:

- **Flashlight.** Ever go on a scout trip? Light beams swirl around the campsite like radiant sabers in a *Star Wars* movie. But most of the time you're better off not using a flashlight to find your way at night. However, when you've lost that one crucial thing you can't go to sleep without, a flashlight is invaluable.

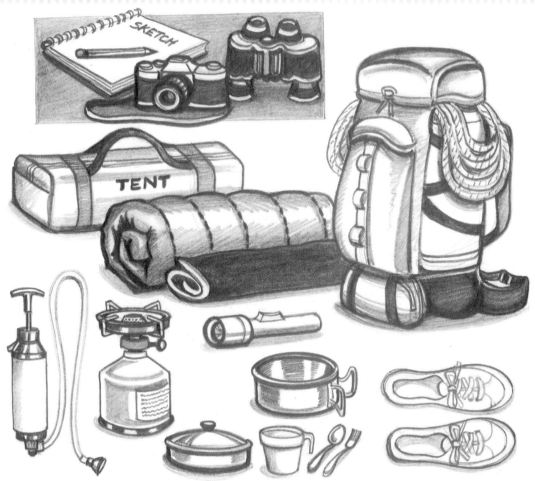

Illustration by Daisy dePuthod

Add this equipment for any overnight hike.

• **Shelter.** A tent, bivy bag, or tarp. Something to keep you dry. (See Chapter 12 for information on tents.)

• **Sleeping bag and pad.** Check the temperature rating on the bag and make sure it's appropriate for the conditions you're likely to encounter. A pad not only makes the hard ground more comfortable, it helps insulate you from the cold. (For more on sleeping bags, see page 126.)

• **Water treatment.** If you're out overnight, you probably don't want to carry all the water you'll need. And, you'll need a system to treat water you find. (For advice on treating water, see page 164.)

• **Stove, fuel, and cookware.** Cooking on open fires can be difficult, and in many places is prohibited. Even if you can make a campfire at night, carry a stove to cook your meals on. (Read more about stoves and cookware on pages 174–186.)

• **Bear bag rope.** Even if there are no bears around, you'll want to protect your food from other critters. Having a small furry creature eat a hole in your $300 tent to get to your candy bars puts a damper on your trip. (See page 20 for more on bear bags.)

• **Shoes.** Not the ones on your feet. Another pair. Give your feet a break by changing their scenery. For crossing streams, a pair of sport sandals is great.

• **Other stuff.** Cameras, binoculars, repair materials, fishing gear, signaling mirror . . . it's up to you.

Getting Help

What would do you do if someone in your party was seriously injured off the beaten path?

Fires big enough to attract attention could be difficult to keep going and just as hard to control. Flares work well, but how many would you need, and do you want to carry the weight?

Assuming you're out of range of cellular phone service and don't have a two-way radio, you could use a signaling mirror. They are simple to use and inexpensive. The limitations are that the sun has to be shining and that people are nearby. For attracting the attention of a pilot high overhead, a signaling mirror works so well that you shouldn't actually practice the technique on a plane unless you've made arrangements beforehand. Although it looks simple to use, a signal mirror requires some practice—preferably before an emergency crops up.

A standard signal mirror has shiny surfaces on both sides and a sight hole in the middle. When using this technique, be very careful not to look directly at the sun. Point the mirror toward, but not directly at, the sun. Look through the sight hole and, with your other arm fully extended in front of you, adjust the angle of the mirror so that light is reflected off the mirror onto your extended hand. Once you can see the bright spot on your hand, slowly adjust your position so your hand is pointing toward the target, with the reflected light still hitting it. Continue to adjust the light until it lands on the target. This isn't difficult to do when the sun is near the target. However, when the sun is behind you and the target is in front, it's much more difficult.

To signal others nearby on the ground, carry a whistle. Whistles are easier on your throat and more effective than yelling. Whistles are also useful at night (when signal mirrors don't work).

STOVES AND FUELS

Ninety-eight percent of long-distance hikers carry stoves, according to extensive field surveys. The most popular stove is the MSR Whisperlite, the first model to incorporate the aluminum fuel bottle as an integral part of the operating stove (see page 176).

Most stoves run on white gas, unleaded auto gas, or refined kerosene, but about 10 percent use butane/propane mixes. A handful rely on alcohol.

PACKS TO BREAK BACKS

This is the list of supplies and equipment recommended for the hearty backpackers of 1898, the gold-rush prospectors who hiked the Chilkoot Trail from Skagway, Alaska, to the Yukon Territory of Canada. They sure didn't travel light.

2 suits of heavy knit underwear
6 pair wool socks
heavy moccasins
2 pairs German stockings
2 heavy flannel overshirts
1 heavy woolen sweater
1 pair overalls
2 twelve-pound blankets
a waterproof blanket
12 bandanna handkerchiefs
a stiff-brim cowboy hat
pack saddles
a pair of rubber boots

a pair of prospector's high land boots
1 mackinaw, coat, pants, shirt
a pair of heavy buck mitts
1 pair leather gloves
a duck coat, pants, vest
6 towels
pocket matchbox, sewing kit, mirror
toothbrush
mosquito netting
1 dunnage bag
a sleeping bag
100 lb. navy beans
150 lb. bacon
400 lb. flour
40 lb. rolled oats
20 lb. corn meal
10 lb. rice
25 lb. sugar
10 lb. tea

20 lb. coffee
10 lb. baking powder
20 lb. salt
1 lb. pepper
2 lb. baking soda
½ lb. mustard
¼ lb. vinegar
2 dozen cans of condensed milk
20 lb. of dried potatoes
5 lb. dried onions
6 tins of beef extract
75 lb. dried fruit
4 pkgs. of yeast
20 lb. candles
1 pkg. tin matches
6 cakes borax
6 lb. laundry soap
½ lb. ground ginger
25 lb. hard tack
1 lb. citric acid
2 bottles Jamaica ginger

Find out from veteran hikers in your area what they recommend, and be prepared before an emergency occurs.

Light Packs and Heavy

There are powerful arguments for keeping your backpack light, but not everybody subscribes to them. Here's veteran California outdoors journalist Gene Rose's take on the

AVERAGE PACK WEIGHTS

In a study of Appalachian Trail through-hikers, author and hiker Roland Mueser found that the average weight of a pack and all gear after the first month was 35 pounds for men and 34 pounds for women. After provisioning, the weight went up to an average of 47 pounds for men and 45 pounds for women. With half of the provisions eaten, the average pack weighed 25 percent of a man's body weight, and 28 percent of a woman's.

For more details, see **Long-Distance Hiking: Lessons from the Appalachian Trail,** by Roland Mueser (Ragged Mountain Press, 1998)

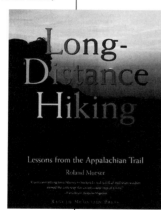

subject. Rose spent much of his working career covering the Sierra Nevada as a writer and photographer. During his 42-year career he reported on many of the major news events of the Sierra, including the first ascent of El Capitan. He is an avid backpacker, hiker, and skier and has hiked most of the world's mountain ranges.

It Walks Like a Man
By Gene Rose

Years ago, Norman Clyde, one of the nation's foremost climbers and pioneer backpackers, was described as the "pack that walks like a man."

In the early part of the century, Clyde was a familiar figure in the mountains of California, often struggling on high to move his 70-pound pack up the trail. He went on to acquire a mountainous reputation as a gung-ho adventurer. He was the elder of the tribe, one who was often identified by the size of his pack.

In the post–World War II years, as recreation exploded over the Sierra, Clyde helped steer many mountain-lovers into backpacking. But despite Clyde's prodigious reputation, he was no model backpacker. He often carried a cast-iron frying pan, a pistol, fishing gear, a camera, and other heavy items such as canned food.

In an era before lightweight frames,

space-age fabrics, and freeze-dried foods, Clyde thought a heavy pack was the price of passage. It was part of the backpacking game: no pain, no gain. In many ways he was an anomaly, a living contradiction to those who believed in going light.

Somewhere along the trail others began looking for a better approach. A heavy pack did not ensure a successful trip; it often preempted it. Going light was the way to go, the early vanguard of the Sierra Club argued. They pointed to John Muir, the early Scottish wanderer who roamed over much of North America subsisting on bread crumbs and tea, using only a small fire for protection from nighttime cold.

Others eschewed John Muir's extreme approach. They pointed to Muir's many close encounters with death, such as when he had to jump into a steaming fumarole atop 14,000-foot Mount Shasta to escape death by freezing.

An avid hiker and skier, Gene Rose was raised in the northern Sierra. A writer and photographer, he wrote extensively about the outdoors for California newspapers and covered the 1960 winter olympics. He has published six books, including *High Odyssey*, the story of one man's 1928 winter exploration of the high Sierra.

Prudent packing

In many ways, the modern revolution in backpacking was led by veterans of World War II, particularly the veterans of the famed U.S. Tenth Mountain Division. Although they had to carry heavy artillery shells and machine guns up the mountainside, they soon realized the importance of prudent packing.

"What you put in your pack is just as important as what you leave out," declared Wilbur Vaughan, a Tenth Mountain veteran who is still on the trail at 70-plus years. "When in doubt, leave it out."

At one point, Vaughan cut off the handle of his toothbrush to reduce weight. And since toothpaste was heavier than tooth powder, he used the latter. A towel became half a towel. A Sierra Club cup served as a bowl, plate, and cup. And who needs a fork? "If you watch the ounces, the pounds will take care of themselves," he said.

Another Tenth Mountain Division veteran, the legendary Paul Petzold of the Tetons and Wind River Range fame, figures most backpackers can do with relatively little. "Necessities are those items that contribute to our safety and comfort without posing a burden in transporting them," he told his followers. "When one must carry a supply of food, clothing, shelter, and equipment on one's own back, selectivity and careful planning are critical."

In preparation for his National Outdoor Leadership School outings, Petzold would have his students separate the contents of their packs into two piles. The first pile comprised those items that each student felt were necessary, while the other pile contained questionable items. Petzold would then reject all the items from the questionable pile, and about half those items the beginners deemed essential.

If a hiker took one of every item that was available at his or her backpacking shop, it would take an entire pack string of horses to carry them.

Epicurean delights

You can simplify and carefully calculate food supplies to save weight, too. Too many backpackers go out with visions of an Epicurean delight rather than of an adventure.

At the other extreme was the hiker I encountered years ago who relied on oatmeal for breakfast and packaged soups for dinner. Lunch consisted of a handful of raisins and nuts. That was his menu for a two-week trip. "Yes, I lost a little weight," he acknowledged, "but I didn't

Anderson Pass, Olympic National Park. Photo by Ed Sobey

starve. Liquids are what should not be shorted."

High altitudes have a way of damping appetites, particularly for the first day or two. At these times, packaged soups with their rehydrating liquids represent the prudent way to circumvent altitude sickness and dehydration.

Today's emphasis on "leave no trace" camping also encourages the go-light approach. The less you carry, the lighter your impact on the land.

In many ways, backpacking is the art of moving across the land in the easiest, most enjoyable way. Louis Stech, a veteran Sierra hiker, describes backpacking as the way that avoids the misery level.

The "pack that walks like a man" has many profiles. Perhaps the most tragic is the young child, headed up the hillside, overburdened, unhappy, and doomed to a lifetime of hating or rejecting something that should have been a positive experience.

A beginner's or child's first backpacking experience should be limited to an overnight campout not far from the family car. Advance preparations are imperative: The child's pack should contain little more than a jacket or a change of clothes. The only thing in excess should be fun.

Backpacking shops are filled with "how-to-do-it" books. Most have practical tips for avoiding mistakes and adversity. It's a good route to take.

Online Information

There is a plethora of information on the Internet about hiking equipment and places to hike. If you don't have access from your home or office, try your local library. Many libraries provide free Internet access.

The Internet is a great place to read product reviews and get information from equipment manufacturers and user groups. For major purchases, check out products on the Web and then compare prices at backpacking stores.

Wherever possible throughout this catalog, we have listed website addresses and phone numbers of manufacturers. Increasingly, manufacturers are displaying their products online, and with the click of a mouse you can see what each has to offer. If they don't offer online catalogs, call to request a printed catalog or find out where you can purchase their products.

Specific Products

The following websites give information on specific products or will put you in touch with the manufacturers.

BaseCamp-Backpacker Magazine: Provides specifications for equipment by manufacturers; www.gearfinder.com or www.bpbasecamp.com

Great Outdoor Recreation Pages (GORP): Articles, equipment, links to nonprofit organizations and government agencies; www.gorp.com

The Lightweight Backpacker: www.isomedia.com/homes/clindsey

The Mining Company: backpacking.miningco.com

Outdoor Action Guide: www.princeton.edu./~rcurtis/

COMPUTER CHECKLIST

Larry Kostal, of Issaquah, Washington, offers a computer disk (or printed copy) of his checklist. His mailing address is P.O. Box 1185, Issaquah, WA 98027-1185.

---

outother.html

Outdoor Link: Locates equipment companies on the Web and links to nonprofit organizations; www.outdoorlink.com

Outdoors Today: Helps you contact the websites of equipment manufacturers; www.outdoors-today.com

REI: Offers product reviews; www.rei.com

Sports Site: Links to manufacturers; www.sportsite.com

Online Ordering

Ordering on the Web is easy. You can order from retail stores, such as REI or L.L. Bean, or directly from the manufacturers. If you are ordering several different products by different makers, it's easier to order from the retail stores online.

Sierra Trading Post sells overstock, close-outs, and irregulars of brand name products at steep discounts. You need to get on their mailing list to receive a current catalog. Their phone number is listed below. Contact: (800) 713-4534

THE GEAR GUY

Log on to the Web and ask the "Gear Guy," Douglas Gantenbein, questions about outdoor equipment. Think of a really tough question and go online at //outside.starwave.com/ outsidestore/gearguy/gearexpert.html

---

Here is a modest sample of the hiking and backpacking companies doing business on the Internet. To find contacts for other companies, check out www.gorp.com or wwwbpbasecamp.com.

American Wilderness: (800) 284-0365; //home.communique.net/~awi

Backcountry Experience: (800) 648-8519; www.bcexp.com

Backcountry Outfitters: (812) 479-6887; www.evansville.net/biz/backpack

Backcountry Store: (800) 409-4502; www.bcstore.com

Bearfoot Traveller: (812) 945-BEAR; www.kyana.com/bearfoot

Campmor: (800) 226-7667; www.campmor.com

Cyberspace Discount Outdoor Store: www.omix.com/rmo

Denali Outdoors: (888) 4DENALI; www.denali1.com

EDGE: //soli.com/edge/contents.htm

Foggy Mountain Shop: (907) 586-6780; www.alaska.net/~foggymtn

Marmot Mountain Works: (800) MARMOT-9; www.marmotmountain.com

Mountain Gear: (800) 829-2009; www.mgear.com

MountainZone: (800) 644-5232; www.mountainzone.com

Muddy River: (816) 753-7093; www.kc-outdoors.com/muddyriver

Online Sports: www.onlinesports.com/

REI: (800) 426-4840; www.rei.com

Rocky Mountain Sports: s2.com/html/rms/rms.html

Sierra Nevada Adventure Company: (209) 532-5621; www.snacattack.com

The Outdoor: (888) 737-5500;
www.theoutdoor.com
Wilderness Furnishings:
(800) 343-3564; www.wildfire.com
Wilderness Outfitters:
(800) 778-3636;
www.redbud.com/wilderness

Your Checklist

Here is a checklist of equipment to consult before every trip. You won't need all of this for one hike, but you can refer to the list to make sure you packed everything you do need.

Photocopy this list and check off each item as you put it in a pile. If you keep the list until you're planning your next trip, it will help you remember what you needed and didn't have, or what you took and didn't need.

Route information
Guide books•maps•compass•GPS

Footwear
Boots•liner socks•outer socks•
camp shoes•sandals

Pack
Backpack•day pack or fanny
pack•pack cover (for rain)

Sleeping gear
Sleeping bag•bivy bag•sleeping
pad•over bag•bag liner•stuffsack

Tent
Tent•poles•rain fly•stakes•
stuffsack•ground cloth

Water
Water treatment system•
backup system•water containers•
camp bucket

Food and cooking
Food•spices•stove and repair kit•
spare fuel and funnel•matches
in waterproof case•fire starters
(two per day)•cookware•
eating utensils•pot holder•
cup and plate•pot scrubber•
biodegradable soap•towel•
plastic bag to haul out trash•
food for one more day

For your health
First-aid kit•vitamins•sun blocker•
insect repellent•bear repellent•
prescription medicines•
toilet paper and trowel in sack

Clothing
Underwear•wicking layer•
insulation layer•wind and rain
protection•bandanna•shorts•
hat for warmth•sun hat•gloves•
gaiters•sunglasses

All the rest
Pocket knife•survival tool•
camera•binoculars•rope or cord•
whistle•flashlight•spare bulb•
spare batteries•hiking staff or poles

Enchanted Valley, Olympic National Park. Photo by Ed Sobey

Hiking Information by Region:

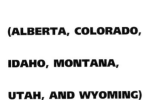

(ALBERTA, COLORADO,

IDAHO, MONTANA,

UTAH, AND WYOMING)

Alberta
Highest point: Mt. Columbia, 12,294 feet.

Government Resources

Access Alberta: travel information:
www.agt.net/public/access/acchomep.htm
Banff National Park: (403) 762-1550
Elk Island National Park: (403) 292-4401
Jasper National Park: (403) 852-6161
Parks Canada:
//parkscanada.pch.gc.ca/parks/alphape.htm

Travel Alberta: (800) 661-8888
Waterton Lakes National Park:
(403) 859-2224;
(403) 859-2445 in summer
Wood Buffalo National Park: (867) 872-7900

Guides and Outfitters

Fortech Adventures: (888) 565-HIKE
Rocky Mountain Hiking: (403) 852-0078
Totem Outdoor Adventures: (403) 465-5960
Ultimate Adventure Camp: (403) 538-3890

The Rockies

Rocky Mountain National Park. Photo by Ed Sobey.

Kent and Donna Dannen (Globe Pequot Press, 1994).

If you are considering exploring the Rocky Mountain National Park with children, **Rocky Mountain National Park: A Family Guide,** by Lisa Gollin Evans (Mountaineers Books, 1991), is the resource you need.

You can walk west from downtown Boulder and, in just a few minutes, bump into deer grazing in the foothills. The trails are described in **Boulder Hiking Trails: The Best of the Plains, Foothills, and Mountains,** by Ruth Carol Cushman and Glenn Cushman (Pruett Publishing, 1995). For hikes around Denver, try **Day Hikes in Denver,** by Robert Stone (ICS Books, 1996).

Other books worth consulting are:
Colorado's Fourteeners: From Hikes to Climbs, by Gerry Roach (Fulcrum, 1992).
The Colorado Trail: The Official Guidebook, by Randy Jacobs (Westcliffe, 1994).
San Juan Mountains: a Climbing and Hiking Guide, by R. Rosengrough and Robert F. Rosebrough (Cordillera Press, 1986).

Colorado

Highest point: Mount Elbert: 14,433 feet.

Reference Material

Hiking Trails of Southwestern Colorado, by Paul Pixler (Pruett Publishing, 1992), guides you through the San Juan and Uncompahgre National Forests. Another good reference is **Hiking Rocky Mountain National Park: Including Indian Peaks,** by

Federal and State Resources

Black Canyon of the Gunnison: (970) 641-2337
Bureau of Land Management, Colorado: (303) 239-3700

Colorado National Monument: (970) 858-3617
Colorado State Office of Tourism:
(800) COLORADO;
www.state.co.us/visit_dir/visitormenu.html
Colorado State Parks: (800) 678-2267;
www.dnr.state.co.us/parks/index.asp
Curecanti National Recreation Area:
(970) 641-2337
Dinosaur National Monument: (970) 374-3000
Elk Range, U.S. Forest Service: (303) 925-3445
Flat Tops Wilderness: (303) 878-4039
Florissant Fossil Beds National Monument:
(719) 748-3253
Great Sand Dunes National Monument:
(719) 378-2312
Gunnison Resource Area: (303) 641-0471
Hovenweep National Monument: (303) 529-4461
La Junta, Forest Service: (719) 384-7411
Mesa Verde National Park: (970) 529-4465
Maroon Bells-Snowmass Wilderness:
(303) 925-3445
Pikes National Forest: (719) 545-8737
Rocky Mountain National Park: (970) 586-1206;
backcountry information: (970) 586-1242
San Isabel National Forest: (970) 925-3445
White River National Forest: (970) 945-2521
U.S. Forest Service, Rocky Mountain Region:
(303) 275-5350

Guides and Outfitters

Adventures Afoot: (800) 294-8218;
e-mail: pam@afoot.com
Adventure Specialists: e-mail: adventur@rmii.com
American Adventures Expedtions: (800) 288-0675
Backcountry Outfitters: (800) 898-2006;
www.itoday.com/backcountry/
Bill Dvorak's Kayak and Rafting Expeditions:
(719) 539-6851; www.vtinet.com/dvorak
Blazing Adventures: (800) 282-7238
Cannibal Outdoors: (970) 944-2559;
www.hinsdale-county.com/hikes.html
Colorado Backcountry Adventures: (970) 926-5299
Elk Mountain Ranch: (719) 539-4430
Frying Pan River Ranch: (800) 352-0980
JML Outfitters: (303) 770-2541; e-mail:

haskettm@aol.com
Keystone Resort: (970) 496-4386;
www.skimountains.com/colorado/keystone.html
Lost Valley Ranch: (303) 647-2311
Noah's Ark Whitewater Rafting: (719) 395-2158;
e-mail: flood@noahsark.com
Pagosa Rafting Outfitters/Wilderness Journeys:
(970) 731-4081
Road Less Traveled:
(800) 488-8483; e-mail: fun@rmi.net
Skyline Guest Ranch:
(970) 728-3757; e-mail: skyline-ranch@toski.com
Wildside Adventures: (970) 471-4902

Llama Packers

Buckhorn Llama: (970) 667-7411
Red Dog Ranch: (970) 728-0401
Timberline Llamas: (303) 526-0092

Clubs and Organizations

Colorado Mountain Club is a mountain of an organization with chapters in several cities, each one offering a range of outdoor activities.
Contact: (303) 279-3080; www.xpert.net/cmc.

The James P. Beckwourth Mountain Club, based in Denver, sponsors a variety of outdoor experiences throughout the year.
Contact: www.ecentral.com/members/jpb/.

Idaho
Highest point: Borah Peak, 12,662 feet.

Reference Material

Ralph Maughan and Jackie Johnson Maughan wrote *Hiking Idaho* (Falcon Press, 1995) to include "something for everyone—from easy day hikes suitable for a picnic with children, to a strenuous climb of Mount Borah,

Idaho's highest mountain."

Trail information about the Sawtooths is available in **Adventures in Idaho's Sawtooth Country: 63 Trips for Hikers and Mountain Bikers,** by Lynne Stone (The Mountaineers, 1990).

Federal and State Resources

Boise National Forest: (208) 364-4100
Bitterroot National Forest: (406) 363-7117
Bruneau Dunes State Park:
(208) 366-7919
Bureau of Land Management, Idaho:
(208) 384-3001
Caribou National Forest:
(208) 236-7500
Chellis National Forest:
(208) 879-2285
City of Rocks National Reserve:
(208) 824-5519
Clearwater National Forest:
(208) 476-4541
Craters of the Moon National Monument: (208) 527-3257
Farragut State Park: (208) 683-2425
Hagerman Fossil Beds National Monument: (208) 837-4793
Hells Canyon National Recreation Area: (541) 523-6391
Hells Gate State Park: (208) 799-5015
Heyburn State Park: (208) 686-1308
Idaho Panhandle National Forest:
(208) 765-7223
Idaho State Department of Parks and Recreation: (208) 334-4199
Idaho State Office of Tourism:
(208) 726-8291
Idaho State Travel Council:
(800) 635-7820 or (800) VISIT-ID
Nez Perce National Forest:
(208) 983-1950
Owyhee Badlands, Bureau of Land

Management: (208) 384-3300
   Payette National Forest: (208) 634-8151
   Ponderosa State Park: (208) 634-2164
   Priest Lake State Park: (208) 443-2200
  Salmon National Forest: (208) 756-2215
Sawtooth National Forest: (208) 737-3200
Sawtooth National Recreation Area:
(208) 726-7672
Targhee National Forest: (208) 624-3151

Guides and Outfitters

For general information on outfitters in Idaho, telephone the Idaho Outfitters' and Guides' Association at (800) 635-7820.

Rocky Mountain National Park. Photo by Ed Sobey.

Boulder Outdoor Survival School: (208) 359-2400

Cooks Idaho Outfitters: (800) 854-6697

Hidden Creek Ranch: (800) 446-3833;
www.nidlink.com/~hiddencreek

Hughes River Expeditions: (800) 262-1882

Idaho Adventures: (800) 789-WAVE;
www.recworld.com/moser.html

Joe Cantrell Outfitting: (208) 753-4501

**Middle Fork Wilderness
Outfitters:** (800) 726-0575;
www.gorp.com/mfwo

Mystic Saddle Ranch:
(888) 722-5432;
www.mysticsaddleranch.com

Pioneer Mountain Outfitters:
(208) 774-3737; (208) 734-3679

Priest Lake Guide Service:
(208) 443-2956;
www.priestlake.org/plgs.html

ROW (River Odysseys West):
(800) 451-6034; www.rowinc.com

Venture Outdoors:
(800)528-5262;
e-mail: venout@micron.net

White Cloud Outfitters:
(208) 879-4574

**White Otter Outdoor
Adventures:** (208) 726-2429

Whitewater Outfitters:
(208) 926-4231; www.lesbois.
com/outdoors/1019.htm

**Worldwide Outdoor
Adventures:** (800) 859-0345;
www.wwoutdooradventures.com

Llama Packers

High Llama Wilderness Tours:
(800) 775-5262

Spindrift Llamas:
(208) 756-6206; e-mail:
73517.3121@Compuserve.com

Venture Outdoors:
(800) 528-LAMA;
www.webpak.net/~venout

Montana

Highest point: Granite Peak, 12,799 feet.

Reference Material

The Hiker's Guide to Montana, by Bill Schneider (Fal-

con, 1994), lists 120 hikes in Glacier National Park, Purrcell Mountains, the Bob Marshall and Beartooths, and the Bitterroot Range. He also includes sections on survival and first-aid kits, tips on dealing with bears and rattlesnakes, and hiking with kids.

For more information on Glacier National Park and Waterton Lakes

National Park (in Alberta), see **Glacier National Park and Waterton Lakes National Park,** by Vicky Spring (The Mountaineers, 1994). Spring lists day hikes, backpack trips, and bicycling trips.

Another good reference is **Bitterroot to Beartooth: Hiking Southwest Montana,** by Ruth Rudner (Random House, 1985).

Federal and State Resources

Beaverhead-Deerlodge National Forest: (406) 683-3900
Bighorn Canyon National Recreation Area: (406) 666-2412
Bitterroot National Forest: (406) 363-3131
Bureau of Land Management, Montana: (406) 255-2904
Custer National Forest: (406) 587-6701 or (406) 657-6361
Flathead National Forest: (406) 755-5401
Gallatin National Forest: (406) 587-6701
Glacier National Park: (408) 888-5441
Helena National Forest: (406) 449-5207
Kootenai National Forest: (406) 293-6211
Lewis and Clark National Forest: (406) 791-7700
Little Bighorn Battlefield National Monument: (406) 638-2622
Lolo National Forest: (406) 329-3750
Montana State Office of Tourism: (800) 548-3390; www.travel.mt.gov
Montana State Parks: (406) 444-3750; //fwp.mt.gov/parks/parks.htm

Nez Perce National Historical Park:
(208) 843-2261
U.S. Forest Service, Northern Region:
(406) 329-3511

Guides and Outfitters

Averill's Flathead Lake Lodge: (406) 837-6977;
e-mail: fll@digisys.net
Big Timber Guides:
(406) 932-4080
Big Wild Adventures:
(406) 821-3747
Cayuse Outfitters:
(406) 222-3168
Flat Iron Outfitting:
(406) 827-3666
Glacier Raft Company:
(800) 235-6781; www.
glacierraftco.com/welcome.html
Glacier Wilderness Guides:
(800) 521-RAFT; e-mail:
glguides@cyberport.net
**Hargrave Cattle and Guest
Ranch:** (406) 858-2284
**Mills Outfitters,
(horse-supported trips):**
(406) 562-3335
Mountain Fit Experience:
(800) 926-5700;
www.mountainfit.com
Pangaea Expeditions:
(406) 721-7719;
www.bigsky.net/pangaea
Rugg's Outfitting:
(406) 822-4240; www.marsweb.
com/rugg/toindex.html
**10,000 Waves—Raft & Kayak
Adventures:** (800) 537-8315;
www.10000waves.com/index.html
Wild Horizons Expeditions:
(406) 821-3747

Llama Packers
Great Northern Llama:
(406) 755-9044

Yellowstone Llamas:
(406) 586-6872;
e-mail: llamas@mcn.net

Utah
Highest point: Kings Peak, 13,528 feet.

Reference Material

The Official Wasatch Hiking Map is published by the
University of Utah (University of Utah Press, 1994).

Rocky Mountain National Park. Photo by Ed Sobey.

Hiking the Southwest's Canyon Country, by Sandra Hinchman (The Mountaineers, 1997), describes 100 hikes in the Four Corners region. She includes short hikes and three-week trips, and provides maps and background information.

High Uinta Trails, by Mel Davis (Wasatch Book Distribution, 1974), is still a useful reference.

Hiking the Escalante, by Reudi Lambrechtse (Wasatch Books, 1985), and *Hiking and Exploring the Paria River,* by Michael Kelsey (Wasatch Books, 1987), collectively cover the entire monument.

Equipment Rental

EZCamp Rentals has equipment for hire and will even set up base camps in southern Utah and northern Arizona. Contact: (888) 4EZ-CAMP; www.ezcamp.com.

Federal and State Resources

Arches National Park: (801) 259-8161
Bryce Canyon National Park:
(801) 644-2672 or (801) 834-5322
Bureau of Land Management, Utah:
(801) 539-4021
Canyonlands National Park:
(801) 834-5322 or (801) 259-3911
Capital Reef National Park:
(801) 259-7164 or (801) 425-3791
Cedar Breaks National Monument:
(801) 425-3791 or (801) 586-9451
Dinosaur National Monument: (303) 374-3000
Glen Canyon National Recreation Area:
(602) 645-8200

Grand Staircase-Escalante National Monument:
(801) 826-5499 or (801) 644-2672
Hovenweep National Monument: (303) 749-0510
Kanab Area Office, Bureau of Land Management:
(801) 586-9451
Manti-La Sal National Forest: (801) 644-2672
Natural Bridges National Monument:
(801) 259-5174
Rainbow Bridge National Monument:
(602) 645-8200
San Juan Resource Area, Bureau of Land Management: (801) 637-2817
San Rafael Swell, Bureau of Land Management:
(801) 587-2141
Timpanogos Cave National Monument:
(801) 756-5239
Uinta National Forest: (801) 636-3600
U.S. Forest Service, Intermountain Region:
(801) 625- 5352
Utah State Division of Parks: (801) 538-7221;
www.nr.state.ut.us/parks/utahstpk.htm
Utah State Office of Tourism: (800) 200-1160
Utah Travel Council: (801) 538-1030
Wasatch-Cache National Forest: (801) 524-5030
Zion National Park: (801) 524-5030 or (801) 772-3256

Guides and Outfitters

Adrift Adventures: (800) 874-4483;
//moab-utah.com/adrift/adventures.html
Buckhorn Llama Company:
(800) 318-9454; e-mail: sslamar@aol.com
Canyonlands Field Institute: (800) 860-5262
Earthspirit Adventures: (801) 644-5457;
e-mail: earthspirit@xpressweb.com
Escalante Canyon Outfitters: (801) 335-7311;
e-mail: ecohike@color-country.net
Falcon's Ledge: (801) 454-3737
Fred's Adventure Tours: (801) 739-4294
Hondoo Rivers and Trails: (800) 332-2696;
e-mail: hondoo@color-country.net
Kaibab Mountain Bike Tours: (800) 451-1133;
www.kaibabtours.com/index.htm
Moki Treks: (801) 259-8033
Nichols Expeditions: (800) 648-8488;
www.nicholsexpeditions.com

Ravenworks Tours: (801) 772-3268
Red Rock'n Llamas: (801) 559-7325
Tag-a-Long Expeditions: (800) 453-3292
The Norwegian School of Nature Life:
(800) 649-5322
The Wilderness School:
(801) 226-7498
Ultimate Adventures:
(888) 483-2787

Clubs and Organizations

The Wasatch Mountain Club
offers hikes for a variety of endurance levels; contact
(801) 463-9842; www.digitalpla.
net/~wmc/index.html
Write **The Great Western Trail
Association** at P.O. Box 1428,
Provo, UT 84602.

Wyoming
Highest point:
Gannett Peak, 13,804 feet.

Reference Material

The Grand Teton Natural History
Association published **Teton
Trails,** by Katy Duffy and Darum
Wile, in 1995.

**Best Easy Day Hikes in Yel-
lowstone,** by Bill Schneider (Falcon Press, 1997), lists 28 hikes
with descriptions and maps. All
the hikes listed are on trails.

**Hiking Wyoming's Wind
River Range,** by Ron Adkison
(Falcon Press, 1996), covers
"nearly all of the wilderness trails
in the range and offers suggestions for extended trips." Adkison
gives extensive descriptions and
accompanies each with maps,

elevation charts, and photographs.

Read also: **Day Hikes in Yellowstone National
Park: 25 Favorite Hikes,** by Robert Stone (ICS Books,
1996).

Rogue River Trail. Photo by Ed Sobey

Federal and State Resources

Bighorn Canyon National Recreation Area:
(406) 666-2412
Bighorn National Forest: (800) 225-5996
Bridger-Teton National Forest: (307) 672-0751
Bureau of Land Management, Wyoming:
(307) 775-6001
Devils Tower National Monument: (307) 467-5283
Fossil Butte National Monument: (307) 877-4455
Glacier National Park: (307) 367-4326
Grand Teton National Park: (406) 888-7800 or
(307) 739-3300
**Lander Resource Aream, Bureau of Land
Management:** (307) 733-2880
Medicine Bow National Forest: (307) 332-7822
Shoshone National Forest: (307) 745-8971
Wind Rivers, Shoshone & Arapaho Fish and Game:
(307) 527-6241
Wyoming State Parks and Historic Sites:
(307) 777-6323
Wyoming Tourism Office: (800) 225-5996

Yellowstone National Park: (307) 332-7207 or
(307) 344-2002

Guides and Outfitters

Absaroka Ranch: (307) 455-2275
Bear Basin Camp: (307) 486-2215
Early Guest Ranch: (800) 532-4055
Haderlie's Tincup Mountain Guest Ranch:
(800) 253-2368
Paradise Guest Ranch: (307) 684-7876
Rawah Guest Ranch: (800) 820-3152
Snake River Kayak & Canoe School: (800) 529-2501
Wyoming Outfitters' Association: (307) 527-7453
Wyoming Rivers and Trails: (888) 978-2333;
www.jacksonholenet.com/WRT

Llama Packers
High Plains Llamas & Alpacas: (370) 537-5292
Wilderness Pack Trips:
(307) 332-5624; e-mail: swoodruf@wyoming.com

CHAPTER

Good for Your Soles

**More backpacking trips are ruined by sore feet
than by all other causes combined. Pounded by
the ground below and the weight of you and your
pack above, your feet receive harsher treatment
than any other part of your body.**

—Chris Townsend,

The Backpacker's Handbook

The Importance of Boots

Boots and socks may be the most mundane equipment for a trip into the backcountry but they are the most important. Footwear is not where you want to scrimp. A good pair of boots properly fitted to your feet can give years of comfortable wear and protection.

Here is some more sage advice from Gene Rose, a veteran Californian journalist:

Boots are Your Passport

By Gene Rose

If there is one piece of equipment all backpackers need, it is a good pair of boots. By any measure, boots serve as the hiker's passport to outdoor life and adventure. A bad pair can lead straight to the proverbial trip from hell.

But don't expect to find the perfect pair, that is, the perfect fit. While some of the new lightweight boots have gone a long way toward meeting the needs of a hardy hiker, the perfect pair of hiking boots has yet to be crafted. As also, the perfect pair of feet.

While a pair of boots might seem fine on a short hike through the woods, terrain, weather, and other conditions often conspire to make them painful farther down the trail. A long downhill pitch can be especially troublesome, as the toes are thrust to the front. Side-hill hiking can put an inordinate

Photo by Ed Sobey

Norwegian welt-stitching

filler cushion

inner sole

Illustration by Daisy dePuthod

Learn to Love Leather

What should you look for in boots? Make sure they're suitable for the job. Lightweight boots and sneakers are fine for day hikes in good weather and you can also use them with lighter loads on well-maintained trails. But, although you save energy by not picking up heavy boots with each footstep, you need better protection from sturdier footwear as the going gets tougher. For backpacking, your feet need leather, or a leather and Gore-Tex combination. For mountaineering, you need a heavier boot, one that is stiff enough to handle a crampon.

It's ideal

Leather is the ideal material for boots because with care it lasts a long time. It conforms to your foot and it can be treated with waterproofing. Gore-Tex boots (which are composed mostly of leather) are good for wet and cold climates as they help your feet pass perspiration.

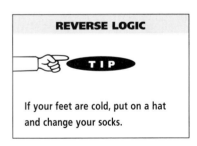

REVERSE LOGIC

TIP

If your feet are cold, put on a hat and change your socks.

amount of pressure on the sides of the feet, and heat build-up can make feet tender and sore, leading to other problems.

Consequently, some experienced hikers shy away from boots with the new microporous moisture barriers that tend to exacerbate heat and moisture build-up.

Hikers should remember that their feet can swell as much as one whole size during an extended hike. In other words, your feet change with the trail; but your boots don't. So attention to your feet is imperative. Tender places—the precursor of blisters—need to be addressed immediately.

On long hot hikes, a good lunch break includes time to bathe your feet and dry out your

socks and boots. At the other extreme, when your feet are cold, a change of socks will help them warm up.

Despite an avalanche of high-tech socks made out of miracle fibers, the old two-sock approach still affords maximum protection. A light sock inside a heavier cushioned sock, capable of wicking away moisture, helps. A good approach is to stop at the first sign of a hot spot and apply some abrasion protection, such as moleskin or an adhesive bandage.

Don't stick with a poor-fitting boot. Some backpacking shops will allow you to return slightly-used boots if you are purchasing a replacement pair. Obviously you need to step out in the best-fitting boot you can find. Happy hiking!

The soles should inspire confidence in you that they will grip even the most slippery surfaces. The fewer seams there are, the drier the boot will stay. Pull out the tongue and see if it will keep water out. Will the top of the boot conform to your leg and keep out pebbles?

Get a good fit

The most important consideration is the fit. Since each manufacturer uses different lasts, some brands of boots will fit your feet better than others. And, although leather will (eventually) conform to your feet, a rub in the store will only get worse after a few miles on the trail.

Boots should be substantially larger than ordinary shoes. In most day-to-day walking you aren't on your feet for long periods, but when you're hiking, you're on your feet most of the time. Your feet swell up and they need more space. You also need more space in front to ensure that your toes don't smash into the end of the boot on downhill stretches. One way to test this fit is to push your feet forward in unlaced boots, until your toes touch the end.

The finger test

If you can insert at least one finger, but not more than two, between the boot heel and your heel, you have enough room. Then, when you have laced the boots tightly, your foot shouldn't slide around inside the boot. You will, however, have wiggle room in the toe and a snug fit at the heel. The store should have an inclined ramp for you to walk on, to make sure your feet aren't sliding inside the boot. With the laces tightened, the tongue should lie comfortably along the top of your foot.

Try walking, to see if foot and boot bend at the same place. And, since your feet probably differ in size, try on both boots and test them for comfort.

Most hiking boots rise above the ankles to give support and they should have a scree collar to keep out all the stuff you kick up during the day's hike.

One more consideration in choosing a boot is the weight. Since you have to lift each foot more than 1,000 times per mile, even a few additional ounces will

STOP AND TIGHTEN

TIP

After climbing up to the mountain pass, your boots and laces have loosened a bit, allowing your feet to slide. Before beginning the descent, tighten the laces to ensure your toes won't ram into the end of the boots. If you feel your toenails hitting, clip them shorter.

mean the expenditure of much more energy. So compare your chosen boots with others in the store, and avoid ones that are heavier for no good reason.

Boot Manufacturers

Alico Sport: (800) 475-4266
AlpinaSports: (603) 448-3101;
www.alpinasports.com
AKU USA: (888) 258-2668
Asolo: (800) 892-2668;
www.asolo.com
B-West Outdoor Specialties:
(800) 293-7855
Boreal: (714) 498-1011;
www.borealuse.com
Cabela's: (800) 237-4444;
www.cabelas.com

GRIPPING BETTER

TIP

Look at almost any hiking boot and you will see the name Vibram on the soles. It was derived from the name of the founder, Vitale Bramani. Vitale was motivated to invent a better sole for climbing boots when he witnessed the death of six climbers in the Italian Alps in 1935. Two years later he came out with a rubber-studded sole. He developed high-traction rubber compounds and new sole designs to improve boots.

Columbia Sportswear:
(800) 622-6953;
www.columbia.com
Danner Shoe: (800) 345-0430
Eastern Mountain Sports:
(888) 463-6367;
www.emsonline.com
Eurovictory Sports:
(800) 520-3876
Five Ten Co: (909) 798-4222

EXO: (303) 443-8283;
www.exosport.com
Fabiano: (617) 268-5625;
//world.std.com/~fabiano/info.html
Garmont USA: (888) 343-5200
GriSport: (905) 793-1252

H.H. Brown Shoe:
www.hhbrown.com
HiTec Sports USA, Inc.:
(800) 521-1698; www.hi-tech.
com/boots
Koflach: (603) 880-6143

Photo by Burt Kornegay, Slickrock Expeditions

Lake of the Woods:
(800) 438-7463
La Sportiva USA: (303) 443-8710;
www.sportiva.com
Legends Footwear:
(800) 948-7245
Limmer Boot: (603) 694-2668
L.L. Bean: (800) 809-7057;
www.llbean.com
Lowa: (203) 353-0116
Merrell Footwear:
(800) 869-3348;
www.merrell.boot.com
Nike: (800) 344-6453;
www.nike.com
Northlake Outdoor Footwear:
(800) 251-3388
One Sport, Inc.: (206) 621-9303
Raichle: (800) 431-2204;
www.oputdoorlink.com/
raichlehiking
Reebok: (800) 843-4444;
www.planetreebok.com
Rockport: (800) 762-5767;
www.rockport.com
Salomon:
(800) 995-3556;
www.salomonsports.
com
Sorel: (800) 667-6735;
www.kaufman.ca
Sportiva:
(303) 443-8710;
www.sportiva.com
Tecnica:
(800) 258-3897;
www.tecnicausa.com
Timberland:
(800) 445-5545
Trezeta USA:
(203) 227-4988
Vasque:
(800) 224-HIKE;
www.vasque.com
Yukon:
(800) 352-3331

Caring for Your Boots

After every trip, clean your boots with a brush and make sure they're dry. If they're wet, stuff them with newspapers or cloth, and renew it every few hours. Don't put them near heat.

Annie Getchell in **The Essential Outdoor Gear Manual** (Ragged Mountain Press, 1995), offers the following advice on treating your boots:

• Break in new boots slightly before treatment.

• Boots should be very dry before conditioning (unless you're applying a water-based treatment).

• If you plan to seam seal boots, do so before waterproofing the leather and allow the sealer to cure fully before treatment.

• Remove bootlaces and meticulously work in the dressing with your fingers, paying special attention to overlapping seams and folds around tongue gussets, where most water penetrates.

• Allow the dressing to cure fully, preferably overnight, before wiping off the excess with a lint-free cloth (chamois or PakTowl). At this point you may wish to apply a second,

thin coat of goop, depending on the condition of your boots.

• Set freshly treated boots in a sunny window or apply moderate heat (from a wood stove or hair dryer) to warm and soften the conditioner. Then polish or buff the boots to seal the dressing—that is, to create a hard, smooth finish.

• If the boots still feel sticky after 24 hours, the dressing has not cured and will pick up dirt rather than protect the boot against it. Rework and buff the boots until the excess conditioner is removed.

DEALING WITH HOT SPOTS

When you feel a hot spot developing on your foot, take care of it before it becomes a blister. Band-Aids may not stay put. Moleskin will do the job, but duct tape also works well and costs a lot less. Socks slide easily over the smooth side of the duct tape while the adhesive holds tight to the skin, stopping the rubbing. You can take the tape off each night to speed healing, but it will adhere well for several days if you leave it on.

Waterproofing Products

When you've conditioned your boots, you can apply a sealer. Sealers will let the boot breathe—letting out water vapor while keeping water out. However, no sealer can completely waterproof boots. Ask at the store where you buy your boots about the type of conditioner and sealer they recommend.

Aqua Seal: (800) 878-1492
Bee Seal: (503) 452-1638

Biwell: (802) 985-5056
Kiwi Camp Dry: (800) 392-7733
Nikwax USA: (800) 577-2700; www.nikwax-usa.com
Scotchgard: (800) 367-7683
Sno-Seal: (803) 531-1820
Tectron: (800) 289-2583

BRAND-NEW BOOTS

The backpack trip heads out on Friday, so Thursday night you go looking for boots, right? Wrong.

Boots and feet need some low-stress quality time to get acquainted. Wear them around the house for a couple of weeks before the big trip. Wear them on a few break-in trips, too, before you tackle a long hike.

To seal the seams of your boots use Seam Grip, or a comparable product.

Boot Repairers

When your boots need repair, first try the retailer who sold them to you. They could be under warranty, and the manufacturer might replace them or repair them for no charge. Alternatively, call local cobblers listed under Shoe Repair in the telephone directory. You might also ask outfitters who they recommend, or contact one of the companies listed here. To find repair shops authorized by Vibram, call (800) VIBRAM-7.

Here are the names and phone numbers of cobblers recognized for quality work:

NOT TOO TOASTY

TIP

Don't put your boots closer to a fire than you'd put your feet.

Carters Cobble Shoppe, Bozeman, Montana: (406) 585-8607
Cobbler & Cordwainer, New Rochelle, New York: (800) 788-2668
Dave Page, Cobbler, Seattle, Washington: (800) 252-1229
Komito Boots, Estes Park, Colorado: (800) 422-2668
Marmot Mountain Works, California: (800) MARMOT-9; www.marmotmountain.com
Mekan Boot Company, Salt Lake City, Utah: (800) 675-2884
Morin Custom Boots and Repair, Idaho Springs, Colorado: (800) 228-BOOT
Mountain Soles, Trout Lake, Washington: (509) 395-2844
Phelps Shoe & Boot Repair, Longmont, Colorado: (303) 776-9762
Progressive Outdoor Footwear Repairs, La Mesa, California: (800) 783-7764
Rocky Mountain Resole, Idaho Springs, Colorado: (800) 228-2668; www.rmresole.com
Viberg Boots, Bremerton, Washington: (360) 373-8502
Wilson's Eastside Sports, Bishop, California: (619) 873-7520

Get the Right Socks

Before you even try on a new pair of boots in a store, you need to get the socks you will use for hiking and backpacking. If you forget to take your hiking socks when you go to buy boots, you can either borrow a pair of over-socks from the store, or purchase the socks you will use. Since you're about to make an investment of $150 to $200 on boots, you might consider spending a few dollars on socks so you can get the exact fit.

Water vapor streams through the 100,000 sweat pores on each foot. At the end of a long hike, your feet might have passed as much as two cups of water. So, if there isn't a puddle of sweat in your boots at the end of the day, where did it go?

More than half of the perspiration leaves the boot at the top, because every time you step, you force puffs of air into and out of the boot. The rest of the sweat passes through the sides of the boot or is absorbed by the socks and the boot.

The job of the sock is to get the moisture away from your skin so it can be passed through the boot. Liner socks will do this job. These are thin, wicking socks that fit snugly on your feet. In addition to moving perspiration, the liners also reduce friction by clinging to your feet and sliding against the outer sock. The outer sock insulates and cushions your foot.

Socks are made of natural fibers such as cotton, silk, and wool. Silk is a good insulator and is used for liner socks. Wool has good insulating properties and keeps feet drier because it absorbs

a lot of moisture—up to 50 percent of its weight. Cotton is great for a short game of racquetball, but unsuitable for day-long hikes on the trail.

Synthetic fibers include nylon, acrylic, polypropylene, and spandex. Nylon provides strength with little weight, and high resistance to wear. Polypropylene excels at wicking water away from your skin and is exceptionally light, but it shrinks and stinks, retaining odors more than other fabrics. Spandex is a highly elastic fiber used with other fibers to give a snug fit. Acrylic material gives warmth, yet is light.

These fibers are modified in a variety of ways to create brand-name fibers used in socks. Cool-Max, Hollofil, Duraspun, Acrylic, Thermax, and ThermaStat were created to provide wicking with

varying degrees of thermal insulation. Eagle Mills socks use Cool-Max fabric. Smartwool uses wool, and Wyoming Wear uses fleece. EcoSpun is made of recycled material, mostly plastic beverage bottles.

For more information contact:

Eagle Mills: (800) 215-9594
SealSkinz: www.dupont.com/sontara.sealskinz
Smartwool: (800) 550-WOOL
Wigwam Socks: (800) 558-7760; e-mail: socks@wigwam.com
Wyoming Wear: (800) 732-2991; e-mail: wyomingwear@wyoming.com

Caring for Socks

Hear what Chris Townsend, one of the world's most experienced backpackers, has to say in **The Backpacker's Handbook** (Ragged

Illustration by Daisy dePuthod

Mountain Press, 1997) about looking after your socks on the trail:

On long trips, I carry three pairs of socks and try to change them every couple of days, though I have worn a pair for as many as 10 days. I like to keep one pair dry for camp wear unless I'm carrying booties or pile socks for that purpose. Clean socks are warmer, more comfortable, and wick moisture better than dirty ones.

Whenever possible, I rinse socks in water taken from a stream or lake, using a cooking pot as a make-shift washbowl. Turning them inside out helps ensure sweat is removed from the inside and the socks can fluff up again. Wool socks take time to dry, so it's often necessary to hang them on the back of the pack to finish the process the next day.

At home, socks should be either hand-washed or put through the wool cycle in a washing machine (inside-out), then line-dried. Non-detergent powders remove less of the wool's natural lanolin. I use Ecover, available from Seventh Generation, or Nikwax Loft, and also add TX.10 in place of fabric conditioner.

Heat is bad for wool socks because it, too, removes lanolin from the wool and can cause synthetics to shrink, especially those containing polypropylene. Socks shouldn't be tumble-dried on a hot setting or draped over a hot radiator or near a fire.

Your Other Footwear

If you carry a pair of light running shoes or sports sandals, you can give your worn-out feet a nice break at the end of the day. These lighter shoes will also protect your feet when you ford streams, and they'll save your boots from getting wet. When a day's hike may entail crossing streams four or five times, it will pay you to strap sports sandals to the outside of your pack—ready to put on when you reach the bank.

Gaiters

Gaiters are of great use if you're going to be walking through deep snow or scree, as they will keep the snow and rocks out of your boots and off your pant legs. The simplest version of gaiters is a cylinder of nylon that fits your over your boot and secures above your calf. To find gaiters, turn to the following companies:

Berghaus Black Diamond:
 (313) 477-8116
Outdoor Research Inc.:
 (800) OR-GEAR; www.orgear.com
Quest: (800) 875-6901
Wild Country:
 (603) 356-5590

Photo by Ed Sobey

Hiking Information by Region:

Devil's Lake State Park, Wisconsin. Photo by Bob Queen, Wisconsin DNR.

(ILLINOIS, INDIANA, IOWA, KANSAS,

MANITOBA, MICHIGAN, MINNESOTA,

MISSOURI, NEBRASKA, NORTH

DAKOTA, OHIO, ONTARIO, QUEBEC,

SASKATCHEWAN, SOUTH DAKOTA,

AND WISCONSIN)

Illinois

Highest point: Charles Mound, 1,235 feet.

You can hike from the Mississippi River to the Ohio River across Illinois on the River-to-River Trail. Some 146 miles long, the trail winds through the Shawnee National Forest. For information and maps, contact the River-to-River Trail Society: (618) 252-6789.

Illinois Hiking & Backpacking Trails

REVISED EDITION

Walter G. Zyznieuski & George S. Zyznieuski

Reference Material

Illinois Hiking & Backpacking Trails, by Walter G. and George S. Zyzieuski (Southern Illinois University Press, 1993) includes updated information on nearly 70 trails, most of which are in state parks.

The U.S. Midwest and Central Canada

Vermilion River National Scenic River: (217) 782-7139

Indiana
Highest point:
Hoosier Hill, 1,257 feet.

Reference Material

Nature Walks in Northern Indiana and *Nature Walks in Southern Indiana,* both by Alan McPherson (Hoosier Chapter/Sierra Club, 1996), are useful reference sources.

Federal and State Resources

Indiana Dunes National Lakeshore: (219) 926-7561
Indiana State Parks: (317) 232-4125
Indiana State Travel Office: (800) 289-6646

Clubs and Organizations

Indiana, although not blessed with mountains, has many organizations to help get you hiking. **Central Indiana Wilderness Club,** P.O. Box 44351, Indianapolis, Indiana 46244, organizes some 30 trips each year. Here are some other clubs devoted to hiking and outdoor recreation:

• **Indianapolis Hiking Club,** 6429 Friendship Circle, Indianapolis, Indiana 46268.

Federal and State Resources

Illinois and Michigan Canal National Heritage Corridor: (815) 740-2047
Illinois State Bureau of Tourism: (800) 223-0121
Illinois State Park Information: (217) 782-7454
Shawnee National Forest: (800) 699-6637

• **Indiana Volksport Association,**
11982 Trolley Road, Indianapolis, Indiana 46236.

• **Southern Indiana Hiking Club,**
2881 Beth Lane, Corydon, Indiana 47112

• **Southern Indiana Outdoor Adventure Club,**
www.evansville.edu/~ma35/sioac/sioac.html

Iowa
Highest point: High Point, 1,670 feet.

Federal and State Resources

Effigy Mounds National Monument:
(319) 873-3491
Iowa State Office of Tourism: (800) 345-IOWA
Iowa State Parks Information: (515) 281-5145

Kansas
Highest point: Mount Sunflower, 4,039 feet.

Federal and State Resources

Kansas State Travel Office: (800) 252-6727
Kansas State Wildlife and Parks: (316) 672-5911
Tuttle Creek State Park: (913) 539-7941

Manitoba
Highest point: Baldy Mountain, 2,730 feet.

The longest trail in the Canadian Shield area of Western Canada is the Mantario Hiking Trail. The route is 36 miles of rugged Precambrian terrain. The trailhead is at Caddy Lake.

Government Resources

Beaudry Provincial Heritage Park: (204) 945-7273
Birds Hill Provincial Park: (204) 222-9151
Clearwater Lake Provincial Park: (204) 627-8218
Hecla Provincial Park: (204) 378-2945

Manitoba Natural Resources (maps and parks information): (800) 214-6497; www.gov.mb.ca/natres
Riding Mountain National Park: (800) 707-8480
Spruce Woods Provincial Heritage Park:
(204) 827-2543
Tall-Grass Prairie Preserve: (204) 945-7775
Travel Manitoba: (800) 665-0040
Turtle Mountain Provincial Park: (204) 534-7204
Wapush National Park: (204) 675-8863
Whiteshell Provincial Park: (204) 369-5246

Guides and Outfitters

Adventure Walking Tours: (204) 675-2147
Riding Mountain Nature Tours: (204) 636-2968

Michigan
Highest point: Mount Arvon, 1,980 feet.

Reference Material

Hiking Michigan, by Mike Modrzynski (Falcon, 1996), lists 50 hikes and several longer trips. It also includes information on the North Country Trail.

Michigan State Parks, by Jim DuFresne (The Mountaineers, 1989), is one of a series of books on state parks. DuFresne also wrote *50 Hikes: Lower Michigan* (Countryman Press, 1991); *Michigan's Porcupine Mountains Wilderness State Park* (Thunder Bay Press,

1995); and **Voyageurs National Park: Water Routes, Foot Paths, and Ski Trails** (Lake States Interpretative Association, 1996).

Federal and State Resources

Fayette State Park: (800) 543-2937
Isle Royale National Park: (906) 482-0986
Keweenaw National Historical Park: (906) 337-3168
Michigan Department of Natural Resources: (906) 644-2603
Michigan State Travel Information Center: (800) 543-2937
Michigan State Parks and Recreation: (517) 373-9900
Pictured Rocks National Seashore: (906) 482-0984
Porcupine Mountain Wilderness State Park: (906) 387-3700
Sleeping Bear Dunes National Lakeshore: (616) 326-5134

Minnesota

Highest point: Eagle Mountain, 2,301 feet.

Reference Material

Guide to Minnesota Outdoors, by Jim Umhoefer (Northword Press, 1992), includes hiking trails and canoe trips. The publisher's telephone number is (715) 356-9800. There are hundreds of miles of trails in **Superior National Forest,** by Robert Beymer (The Mountaineers, 1989). The book covers trails, water sports, biking, and skiing.

Ice Age Trail, Wisconsin. Photo by Ice Age Park & Trail.

Federal and State Resources

Chippewa National Forest: (800) 657-3700
Grand Portage National Monument:
(218) 335-2226
Minnesota State Office of Tourism: (800) 657-3700
Minnesota State Parks: (800) 246-2267
Mississippi National River and Recreation Area:
(612) 290-4160
Pipestone National Monument: (507) 825-5464
Saint Croix National Scenic Riverway:
(507) 825-5464
Superior National Forest: (218) 387-2788
Tettegouche State Park: (218) 720-5440
Voyageurs National Park: (218) 226-3539 or
(218) 283-9821

Clubs and Organizations

Contact the **Kekekabic Trail Club** at (800) 818-HIKE.
The Minnesota Rovers is an outdoor club with 350
members who backpack, hike, climb, bike, and canoe.
They operate a hotline on their activities at
(612) 257-7324.

Missouri

Highest point: Taum Sauk Mountain, 1,772 feet.

The **Missouri Department of Conservation** prints
booklets including the free "Discover Outdoor Missouri." It includes a map showing 835 conservation

areas, state parks, and regulations for use. Contact:
(573) 751-4115; www.conservation.state.mo.us.

Katy Trail, converted from a rail line, will include
235 miles from Clinton to St. Charles. About 200 miles
are open already for hiking and biking.
Contact: (800) 334-6946.

Federal and State Resources

Castlewood State Park: (314) 527-6481
Crowder State Park: (816) 359-6473
Cuivre River State Park: (573) 528-7247
Dillard Mill State Historic Site: (573) 244-3120
Grand Gulf State Park: (573) 548-2201
Graham Cave State Park: (573) 564-3476
Hawn State Park: (573) 883-3603
Katy Trail State Park: (800) 334-6946
Johnson's Shut-Ins State Park: (573) 546-2450
Lake Wappepello State Park: (573) 297-3232
Mark Twain National Forest: (573) 364-4621
Mark Twain State Park: (573) 565-3440
Mastodon State Historic Site: (314) 464-3079
Missouri State Office of Tourism,
catalogs: (800) 877-1234;
information: (573) 751-4133
Missouri State Parks: (800) 344-6946;
www.dnr.state.mo.us/dsp/homedsp.htm
Ozark National Scenic Riverways: (314) 323-4236
Pershing State Park: (816) 963-2299
Prairie State Park: (417) 843-6711
Rockwoods Reservation: (314) 458-2236
Runge Conservation Nature Center: (573) 526-5544
St. Francois State Park: (573) 358-2173

St. Joe State Park: (573) 431-1069
Taum Sauk Mountain State Park: (573) 546-2450
Trail of Tears State Park: (573) 334-1711
Washington State Park: (314) 586-2995
Watkins Mill State Park: (816) 580-3387
Weston Bend State Park: (816) 640-5443

Nebraska

Highest point:
Panorama Peak, 5,426 feet.

Federal and State Resources

Agate Fossil Beds National Monument:
(308) 668-2211
Missouri National Recreation River: (402) 336-3970
National Park Service, Midwest Region:
(402) 221-3471
Nebraska Parks: (800) 334-6946
Nebraska State Office of Tourism: (800) 228-4307
Niobrara National Scenic Riverway: (402) 336-3970
Scotts Bluff National Monument: (308) 436-4340

North Dakota

Highest point: White Butte, 3,506 feet.

This is one of the few places where you can hike with (or least near) buffalo or American bison. Other spectacular wildlife includes bighorn sheep, wild horses, moose, and antelope. The variety of wildlands ranges from badlands in the west, to prairies, forests, and the Red River Valley.

Federal and State Resources

Beaver Lake State Park:
(701) 452-2752
Cross Ranch State Park:
(701) 794-3731

Fort Abraham Lincoln State Park: (701) 663-9571
Fort Ransom: (701) 973-4331
Fort Stevenson: (701) 337-5576
Icelandic State Park: (701) 265-4561
International Peach Garden: (701) 263-4390
Lake Metigoshe State Park: (701) 263-4651
Lewis and Clark State Park: (701) 859-3071
North Dakota State Parks and Recreation:
(701) 328-5357
North Dakota State Tourism Office:
(800) 437-2077; www.ndtourism.com
Theodore Roosevelt National Park: (701) 623-4466
Turtle River State Park: (701) 594-4445

Ohio

Highest point: Campbell Hill, 1,550 feet.

Reference Material

Hikers in the Buckeye state can look to *50 Hikes: Ohio,* by Ralph Ramey (Countryman Press, 1997). Ramey also wrote *Walks and Rambles in Southwestern Ohio:*

Devil's Lake State Park, Wisconsin. Photo by Bob Queen, Wisconsin DNR.

From the Stillwater to the Ohio River (Backcountry, 1994).

Hiking Ohio, by Robert Folzenlogen (Willow Press, 1990), lays out 100 day hikes, all less than 12 miles. Folzenlogen describes the geology of the area, and includes a map and photo for each hike.

If you walk along the Cayahoga River south of Cleveland, you'll find it hard to see how this river caught fire some years ago. The lush vegetation and serenity are in stark contrast to the formerly flammable river a few miles downstream in industrial Cleveland.

Other references include:

Beyond Cleveland on Foot: 57 Hikes in Northeast Ohio's Lake, Geauga, Portage, Summit, Medina, Lorain, and Erie Counties, by Patience Cameron (Gray & Company, 1996). *Backpack Loops and Long Day Trail Hikes in Southern Ohio,* by Robert H. Ruchhoft (Pucelle Press, 1984). *Walks and Rambles in Ohio's Western Reserve: Discovering Nature and History in the Northeastern Corner,* by Jay Abercrombie (Backcountry Publications, 1996).

Federal and State Resources

Cuyahoga Valley National Recreation Area: (216) 526-5256

Metropolitan Parks, Summit County: (216) 867-5511

Ohio State Office of Tourism: (800) BUCKEYE

Ohio State Parks, information: (614) 265-7000; reservations: (800) AT-A-PARK

Devils Lake State Park, Baraboo, Wisconsin. Photo courtesy of Wisconsin Division of Tourism.

Clubs and Organizations

You can drive across this state in a long morning, but it would take months to hike the entire Buckeye Trail. It's a tight squeeze to fit 1,200 miles of trail in a state this small, but the **Buckeye Trail Association** did it. They can provide information and maps. Contact: (800) 282-5393; P.O. Box 254, Worthington, Ohio 43085.

Ontario
Highest point: Ishpatina Ridge, 2,275 feet.

The Bruce Trail
One of several long-distance trails in Canada, the Bruce Trail has 800 kilometers of hiking trails on the Niagara Escarpment between Niagara Falls and Tobermory, in Ontario. Contact: (800) 665-HIKE; www.brucetrail.org/main.htm

Government Resources

Algonquin Provincial Park: (705) 633-5572;

http://nrserv.mnr.gov.on.ca/MNR/parks/algo.htm
Frontenac Provincial Park: (613) 376-3489
Half Way Lake Provincial Park: (705) 965-2702; or (705) 688-3161 in winter
Killarney Provincial Park: (705) 287-2900
Lake Superior Provincial Park: (705) 856-2284
Ontario Parks, hiking information: http://nrserv.mnr.gov.on.ca/MNR/parks/hiking.html
Pukaskwa National Park: (807) 229-0801
Sleeping Giant Provincial Park: (807) 977-2526
Travel Ontario: (800) 668-2746; www.travelinx.com

Guides and Outfitters

Black Feather: (800) 5-RIVER-5

Quebec
Highest point: Mt. d'Iberville, 5,322 feet.

Government Resources

La Mauricie National Park: (819) 536-2638

Quebec Tourism: (800) 363-7777; www.tourisme. gouv.qc.ca/anglais/tourisme_a/geo_a.html. For a listing of campgrounds in Quebec and other provinces, go to www.campsource.com.

Saskatchewan
Highest point: Cypress Hills, 4,816 feet.

Government Resources

Check the Web page for park information: www.gov.sk.ca/serm/www/parkfact/Intro.htm
Prince Albert Park: (306) 663-4522
Trade and Convention Center: (800) 667-7191

South Dakota
Highest point: Harney Peak, 7,242 feet.

Reference Material

Hiking South Dakota's Black Hills Country, by Bert and Jane Gildart (Falcon Press, 1996) lists hiking trails, trail etiquette, hiking with children, and clothing.

Exploring the Black Hills & Badlands, by Hiram Rogers (Johnson Books, 1993) covers hiking, biking and skiing in this area contained in South Dakota, North Dakota, and Wyoming.

Federal and State Resources

The 111-mile Centennial Trail, used by hikers, bikers and horseback riders, runs the length of the scenic

Black Hills. The natural surface trail passes through pine forests and sweeping prairies. For information, call the Black Hills National Forest at the number below.

Another long-distance trail is now under construction. About 60 miles of the planned 110-mile George S. Mickelson Trail have been completed. The trail will run from Deadwood to Edgemont. Contact the Department of Game, Fish, and Parks: (605) 773-3391.

Badlands National Park: (800) 843-1930
Black Elk Wilderness: (605) 433-5361
Black Hills National Forest: (605) 673-2251;
campsite reservations: (800) 280-2267
Buffalo Gap National Grasslands: (605) 279-2125
Custer State Park: (605) 255-4515
Fort Pierre National Grasslands: (605) 224-5517
Grand River National Grasslands: (605) 374-3592
Jewell Cave National Monument: (605) 673-2288
Mount Rushmore National Memorial: (605) 574-2523
South Dakota Tourism: (800) 732-5682
    South Dakota State Parks and Recreation: (605) 773-3391; reservations: (800) 710-CAMP
    Wind Cave National Park: (605) 745-4600

Wisconsin
Highest point: Timms Hill, 1,952 feet.

Reference Material

Walking Trails of Southern Wisconsin, by Bob Crawford (University of Wisconsin Press, 1994), is a pocket guide to the trails and natural history of the region. Crawford also wrote ***Walking Trails of Eastern and Central Wisconsin*** (University of Wisconsin Press, 1997).

Federal and State Resources

Apostle Islands National Lakeshore: (715) 779-3397
Black River State Forest: (715) 284-1400
Bong State Recreation Area: (414) 878-5600
Brule River State Forest: (715) 372-4866
Chequamegon National Forest: (715) 762-2461

Devil's Lake State Park: (715) 284-1400
Flambeau River State Forest: (715) 332-5271
Gandy Dancer State Trail: (715) 349-2157
Governor Knowles State Forest: (715) 463-2898
Ice Age, North Country, and Lewis and Clark National Trails: (608) 264-5610
Kettle River Moraine State Forest, North: (920) 626-2116; **South:** (414) 594-6200
Northern Highland-American Lakes State Forest: (715) 356-5211
Saint Croix National Scenic Riverway: (715) 483-3284
Wisconsin Parks and Recreation: (608) 266-2181; //badger.state.wi.us/agencies/tourism/guide/parks00.htm
Wisconsin State Office of Tourism: (800) 432-TRIP; http://tourism.state.wi.us/
U.S. Forest Service: (414) 297-3693
Wild Rivers State Trail: (800) 523-6318

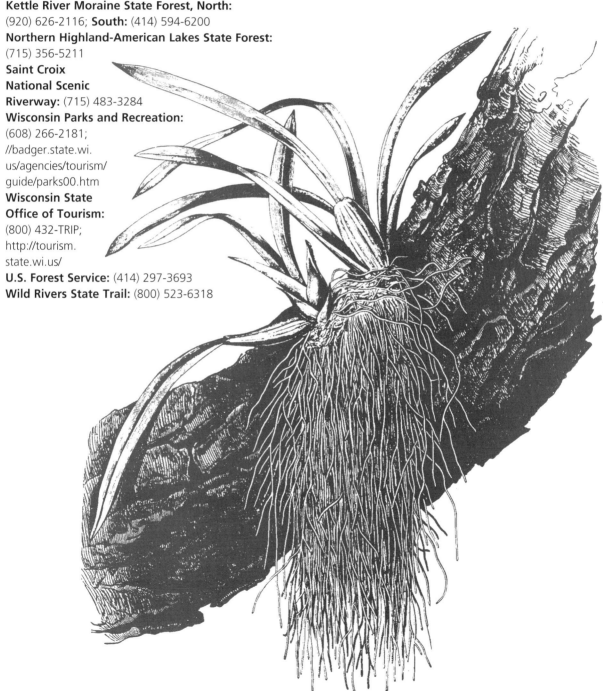

CHAPTER 12

Portable Castles

Climb the mountains and get their good tidings.
Nature's peace will flow into you as sunshine flows
into trees. The winds will blow their own freshness
into you, and the storms their energy, while cares
will drop off like autumn leaves.

—John Muir, John Muir In His Own Words,
compiled by Peter Browning

If your home is your castle, then your tent is your mobile castle. It's your shelter, your sanctuary. It's the place to lay out your clothing and equipment, to read on a rainy evening, and to sleep comfortably while bloodthirsty mosquitoes buzz inches away outside.

Your need for a tent depends on the weather and the number of bugs around. In some cases, backpacking without a tent is preferable. If it's not likely to rain, you can get by with a bivouac (bivy) bag or a plastic tarp. For good protection against the elements, however, a tent is essential.

Choosing Your Tent

For most backpacking trips, a three-season (spring through fall) tent will suffice. Only if you're venturing into Alpine or winter conditions do you need a sturdier—and more expensive—mountaineering tent.

There are many models and manufacturers to choose from, so you'll have no problem finding one to fit your needs. Free standing tents are now the most popular types. The advantages are that you can use them on loose sand or solid rock, where it would be difficult or impossible to stake down a normal tent efficiently. If the wind is blowing, a freestanding tent will still need the odd stake here and there, or a line to a rock or tree. A light tent in a moderate breeze makes a great kite that can cartwheel across the meadow before you can catch it. But it doesn't depend on stakes all around to keep it upright.

Tents that don't stand by themselves require multiple stakes and guy ropes that will trip the clumsy frequently and even the cautious every now and then. Staked tents work well, however, and are less expensive.

Tents for backpacking should protect you from rain and allow condensation to escape from the inside. The usual way to accomplish this is to have a tent that "breathes," with a waterproof rain fly over it, and a gap of an inch or two between them.

Some tents use a single layer of breathable fabric such as Gore-Tex, and forgo the rain fly, but this seems to work better on smaller tents.

The bottom of the tent should be made of a waterproof material such as urethane-coated nylon. Although the manufacturers may say you don't need a ground cloth underneath, we still recommend one for added protection. Don't let the ground cloth extend beyond the sides of the tent, though, or it will collect rain running down the sides of the tent and concentrate it in puddles that could leak into your tent.

Consider the layout and size of the tent. How many people will be using it? Are they so tall that they need higher-than-average headroom? It's tough to pull on a sweater sitting up in a cramped tent. Is there room to store equip-

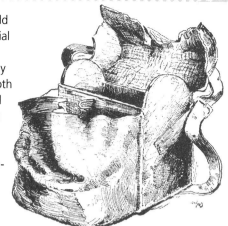

ment? Many tents have vestibules for this purpose. Will you be able to cook in the entryway of the tent in really crummy weather? What will the air circulation be like on a hot summer evening? Are the openings big enough? Some tents have net pockets attached to the inside so you can store a flashlight and find it in the middle of the night.

The only moving part of a tent, and the part most likely to fail, is the zipper. Make sure it is sturdy enough to handle the job. Ask the salesperson about the quality of the zipper in the tent.

Aside from zippers, the biggest problems with tents are the poles. Will they poke through the fabric sleeves the first time you set up the tent? Poles are made of aluminum rods or hollow fiberglass, usually connected internally with elastic bands. Although poles are remarkably strong in compression, you can easily bend or break one by grabbing it carelessly when you want to pick up the tent to shake it out. You can crunch a pole, too, by walking on it on uneven ground, so don't leave poles lying about.

Before buying a tent, ask if you can set it up in the store. Does it

take a doctoral degree in engineering to figure it out? How long does it take *you?* Does the construction impress you with its durability? How are the guy lines set up? Did the manufacturer include fittings to make it easy to shorten or lengthen the guy lines? Do they hold?

Here are some sources of tents:

American Camper:
(913) 492-3200
Bibler Tents: (303) 449-7351;
www.biblertents.com
Cabela's: (800) 237-4444;
www.cabelas.com
CampTrails: (888) 245-4985;
www.jwa.com
Diamond Brand: (800) 258-9811
Eastern Mountain Sports:
(888) 463-6367;
www.emsonline.com
Eureka: (888) 245-4984;
www.jwa.com
Ferrino: (800) 566-0690;
www.electriciti/~eccamp
Garuda Mountaineering:
(406) 587-4153
Integral Designs: (403) 640-1445;
www.agt.net/public/integral
Jack Wolfskin: (800) 847-1460;
www.jwa.com
Kelty: (800) 423-2320;
www.kelty.com
L. L. Bean: (800) 809-7057;
www.llbean.com

Rocky Mountain National Park. Photo by Ed Sobey

Lowe Alpine: (303) 465-0522;
www.lowealpine.com
Marmot: (707) 544-4590;
www.marmot.com
Moss Tents: (800) 859-5322;
www.mosstents.com
Mountain Hardwear:
(510) 559-6700;
www.mountainhardwear.com
Mountainsmith: (800) 426-4075
Noall Tents: (909) 659-4219
Outbound/Safesport:
(800) 433-6506
Peak 1: (800) 835-3278
Quest: (800) 875-6901
REI: (800) 426-4840; www.rei.com

Sierra Designs: (800) 635-0461;
www.ecotravel.com/sierradesigns
Stephensons-Warmlite:
RD 4 Box 145, 22 Hook Road,
Gilford, NH 03246
The North Face: (805) 379-3372;
www.clubhousegolf.com/
northface.htm
VauDe Sports: (800) 447-1539
Walrus: (800) 550-8368
Wild Country: (802) 985-5056
Wilderness Experience:
(406) 587-3522; www.wildx.com

Tent Stakes

The most overlooked items of your equipment, and probably the most often lost, are tent stakes. You may sometimes gain one or two over the camping season, finding "spares" left behind by others, but it's more likely that you'll lose one or two.

Tent stakes come in a variety of materials, shapes, and lengths. In general, the more surface area you can push into the ground—in other words, the broader and flatter they are—the better the stakes will hold, but the harder they are to pound in.

On beach sand, you need lots of area. In rocky ground, you'd be lucky to knock in a big stake more than a few inches, so what you need there is a long, skinny, steel stake. If you don't know what conditions to expect, carry a few different kinds of stakes.

As with all backpacking equipment, weight matters. So the goal is to choose the best-holding and lightest stakes.

Stakes are made of plastic, steel, aluminum, and titanium. Plastic stakes are bulky and, if you whack them hard enough, they'll break. Steel won't break easily, but weighs more than other stakes. Aluminum stakes are light and compact, but bend easily. Titanium stakes are the strongest and lightest—and the most expensive by far.

Aluminum stakes are usually long rods with pointed ends. They hold well in compacted soils, but pull right out of sand. T-stakes, made of aluminum, steel, or plastic in the shape of a capital T, hold better in loose soil, but are difficult to drive into compacted or rocky soil. For camping in snow, you need a wider stake, and for camping on ice, you need an ice screw.

These firms are sources of tent stakes:

Kelty: (800) 423-2320; www.kelty.com
Reliance: (800) 665-0258
Simon Metals: (888) 638-2599
Suka Sales: (805) 445-8434

Pitching Your Tent

Picking the best spot to pitch your tent is an art. Pitch it under the trees and you'll stay warmer, but what's likely to fall on the tent?

Branches, bird droppings, and pine cones. When we were camping in Costa Rica, we had coconuts fall all around our tent.

In hot weather, pitch your tent so it catches the breeze through your vent and door. Or, if the wind is blowing fiercely, look for shelter in the lee of rocks or in a slight depression.

PLASTIC KNOTS

If your tent or tarp requires a taut-line hitch, but you don't want to tie one, you can purchase plastic or metal slides that do the same thing. Check out your backpacking store.

Don't pitch it on game trails or hiking trails, of course, or closer to water than 100 feet. In some areas, managers require you to camp at least 200 feet from streams, lakes, and rivers. It's better to find out before you pitch your tent than have to move it when the ranger comes along.

If there are designated camping areas, use them. If not, figure out what areas will be affected least

MIDNIGHT RAIN FLY TEST

You know it will happen, so think about the Midnight Rain Fly Test when purchasing a tent.

You and your hiking partner decide to leave off the rain fly because the skies are clear. Then, just past midnight, the crack of thunder awakens you to a downpour.

Just how fast can two people get out of the tent, set up the rain fly, and get back in? Know before you go.

The taut-line hitch, also well known as the rolling hitch. First take a turn around the guy line . . .

. . . then add a second pass below the first . . .

. . . and finish off by tying a half-hitch above both.

Photos by Ed Sobey

by your setting up tents. Preferably, you won't set up on soft vegetation.

GREEN HEAT

 **TIP**

If the skies are clear, camp under trees. Clear nights are cold nights, but trees reflect radiated heat back to the ground, keeping you warmer.

You want to pitch on flat or slightly sloping ground, not at the bottom of a rise where water will wash down the hill into your tent. A slight slope drains water away from your tent and lets you rest with your head higher than your feet, a position most people prefer. Place your eating and cooking areas well away from the sleeping tent, since the sweet smells of your dinner might attract uninvited company.

Once you have found the best site, lay down the ground cloth and roll around on top of it to find all the sharp rocks, roots, and pine cones you couldn't see. After clearing them away, or changing your site, pitch your tent on top of the ground cloth. If you do that as soon as you arrive at your camp for

the evening, you will have shelter ready when you need it.

MAKING SPACE INSIDE

Tired of the clutter on the floor of your tent?

You can hang miscellaneous items from the roof of your tent with Gear Loft (The North Face) or REI's Tent Attic. These space creators clip onto the ceiling loops of your tent.

Make sure that the product you buy will work in your tent; the label lists the tent models.

Caring for Your Tent

With only a few minutes of maintenance after each use, your tent will last for years. Its biggest enemy is mildew.

Make sure it is completely dry before storing it away, and clean out dirt from the inside by turning the tent inside out and shaking it

well. After several uses, you may want to wash it in a bath tub with mild soap, rinse it well, and dry it completely.

Take care of the zipper. Keep it clean and don't force it along its track. If you damage it, you'll have a lot of stitching to do to install a new one. If you don't want to sew it yourself, check your telephone directory for companies that do custom tent or canvas work. Or, see the list of companies that repair outdoor gear on page 120.

Use a ground cloth under your tent to protect the underside. Cut a piece of plastic, available at hardware stores, to the size and shape of your tent's footprint. Fold up the ground cloth and carry it in a grocery store plastic bag to keep the dirt and moisture away from the other stuff in your pack.

Stuff your tent loosely in its sack so air can circulate around it; don't fold it tightly. When storing

Photo by Ed Sobey

Rolling around on top of the ground cloth will soon locate all the rocks and sharp stones you couldn't see before.

your tent, pile it loosely in a cardboard box, rather than leaving it in its stuff sack.

Tent Repairs

Here are companies that repair tents, backpacks, and sleeping bags:

Appalachian Outfitters, Oakton, Virginia: (703) 281-4324
Black's Camping-Sports Sewing Shop, Toronto, Ontario: (416) 603-0744
Boulder Mountain Repair, Boulder, Colorado: (303) 499-3634
Carter's Cobble Shoppe, Bozeman, Montana: (406) 585-8607
Cyrex Accessories, Calgary, Alberta: (403) 243-7086
Everett Tent & Awning, Everett, Washington: (800) 797-8213
Froze-to-Death, Billings, Montana: (406) 252-5428
Needle Mountain Designs, Evergreen, Colorado: (800) 795-2941
Northwest Garment and Gear Repair, Seattle, Washington: (206) 545-8683
Patty Spiro Sewing/Outdoor Gear Repair, Balsam Grove, North Carolina: (704) 862-3278
Rainy Pass Repair, Seattle, Washington: (800) 733-4340
Ragged Mountain Equipment, Intervale, New Hampshire: (603) 356-3042
Ralph's Tent & Tarp, Coon Rapids, Minnesota: (612) 421-7053
Stitchlines, Englewood, Colorado: (303) 781-9044
Sunshine Tent Pole Specialists, Calabasas, California: (818) 222-5217
Super Stitches, Youngstown, Ohio: (216) 743-6865

TA Enterprises, Vancouver, Washington: (206) 260-9527
Tent City, Fresno, California: (209) 292-1221
Tent Repair Services, Camden, Maine: (207) 236-0997
The Grant Boys, Costa Mesa, California: (714) 645-3400
Wilderness Workshop, Highland Park, California: (213) 256-0723

ZRK Enterprises, McCall, Idaho: (800) 735-4620

Tarpaulins

One alternative to a tent is a tarp. On a clear night, when you unfold a tarp and lay your sleeping bag on top, you're done setting up your shelter. The tarp also gives you a convenient place to lay out your gear and to pile up your stuff while you look for that

Photo by Burt Kornegay, Slickrock Expeditions.

little item that wiggled down to the bottom of your pack. In the middle of the night, if a drizzle starts, pull one side of the tarp over your bag and go back to sleep. If a gullywasher erupts, you may have to plead to move into a companion's tent and endure the taunts of "I told you so." No matter. You will have spared yourself considerable weight in your pack and the inconvenience of setting up and taking down a tent.

Tarps have lots of other uses as well. For extra versatility, tarps should have grommets set in reinforced corners and mid-sections. If the grommets pull out you can use the stone trick. Wrap a corner of the tarp around a pebble or a small fir cone, and tie your line around the wrapped pebble. It holds well, and works for tarps that never had grommets in the first place.

You can purchase tarps from one of the following outdoor equipment manufacturers, or from a hardware store:

Black Diamond: (801) 278-0301
Campmor: (800) CAMPMOR; www.campmor.com
Moss Tents: (800) 859-5322; www.mosstents.com
North Face: (805) 379-3372; www.clubhousegolf.com/ northface.htm
REI: (800) 426-4840; www.rei.com
Quest: (800) 875-6901

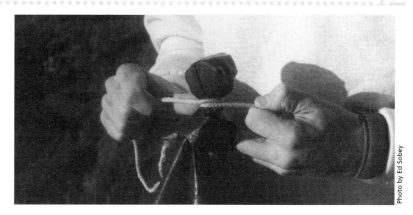

Photo by Ed Sobey

A pebble wrapped in a corner of a tarpaulin and held fast with a clove hitch, makes an excellent substitute for a grommet.

Hiking Information by Region:

(ARIZONA, NEVADA,

AND NEW MEXICO)

Arizona

Highest point: Humphreys Peak, 12,633 feet.

Reference Material

On Foot in the Grand Canyon, by Sharon Spangler (Pruett Publishing Company, 1991), is a guide for hiking the trails of the South Rim. Spangler includes maps and trail information.

Hiking the Grand Canyon, by John Annerino (The Sierra Club, 1993), covers natural history, Native Americans, and geology as well as giving trail descriptions.

REGION
CHAPTER

The Southwest

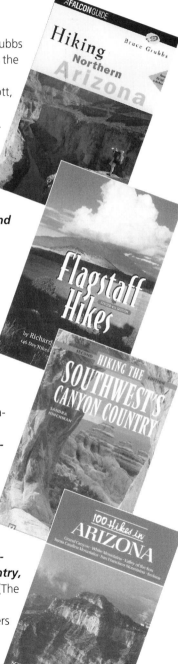

Hiking Northern Arizona, by Bruce Grubbs (Falcon, 1994), covers the area bounded by the Grand Canyon, Prescott, Camp Verde, Payson, Sedona, and Flagstaff. It includes 200 hiking trails and routes.

There's great information on local hikes in **Day Hikes and Trail Rides in and around Phoenix,** by Roger and Ethel Freeman (Gem Guides Book Company, 1991); **Tucson Hiking Guide,** by Betty Leavengood (Pruett, 1997); and **Flagstaff Hikes,** by Richard Mangum and Sherry Mangum (Hexagon Press, 1995).

Hiking the Southwest, by Dave Ganci (Sierra Club Books, 1987), covers Arizona, New Mexico, and West Texas.

Hiking the Southwest's Canyon Country, by Sandra Hinchman (The Mountaineers, 1990), covers the Four Corners area.

Another good reference is Scott S. Warren's **100 Hikes**

in Arizona (The Mountaineers, 1994).

Equipment Rental

EZCamp Rentals rents equipment and sets up base camps in southern Utah and northern Arizona. Contact: (888) 4EZ-CAMP; www.ezcamp.com

Federal and State Resources

Arizona State Lands Department, permits: (602) 542-4631
Arizona State Office of Tourism: (602) 542-8687
Arizona State Parks, permits: (602) 542-4174; **information:** (602) 542-8687; www.pr.state.az.us
Bureau of Land Management, Arizona: (602) 650-0500
Canyon de Chelly National Monument: (602) 674-5436
Coconino National Forest: (520) 527-7400
Coronado National Forest: (520) 670-6483
Coronado National Memorial: (520) 366-5515
Glen Canyon National Recreation Area: (602) 645-8200
Grand Canyon National Park: (520) 638-7888
Huachuca Mt., U.S. Forest Service: (602) 458-0530
Kaibab National Forest: (520) 635-2681
Lake Mead National Recreation Area: (702) 293-7920
Organ Pipe National Monument: (602) 387-6849
Petrified Forest National Park: (520) 524-6228
Pipe Springs National Park: (602) 643-7105
Prescott National Forest: (520) 636-2302

Saguaro National Park, permits: (520) 670-6680
Superstition Mountain: (602) 835-1161
Tonto National Forest: (602) 225-5200

Guides and Outfitters

Adventure/Discovery Tours: (800) 774-1926
Canyon Explorations: (800) 654-0723;
songbird.com/canyonx
Grand Canyon Field Institute: (520) 638-2485;
www.thecanyon.com/fieldinstitute
Sky Island Treks: (520) 792-1083
WilderWalk Grand Canyon Adventures:
(520) 722-9123;
www.gorp.com/wilderwalk/default.htm

Clubs and Organizations

The **Huachuca Hiking Club (HHC)** is based in south-eastern Arizona. It organizes hikes, camping, and volunteer trail maintenance. Contact:
www.primenet.com/~tomheld/hhc.html

The **Arizona Trail Association** is working to complete the Arizona Trail. Contact:
www.primenet.com/~aztrail/ata_info.html

Nevada
Highest point: Boundary Peak, 13,143 feet.

Reference Material

Hiking the Great Basin, by John Hart (Sierra Club Books, 1991), includes hikes in the High Desert regions of California, Oregon, Utah, and Nevada. Hart also discusses wilderness issues of the region, the landscape, and information for hiking in the deserts.

Hiker's Guide to Nevada, by Bruce Grubbs (Falcon Press, 1995), details 50 hikes.

Federal and State Resources

Bureau of Land Management, Nevada:
(702) 861-6500
Desert National Wildlife Refuge: (800) 237-0774
**Red Rock Canyon National Conservation Area,
Bureau of Land Management:** (702) 646-3401
Great Basin National Park: (702) 234-7331
Lake Mead National Recreation Area:
(702) 293-7920
Nevada State Office of Tourism: (800) 638-2328
Nevada State Parks: (702) 687-4387

Guides and Outfitters

Sky's the Limit: (800) 733-7596;
www.skysthelimit.com

New Mexico
Highest point: Wheeler Peak, 13,161 feet.

Reference Material

75 Hikes in New Mexico, by Craig Martin (The Mountaineers, 1995).
Guide to the Hiking Areas of New Mexico, by Mike Hill (University of New Mexico Press, 1995).
The Gila Wilderness Area, by John Murray (University of New Mexico Press, 1988).

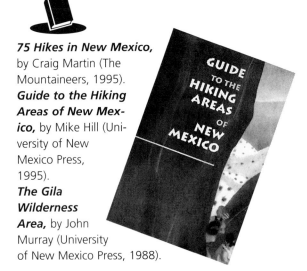

Federal and State Resources

Aztec Ruins National Monument: (505) 334-6174
Bandelier National Monument: (505) 672-0343
Bureau of Land Management, New Mexico:
(505) 438-7501

Capulin Volcano National Monument:
(505) 278-2201
Carlsbad Caverns National Park:
(505) 285-4641 or (505) 785-2251
Chaco Culture National Historical Park:
(505) 786-7014
El Malpais National Monument: (800) 545-2040
El Morro National Monument: (505) 783-4226
Fort Union National Monument: (505) 425-8025
Gila Cliff Dwellings National Monument:
(505) 536-9461
National Park Service, Southwest Region:
(505) 988-6012
New Mexico State Office of Tourism:
(800) 545-2040
New Mexico State Parks and Recreation:
(505) 827-7173; www.emnrd.state.nm.us/nmparks
Pecos National Historic Park: (505) 757-6414

Petroglyph National Monument: (505) 766-8375
Salinas Pueblo Missions National Monument:
(505) 847-2585
U.S. Forest Service, Southwestern Region:
(505) 842-3292
White Sands National Monument:
(505) 497-6124

Guides and Outfitters

Derringer Outfitters and Guides:
(505) 773-4860; www.viva.com/nm/derringer.html
Known World Guide Service:
(800) 983-7756; www.knownworldguides.com
Kokopelli Rafting Adventures: (800) 879-9035
Santa Fe Rafting Company: (800) 467-RAFT

Z-Z-Z-Time

When you're backpacking, you need a good night's sleep to replenish your energy and repair the wear and tear your body has suffered during the day. Experienced through-hikers on long trails go to bed as daylight fades, and average about nine hours of sleep a night. Beginners often need more.

How do you get a great night's sleep in the outdoors? Z-Z-Z-Time equipment shields you from cold, rain, rocks, and pebbles.

Sleeping Bags

Backpackers often use mummy bags, named for their shape, but there's no reason why you shouldn't use the traditional rectangular bag. These are less expensive, but since there is more free air around the feet, they're heavier for the warmth they provide.

The major choice facing you concerns the amount and type of insulation in the bag. Bags come in three weights: the summer-temperature type, the three-season type, and the cold-weather models. It doesn't make sense to spend money on a heavier, winter-weight bag and then to be so warm that you sleep on top of it. Buy the temperature-rated bag that fits your style of camping and the season of the year.

As for insulation, down is tops, pound for pound. The caveat is that its insulating qualities deteriorate when it's wet. Drop a down-filled bag in a river, and you end up with a very heavy, hard-to-dry, ineffective, and uncomfortable

Come to the woods, for here is rest.

There is no repose like that of the green

deep woods.

—**John Muir,** *John Muir In His Own Words,*

compiled by Peter Browning

Photo by Burt Kornegay, Slickrock Expeditions.

sleeping bag. You should protect any sleeping bag from rivers and rain, but protect down bags especially well.

Down comes in different grades, depending on the percentage of feathers among the down. The feathers add little to the insulation so the higher the percentage of down in the fill, the warmer the bag will be.

Photo by Ed Sobey

A mummy bag laid on top of a traditional rectangular sleeping bag.

THE WONDER OF DOWN

Down is nature's wonder insulating material. It's the fluffy under-plumage of ducks and geese, an intricately woven mass of thin fibers that trap tiny pockets of air.

The best down has few feathers mixed in with it, so the more quills you can feel in a down bag, the more feathers it has, and the lesser the quality.

Goose down is warmer than duck down, weight for weight, and therefore more expensive. If you hike regularly, a down bag is a good investment. It's estimated that the average down bag lasts 12 years, while a synthetic one loses much of its insulating qualities after only four years.

The greater the volume of the down for its weight, the better it retains heat, so manufacturers measure the loft of down in cubic inches per ounce. A popular standard for sleeping bags is 550 cubic inches of down per ounce. Higher loft provides more insulation and costs more. The maximum loft available is 800 cubic inches per ounce.

The alternatives to down are any of the many synthetic fills.

These include Hollofil, Lamilite, Microloft, Primaloft, Thinsulate, Polarguard, ExcelLoft, Liteloft, and Quallofil.

BASIC FILLINGS

There are basically two types of synthetic insulation for sleeping bags: short-staple fibers and continuous-filament fibers.

The best-known continuous-filament fill is Polarguard, the latest version of which claims to be 20 percent lighter than previous versions.

The latest top-quality short-staple fibers are Micoloft, Primaloft, and Thinsulate Lite Loft. All three are reportedly superior to the old standbys, Quallofil and Hollofil.

Hollofil is made of hollow polyester fibers. Liteloft mimics down with interweaving fibers. Synthetics cost less than down, at least $20 to $40 dollars less per bag, and are easier to care for. They retain some of their insulating qualities when wet, and dry faster than down does but they won't provide a comfortable night's sleep when they're wet.

Synthetic fill may not be such a bargain in the long run. The fill loses its insulating qualities much sooner than down does, and you will have to buy two or three synthetic-fill bags to equal the life of a down bag.

Your final choice is about the material of the shell. Nylon and polyester work well. They are tough, keep out moisture, and don't absorb odors. Some manufacturers use breathable materials or a mix of cotton and polyester.

What else should you look for? The zipper can fail, so make sure it is durable. Having two slides on the zipper lets you open part of the bag when you're warm but don't want to open the bag completely. To keep a cold zipper from your skin and to block air from moving through the teeth of the zipper, the bag should have a draft tube covering the zipper. For colder weather, bags should have a hood with a drawstring.

Bags are graded by their thermal insulation, and you should pick the grade of bag that's right for the weather conditions you are likely to encounter. Of course, one person may be warm in a bag while the person in the next tent in the same model bag is shivering, so you need to take account of your thermal signature: Do you like more or fewer blankets than others? Choose your bag accordingly. Some manufacturers make extra-long and extra-short bags.

The following companies manufacture and/or supply sleeping bags:

ALPS: (800) 344-2577
Bibler Tents: (303) 449-7351
Cabela's: (800) 237-4444;
www.cabelas.com
Camp 7: (714) 545-2204
Caribou: (800) 824-4103;
www.caribou.com

Cascade Designs:
(800) 531-9531;
www.cascadedesigns.com
Eastern Mountain Sports:
(888) 463-6367;
www.emsonline.com
Ensign Mountaineering:
(800) 560-7529
Feathered Friends:
(206) 328-0887;
www.halcyon.com/featherd

Ferrino: (800) 566-0690;
www.electriciti/~eccamp
Integral Designs:
(403) 640-1445;
www.agt.net/public/integral
Jack Wolfskin: (800) 847-1460;
www.jwa.com
Kelty: (800) 423-2320;
www.kelty.com
Lafuma America: (800) 514-4807

Liberty Mountain Sports:
(503) 685-9600
L.L. Bean: (800) 341-4341;
www.llbean.com
Marmot: (707) 541-2166;
www.marmot.com
Mont Adventure Equipment:
(303) 384-9148
Moonstone Mountaineering:
(800) 822-2985
Mountain Hard Wear:
(510) 559-6700;
www.mountainhardwear.com
Outbound: (800) 433-6506
Peak 1: (800) 835-3278
REI: (800) 426-4840;
www.rei.com
Sierra Designs:
(800) 736-8592;
www.ecotravel.
com/sierradesigns
Slumberjack:
(800) 233-6283
Stephensons-Warmlite:
RD 4 Box 145,
22 Hook Road,
Gilford, NH 03246
Texasport:
(713) 464-5551;
www.texasport.com
The North Face:
(805) 379-3372;
www.clubhousegolf.
com/northface.htm

Photos courtesy of Cascade Designs and L.L. Bean

THREE VOICES

Here by the camp-fire's flicker,
Deep in my blanket curled,
I long for the peace of the pine-
gloom,
When the scroll of the Lord is
unfurled,
And the wind and the wave are
silent,
And world is singing to world.
—Robert Service, The Three Voices

VauDe Sports: (800) 447-1539
Walrus: (800) 550-8368
Wenzel: (800) 325-4121
Western Mountaineering:
(408) 287-8944
Wiggy's: (800) 748-1827

GIVE IT AIR

When you're on a long hike, you find that your sleeping bag benefits from being aired whenever possible.

This is particularly true of down bags, which are likely to absorb more moisture overnight than synthetic bags do. Without regular airing, you'll end up with a heavy, soggy bag that won't keep you warm, and smells terrible.

Cleaning Your Bag

Sleeping bags don't like being washed, so do your best to keep yours clean, inside and out, for as long as possible. You can keep the inside clean by using a bag liner that's removable for washing. You can keep the outside clean by removing spots with a brush and water or mild soap and water.

When is it absolutely necessary to wash it? Your nose will probably tell you if someone else hasn't mentioned it already, but another indication that your bag needs cleaning is that it doesn't keep you as warm as it used to.

When you do wash your bag, check the instructions attached to it. Don't have the bag dry-cleaned because the chemicals used in dry cleaning can ruin the insulation. Some manufacturers will tell you to wash it in a bathtub, others in a front-loading washing machine. Use soap sparingly and don't use any other chemicals. Let it tumble-dry, or, if you live in a dry environment, let it air dry outside, lying on a clean tarp, not on a clothes line.

Make sure it is dry before storing it loosely in a cardboard box or a cloth bag so the down or synthetic material retains its loft.

Extra Warmth

Sometimes you have to put up with a bag that's a few inches too long. Your feet will stay warmer then if you close off the end of the bag with a belt or rope. You could also jam clothing into the foot end of the bag to reduce the amount of cooling air down there.

Unroll the bag as soon as possible after making camp, so the insulation springs back to its full

fluffiness, or loft. Keep extra clothing, a watch cap and sweater, inside your bag or inside a stuffsack, for a pillow. If you wake up cold, you will know where to find them.

To add insulation to your bag, use a liner. If you keep your bag dry, and let it air out and sun dry at every opportunity, you should have no trouble staying warm at night, particularly if you sleep on a pad or mattress to reduce your heat loss to the ground.

Sleeping Bag Liners

Liners can extend the temperature range of your sleeping bag and let you keep the inside clean. You can make your own liner from fleece (for warmth) or cotton (ease of washing), or purchase one. A cotton liner can add insulation that will raise your temperature by about 5°F; silk adds 2°F or 3°F more; flannel adds as much as 12°F. On long trips, a liner lets you wash the fabric that's next to your skin; a clean liner is truly one of life's finest luxuries on a long trail.

You can buy bag liners from:

Design Salt: (800) 254-7258; www.designsalt.com
Feathered Friends: (206) 328-0887; www.halcyon.com/featherd

Sleeping Bag Repairs

See the list of repair companies in Chapter 12. For repairs to sleeping pads, return the product to the company that manufactured it.

Insulating Pads

When you hunker down in your sleeping bag for a warm night's rest, you compress the insulation in the bag

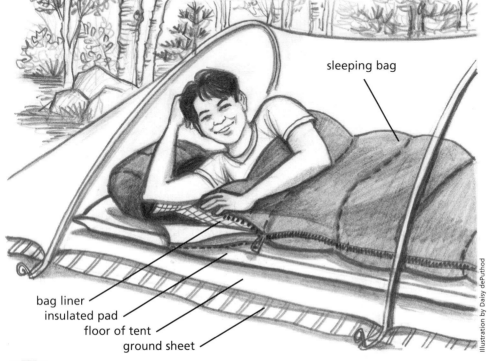

beneath you. That puts you in close contact with the cold ground. You actually need more insulation under you than you do on top. And the way to get it is by sleeping on a pad.

Pads not only insulate you from the ground, they also give you a softer surface to sleep on. Pads weigh very little, but they do take up considerable room in or on your pack. Old-style inflatable air mattresses were uncomfortable, had poor insulating qualities, and tended to

sleeping bag

bag liner
insulated pad
floor of tent
ground sheet

bounce you off if you made any sudden moves in your sleep. Modern pads are much better, and offer you two choices: closed-cell foam

FROM AEROSPACE TO THERM-A-REST

Two former Boeing aircraft engineers, Jim Lea and Neil Anderson, designed a lightweight backpacking mattress after being laid off in 1971. Their innovation was to make it self-inflating. The easy-to-use mattress kept campers comfortable and warmer, while adding very little weight to their packs.

The men formed Cascade Designs just as a big surge in backpacking occurred. Riding the surge, the company has expanded into other products including sleeping bags, dry bags, water containers, hiking staffs, backpacking ovens, medical kits and other gear.

Great ideas, solid engineering, and great timing have contributed to Cascade Designs' success.

Photo by Ed Sobey

pads, and self-inflating mattresses. (You can rule out open-cell foam pads—they absorb water.)

Closed-cell foam pads are tough and inexpensive. Unroll one and lay your sleeping bag on top, and you're ready for bed. Roll it up in the morning and secure it with a rubber band or nylon strap, and then attach it to the outside of your pack. It takes only seconds, and provides at least Motel 6 comfort.

For Sheraton comfort, invest in a self-inflating mattress. These cost more and have parts that break, but they are softer and give better insulation. If you open the air valve while the mattress is rolled up it will gradually unroll itself, sucking

in air as it goes. This process takes a few minutes, after which you merely twist the air valve shut and the mattress is ready. In the morning, you open the valve and slowly roll it up, forcing air out as you roll. Closing the valve after you've expelled the air tends to keep it rolled up.

Sharp rocks or sticks can poke holes in an inflatable mattress, which you can repair with nylon repair tape (or spinnaker tape from a ship's chandler). Valves can break, but are usually reliable. Neither problem, of course, can occur with closed-cell foam pads.

Storing pads and mattresses requires you to leave them unconstricted. Take off any bindings, open the valve of the mattress, and store loosely.

When your closed-cell foam pad

finally needs to be retired, you can find lots of uses for it. In states with fire ants, hikers carry squares of foam pads to sit on. For some reason, the ants don't climb onto the foam. Pieces can become knee pads for canoeing or pads for knee braces in kayaks.

The following firms manufacture and sell sleeping pads:

Artiach: (800) 569-4110
Cascade Designs, Therm-a-Rest: (800) 531-9531; www.cascadedesigns.com
Skinman: (800) 569-4110; www.mindspring.com/ ~amsupply/camp.htm
Slumberjack: (800) 233-6283

Bivouac Bags

Under most conditions, the best roof for your bedroom is the sky. This commonsense arrangement saves weight, time, energy, and money.

—Colin Fletcher, The Complete Walker III

For less than two pounds of weight and less space than a stove takes up, bivouac (bivy) bags let you leave the tent behind. They also let you set up camp in seconds: no tent poles or stakes, just lay out the bivy bag and stuff your sleeping bag inside. In the morning, it takes only seconds to pack up the bag and be on your way.

The disadvantage is that a bivy bag sleeps only one person. If you camp with two or three, a tent is more economical to purchase, and less bother to carry if you can divide the weight among the campers. Tents also give you room

Photo by Ed Sobey

A bivouac (bivy) bag weighing less than two pounds can substitute for a tent inside to sit up and put on your clothes when it's pouring rain outside. They also give you space to lay out clothing and gear, and keep things under shelter.

If you're shopping for a bivy bag, make sure the bottom is waterproof. When you wake up to find yourself bridging several tiny streams or puddles, you still want your sleeping bag to be dry inside. The top of the bag should be a breathable material so you're not soaking in your own perspiration all night. Check out the cover for your head and see if it offers protection against bugs.

The following companies make bivy bags:

Feathered Friends: (206) 328-0887; www.halcyon.com/featherd
Outdoor Research: (800) 421-2421; www.orgear.com

REI: (800) 426-4840; www.rei.com

Before taking your bivy bag on its first hike, seal the seams. Pitch it on top of a ground cloth to protect the fabric. Take your sleeping bag out when you get up in the morning. If the weather is dry, let your bivy bag air before stuffing it in its sack. Make sure the bivy bag is dry before storing it.

Pillows

Most people sleep better with a pillow, but it's an awful waste of space to take an ordinary pillow backpacking. Inflatable pillows are popular with some people, but most hikers use a stuffsack filled with the clothes they'll need when they wake up. If you need the feel of cotton on your face, take along a pillowcase and stuff it full of soft things.

Cascade Designs makes a Pocket Pillow that you stuff with

clothing. Pillows with more insulation include those made by the SYZYGY Design Group and J. Kraemer.

The following companies make camping pillows:

Cascade Designs:
(800) 531-9531;
www.cascadedesigns.com
J. Kraemer, Outters Camp Outdoor Pillow: (612) 439-7175
SYZYGY Silver Cloudz:
(800) 472-3492

Insect Screens

A bug screen lets you get a good night's rest in mosquito territory. EPCO Design makes SleepScreens and TropicScreens, free-standing net tents, with poles.
Contact: (360) 468-4121; www.epco.com/~larry.

Photo courtesy of Cascade Designs

Hiking Information by Region:

(ALABAMA, ARKANSAS, FLORIDA,

GEORGIA, KENTUCKY, LOUISIANA,

MISSISSIPPI, OKLAHOMA, TENNESSEE,

AND TEXAS)

Alabama

Highest point:
Cheaha Mountain, 2,407 feet.

Reference Material

One of the few guide books
on hiking in Alabama is
Alabama Trails by Patri-
cia Stenger Sharpe (Uni-
versity of Alabama Press, 1993).

Federal and State Resources

Most of the state parks have hiking trails, and the fol-
lowing list includes the larger parks.
Alabama State Parks: (334) 242-3151
Alabama State Parks Reservations: (800) ALA-PARK;
www.vten.com
Alabama State Tourism & Travel: (800) 252-2262
Bankhead National Forest: (205) 489-3427
Cheaha State Park: (205) 488-5111
Conecuh National Forest: (334) 222-2555

Southern and Southeastern U.S.A.

Big Bend National Park. Photo by Burt Kornegay, Slickrock Expeditions.

Clubs and Organizations

There are two hiking organizations in Alabama. The **Alabama Trails Association** can be reached through its Web page: www.auburn.edu/~hudsojt/begin.html.

The Vulcan Trail Association is based in Birmingham, and promotes hiking, backpacking, bicycling, and self-propelled water sports: www.mindspring.com/~vta.

Arkansas

Highest point:
Magazine Mountain, 2,753 feet.

Reference Material

Two guides to hiking Arkansas are:

DeSoto State Park: (205) 845-0051
Lake Guntersville State Park: (205) 571-5444
Little River Canyon National Preserve:
(205) 997-9239
Natchez Trace Parkway: (800) 305-7417
Oak Mountain State Park: (205) 620-2520
Russell Cave National Monument: (205) 495-2672
Talladega National Forest: (205) 463-2272
Tuskegee National Forest: (334) 727-2652
Wind Creek State Park: (205) 329-0845

Arkansas Hiking Trails: A Guide to Seventy-Eight Selected Trails in the Natural State, by Tim Ernst (Wilderness Visions Press, 1994); and *Ozark Highlands Trail Guide,* by Tim Ernst (Wilderness Visions Press, 1990).

For day hikes in the Ozark National Forest, check out www.yournet.com/dayhike.htm

Federal and State Resources

Arkansas has more than 250 hiking trails scattered through the state's Corps of Engineers recreation areas, national forest areas, national parks, and state parks.

The **Ozark Highlands Trail** is a long-distance National Recreation Trail. It crosses the Ozark National Forest in Arkansas. Starting at Lake Fort Smith State Park on Highway 71, the trail trends east for about 160 miles across the Boston Mountain, Pleasant Hill, and Buffalo Ranger Districts.

Thirty-four of the 48 state parks have hiking trails. Listed here are the major ones:

Arkansas State Department of Parks and Tourism: planning kit, (800) NATURAL; information, (501) 682-7777; www.arkansas.com or www.state.ar.us
Arkansas State Parks: (501) 682-1191; trail information, (501) 682-1301; www.arkansas.com/stateparks/index.html
Buffalo National River: (501) 741-5443

Delta Heritage Trail State Park: (501) 628-4714
Forest Service Campground Reservations: (800) 280-2267
Hot Springs National Park: (501) 624-3383
Ouachita National Forest: (501) 321-5202
Ozark-St. Francis National Forest: (501) 968-2354

Falls Creek Falls, Citico Creek Wilderness, Cherokee National Forest, Tennessee. Photo by Burt Kornegay, Slickrock Expeditions.

Longer Trails

Buffalo River Trail, 36 miles: (501) 741-5443
Eagle Rock Loop Trail, 27 miles: (501) 356-4186
Ozark Highlands Trail, 178 miles: (501) 968-2354
Womble Trail, 39 miles: (501) 326-4322

Equipment Rental

Three of Arkansas's state parks have a Rent-a-Backpack program. They are:

Devil's Den State Park, West Fork: (501) 761-3325
Lake Fort Smith State Park, Mountainburg:
(501) 369-2469
Pinnacle Mountain State Park, Roland:
(501) 868-5806

Clubs and Organizations

Ozark Highlands Trail Association: (501) 442-2799;
//wilderness.ArkansasUSA.com/ohta.html

Florida

Highest point: Britton Hill, 345 feet.

Hiking in Florida is best in winter. The weather can be cool and dry then, and insects are less active.

Reference Material

You may not picture Florida as a state with great hikes, but Elizabeth F. Carter outlines dozens of them. Her book *A Hiking Guide to the Trails of Florida* (Menasha Ridge Press, 1987) outlines trips from the Appalachian foothills, through coastal lowlands and snow-white beaches, to sweeping prairies.

Federal and State Resources

For a free directory of recreation areas within national

forests in Florida, contact the National Forest Service at (407) 644-5377.

Apalachicola National Forest: (904) 926-3561
Arthur R. Marshall Loxahatchee National Wildlife Refuge: (407) 734-8303
Avon Park Air Force Range: (813) 452-4223
Big Cypress National Preserve: (813) 695-4111
Biscayne National Park: (305) 247-2044
Blackwater River State Forest: (904) 957-4201
Bull Creek Wildlife Management Area: (407) 846-5311
Canaveral National Seashore: (407) 267-1110
DuPuis Reserve State Forest: (407) 924-8021
Everglades National Park: (305) 247-6211
Florida State Forests: (850) 488-4274

Florida State Game and Fresh Water Fish Commission: (850) 488-4676
Florida State Office of Greenways and Trails: (850) 487-4784
Florida State Office of Tourism: (888) 735-2872
Florida State Park Service: (850) 488-7326
Gainesville-Hawthorne Rail Trail: (904) 466-3397
Guana River State Park: (904) 825-5071
Gulf Islands National Seashore: (904) 934-2600
Hickory Hammock Trail: (800) 432-2045
Highlands Hammock State Park: (813) 386-6094
Jay B. Starkey Wilderness Park: (813) 834-3247
Jonathan Dickinson State Park: (407) 546-2771
Lake Kissimmee State Park: (813) 696-1112
Lake Woodruff National Wildlife Refuge: (904) 985-4673
Lower Hillsborough Wilderness Park: (813) 975-2160
Merritt Island National Wildlife Refuge: (407) 861-0667
Mike Roess Gold Head Branch State Park: (904) 473-4701
Myakka River State Park: (813) 361-6511
National Forests in Florida: (850) 942-9300
Ocala National Forest: (904) 625-2520
Orlando Wilderness Park: (407) 246-2800
Paynes Prairie State Preserve: (904) 466-3397
San Felasco Hammock State Preserve: (904) 955-2008
St. George Island State Park: (904) 927-2111
Three Lakes Wildlife Management Area: (407) 436-1818
Timucuan Ecological and Historic Preserve: (904) 221-5568
Tosohatchee State Reserve: (407) 568-5893
Wekiwa Springs State Park: (407) 884-2009
Withlacoochee State Trail: (904) 394-2280
Withlacoochee State Forest: (904) 754-6777

Clubs and Organizations

Florida Trail Association: (904) 378-8823
Rails-to-Trails Conservancy:
2545 Blairstone Pines Drive, Tallahassee, FL 32301
Florida Sierra Club:
462 Fernwood Road, Key Biscayne, FL 33149
Florida Audubon Society: (407) 260-8300

Georgia

Highest point: Brasstown Bald, 4,784 feet.

Reference Materials

Donald Pfitzer's *Hiking Georgia* (Falcon Press, 1996) includes 675 miles of hiking, ranging from one-hour jaunts to the 80-mile section of the Appalachian National Scenic Trail.

Federal and State Resources

Chattahoochee National Forest: (706) 782-3320
Chattahoochee River National Recreation Area: (404) 399-8070
Cumberland Island National Park: (912) 882-4336
Georgia State Office of Tourism: (800) 847-4842
Georgia State Parks: (404) 656-3530; www.ganet.org/dnr/parks
National Park Service, Southeast Region: (404) 331-5187
U.S. Forest Service, Southern Region: (404) 347-2384

Kentucky

Highest point: Black Mountain, 4,145 feet.

Kentucky has two major backpacking trails: the **Sheltowee Trace** and the **Jenny Wiley Trail.** Although they don't intersect, they are connected by a two-mile trail called the Dry Branch Connector. The Sheltowee Trace is a 254-mile trail that extends the length of the Daniel Boone National Forest, from just north of Morehead, Kentucky to Pickett State Park, just inside the Tennessee state line. It is managed by the U.S. Forest Service. Contact: (606) 745-3100.

The **Jenny Wiley Trail** is managed by the Kentucky Department of Parks. The trail runs 163 miles from

Jenny Wiley State Park to South Portsmouth. Contact the State Naturalist: (502) 564-5410.

The **Redbird Crest Trail** covers over 51 miles in Clay and Leslie Counties, within the Daniel Boone National Forest. Contact the Redbird Ranger District: (606) 598-2192.

Reference Materials

Topographic maps are offered for sale by the Kentucky Department of Commerce (Map Sales) and by the Kentucky Geological Survey at the University of Kentucky.

Hiking Kentucky: Scenic Trails of the Bluegrass State, by Darcy Folzenlogen and Robert Folzenlogen (Willow Press, 1995), is a useful source of information.

Federal and State Resources

Big South Fork National River and Recreation Area: (615) 879-4890

South Fork Citico Creek, Citico Creek Wilderness, Cherokee National Forest, Tennessee. Photo by Burt Kornegay, Slickrock Expeditions

Carter Caves State Resort Park: (606) 286-4411

Central Kentucky Wildlife Area: (606) 986-4130

Clay Wildlife Area: (606) 289-2564

Cumberland Falls State Resort Park: (606) 528-4121

Cumberland Gap National Historic Park:
(606) 248-2817

Curtis Gates Lloyd Wildlife Area: (606) 986-4130

Dale Hallow Lake State Resort Park:
(502) 433-7431

Daniel Boone National Forest: (606) 745-3100

Green River State Park: (502) 465-8255

Higginson-Henry Wildlife Area: (502) 389-3580

Jenny Wiley State Park: (606) 886-2711

John A. Kleber Wildlife: (502) 535-6335

Kentenia State Forest: (606) 337-3011

Kentucky Ridge State Forest: (606) 337-3011

Kentucky State Department of Parks:
(800) 225-7275

Kentucky State Geological Survey:
(606) 257-5500

Kentucky State Map Sales: (502) 564-4715

Kentucky State Natural Preservers Commission:
(502) 573-2886

Kentucky State Naturalist: (502) 564-2172

Kentucky State Travel Department: (800) 225-TRIP

Land Between the Lakes: (502) 924-5602

Lapland Wildlife Area: (502) 547-6856

Mammoth Cave National Park: (502) 758-2251

Michael Tygart Trail: (502) 564-2172

Mullins Wildlife Area: (606) 428-3193

Natural Bridge State Resort Park: (606) 663-2214

Otter Creek Park: (502) 583-3577

Taylorsville Lake State Park: (502) 477-8713

Tygarts State Forest Trail: (606) 784-7504

Western Kentucky Wildlife Area: (502) 488-3233

Yellowbank Wildlife Area: (502) 547-6856

Private Trail Agencies

South Kentucky Trails, Inc., is a private trail agency that manages 45 miles of trails in Edmondson and Logan Counties. Contact: (502) 842-7659.

Other non-government trail agencies include:

Berea College Forest Trails: (606) 986-4336
Bernheim Arboretum and Research Forest: (502) 955-8512
Buffalo Trace: (606) 546-6894
Dan Beard Trail: (513) 961-2336
Little Shepherd Trail: (606) 573-4717
Massacre Trail: (502) 245-4021
Munfordville Battlefield Trek: (502) 524-2892
Ohio River Trail: 2400 Windson Forest Drive, Louisville, KY 40272
Ox Cart Trail: (502) 368-9049
Road Runner Trail: (502) 361-7503
Wah-La-Ha Buffalo Trail: (502) 223-7277

Louisiana

Highest point: Driskill Mountain, 535 feet.

Louisiana's longest hiking trail is the **Wild Azalea National Recreation Trail** in the Kisatchie National Forest. The trail is 31 miles of pine and hardwoods brightened by azaleas and dogwoods.

The state's hiking trails are described on a personal webpage: //cust.iamerica.net/sandcroc/trails.htm.

Federal and State Resources

Ben's Creek Wildlife Management Area: (504) 765-2360
Boeuf Wildlife Management Area: (318) 757-4571
Grand Cote National Wildlife Refuge: (318) 253-4238
Kisatchie National Forest: (318) 473-7160
Loggy Bayou Wildlife Management Area: (318) 371-3050
Louisiana State Office of Tourism, catalogs: (800) 633-6970;

information: (800) 261-9144
Louisiana State Parks: (504) 342-8111

Mississippi

Highest point: Woodall Mountain, 806 feet.

Reference Materials

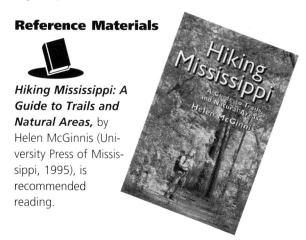

Hiking Mississippi: A Guide to Trails and Natural Areas, by Helen McGinnis (University Press of Mississippi, 1995), is recommended reading.

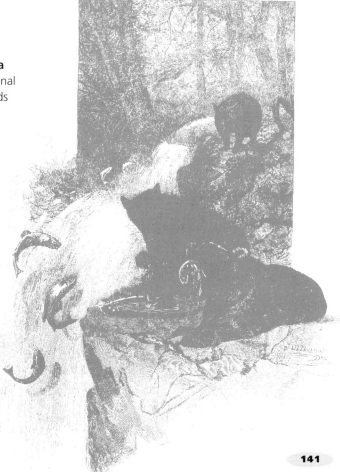

Federal and State Resources

Gulf Islands National Seashore: (904) 934-2600
Natchez Trace National Scenic Trail: (601) 680-4003
Mississippi State Office of Tourism: (800) 927-6378
Mississippi State Parks and Recreation:
(601) 961-5099

Oklahoma
Highest point: Black Mesa, 4,973 feet.

Federal and State Resources

Beavers Bend Resort State Park: (405) 494-6556
Chickasaw National Recreation Area:
(405) 622-3163
Foss State Park (under construction):
(405) 592-4433
Great Plains State Park Bike Trail: (405) 569-2032
Greenleaf State Park: (918) 487-5622
Oklahoma Tourist and Recreation Department:
(800) 652-6552
Ouachita National Forest: (501) 321-5202
Sequoyah State Park: (918) 772-2108
Wichita Mountains National Wildlife Refuge:
(405) 429-3222
Winding Stair National Recreation Area:
(918) 653-2991

Tennessee
Highest point: Clingmans Dome, 6,643 feet.

The Great Smoky Mountains is the most-visited national park in America.

Reference Materials

Hiking Great Smoky Mountains, by Rodney and Priscilla Albright (Globe Pequot, 1994), is a guide to 80 less strenuous hikes.

Trailhead sign in the Citico Creek Wilderness, Cherokee National Forest, Tennessee. Photo by Burt Kornegay, Slickrock Expeditions.

The Best Overnight Hikes in the Great Smoky Mountains, by James Andrews and Kenneth Wise (University of Tennessee Press, 1997), deals with backpacking in the Smokies.

Tennessee Trails: Hikes Along the Appalachian Trail, Trail of the Lonesome Pine, Cherokee National Forest Trail and Many Others, by Evan Means (Globe Pequot Press, 1994), lists more than 100 hiking and backpacking trials outside the Great Smoky Mountains National Park.

Other useful references are **Wilderness Trails of Tennessee's Cherokee National Forest** by William H. Skelton (University of Tennessee Press, 1993) and **Tennessee Hiking Guide** by Robert S. Brandt (University of Tennessee Press, 1988).

Federal and State Resources

Big South Fork National River and Recreation Area: (615) 569-9778
Cherokee National Forest: (423) 253-2520
Cumberland Gap National Historic Park: (606) 248-2817
Great Smoky Mountain National Park: (615) 436-5615; (615) 436-1200
Nachos Trace National Scenic Trail: (601) 680-4003
Obed Wild and Scenic River: (615) 346-6294

Tennessee State Office of Tourism, catalog: (615) 741-2158
Tennessee State Parks: (888) TN-PARKS

Guides and Outfitters

Alpha Adventures YMCA: (423) 984-5519; e-mail: ymcamontvale@juno.com
Ocoee Inn Rafting: (800) 272-7238
Outdoor Adventures Rafting: (800) 627-7636
The Ocoee Adventure Center: (888) 723-8622

Clubs and Organizations

The **Tennessee Eastman Hiking and Canoeing Club** is an outdoors club that offers a full program of day

Limestone caves, Big Bend National Park, Texas. Photo by Burt Kornegay, Slickrock Expeditions.

Photo by Burt Kornegay, Slickrock Expeditions.

hikes, backpacking trips, paddling trips, and other outdoor activities to club members and the public. Contact: //home.tricon.net/tehcc

Texas

Highest point: Guadelupe Peak, 8,749 feet.

Reference Materials

Hiking Big Bend National Park, by Laurence Parent (Falcon Press, 1996), describes the state's number one hiking and backpacking destination. Parent lists 47 trails, with information on the difficulty of each, traffic likely to be encountered, elevation, and maps needed.

Hiking and Backpacking Trails of Texas, by Mickey Little (Gulf Publishing, 1995), lists 80 hikes in parks and wilderness areas.

Hiking Carlsbad Caverns and Guadeloupe Mountains National Park, by Bill Schneider (Grand Teton Natural History Association, 1996), covers western Texas and eastern New Mexico.

Federal and State Resources

Alibates Flint Quarries National Monument: (806) 857-3151
Amistad National Recreation Area: (512) 775-7491
Big Bend National Park: (800) 888-8839
Big Bend Ranch State Park: (915) 477-2251
Big Thicket National Preserve: (915) 229-3416
Chamizal National Memorial: (915) 534-6668
Davy Crockett National Forest: (409) 839-2691
Guadeloupe Mt. National Park: (409) 639-8620
Lake Meredith Recreation Area: (806) 857-3151
Padre Island National Seashore: (512) 937-2621
Rio Grande Wild and Scenic River: (915) 472-2511
Texas State Office of Tourism: (800) 888-8-TEX
Texas State Parks and Wildlife: (800) 792-1112;
www.tpwd.state.tx.us

Guides and Outfitters

Big Bend River Tours: (800) 545-4240
Texas River Expeditions: (800) 839-7238;
www.texasriver.com

Clubs and Organizations

The Lone Star Trail Hiking Club, affiliate of the American Hiking Society, organizes trail-maintenance outings and hikes. Contact them online through the Texins Outdoor Club:
www.outdoorclub.org

Photo by Burt Kornegay, Slickrock Expeditions.

CHAPTER 16

Choosing a Backpack

There is such a large selection of packs available that you might find it intimidating to have to choose one.

So let's start with the very basics: the size and the type of the bag you need. First figure out what you will use the pack for—day hikes, weekend backpack trips, week-long treks, or a season-consuming expedition. That will give you an idea about the size you need.

What Size?

To determine the volume of a pack, manufacturers fill them with dried beans, which they then pour out and measure. This is not an exact science, so you might expect that two manufacturers would get different estimates of volume, depending on how they conduct the measurement, but this method does give a you a pretty good idea of the bag's capacity.

Here are some rules of thumb to go by. Volumes of packs are given in cubic inches:

Day hike, 1,800 to 2,500.
Rucksacks, 2,500 to 3,500.
Weekend backpacking, 4,800 to 5,200.
Week-long treks, 5,900 to 6,300.
Expeditions, 7,200 to 9,000.

Your own size matters, too. Packs come in several sizes that depend on the length of your torso. Height, per se, is not a criterion, but body length is. As a general rule, you'll find packs in these sizes:

Two kinds of backpacks—one with an internal frame (left) and another with an external frame.

FRAME SIZE	HIKER'S HEIGHT
Junior	4'10" or less
Regular	4'10" to 5'6"
Tall	over 5'6"

What Type?

One of the first questions sales people will ask you is whether you want a pack with an internal frame or an external frame. Each has ardent supporters. An external-frame pack has an aluminum frame to which the bag or pack is attached. You could take the bag off and replace it with another bag if you wished, or you could lash equipment or supplies to the frame.

Internal-frame packs have a frame built into the pack; you can't see it unless you go digging through the sleeves in the pack. The frames are made of aluminum, carbon composites, or plastic.

How do you choose between them? You can't really go badly wrong with either, but here are some pointers to help you make a choice:

Internal-Frame Packs

• fit closer to your back, giving you greater comfort and better stability on difficult terrain.

• flex with your body as you move and climb.

• have few compartments; you must dig through everything to find the one thing you need at the bottom.

• with compression straps, allow you to reduce the volume of the pack for smaller loads.

External-Frame Packs

• provide comfort and stability sufficient for most trail hiking.

• provide air space between your back and the pack, keeping your back cooler and sweat-free.

• have lots of compartments; everything is in its proper place and easy to find.

• cost less.

Hipbelts

In *The Backpacker's Handbook* (Ragged Mountain Press, 1997), author and adventurer Chris Townsend describes the hipbelt of the backpack as its most important part, and the one he always examines first.

"A well-fitting, well-

padded hipbelt transfers most of the pack weight (at least 75 percent, and preferably 95 percent) from the shoulders and back to the hips, allowing the backpacker to stand upright and carry a properly balanced load in comfort for hours," Townsend says.

Veteran long-distance hiker Chris Townsend says he hasn't used a traditional external-frame pack since the early 1980s. "For most purposes, I would choose internal-frame packs: They're more stable than all but a few externals, easier to carry around when you're not on the trail, less prone to damage, and comfortable with medium loads (from 30 to 45 pounds). If you carry more weight than that, pack choice becomes more critical."

"A good hipbelt is well padded, with two or more layers of foam at least a half-inch thick. The inner layer should be soft, so that it molds to your hips and absorbs shock; the outer layer should be stiff, so that the belt doesn't distort under the weight of a heavy load."

If you're on a tight budget, you can buy a used external-frame pack at a garage sale and add a first-class hipbelt. It even makes sense to buy the belt first and then go searching for the pack to attach it to. You can always upgrade the frame later.

Anatomical efficiency is a major reason why hipbelts are so good. Shoulder straps transfer weight from the pack across the shoulders, down the spine, through the pelvis to the hip sockets and down through the legs to the feet. At each joint along the way, muscles, cartilage, tendons, and ligaments support the weight of the pack. And each joint is a potential weak link. But a good hipbelt puts most of the weight directly on the hips, reducing fatigue on the other parts.

Suspender Packs

A new approach to day packs is the suspender pack, made by TrekNology. This pack rides in the small of your back, suspended from your shoulders. It is recommended for trail runners and people packing skis.

Photo by James W. Kay. Courtesy of Jansport.

The following companies manufacture backpacks:

Arc'Teryx: (800) 985-6681
Brenthaven: (800) 803-7225
Camp 7, Inc.: (714) 545-2204
CampTrails: (888) 245-4985;
www.jwa.com
Caribou Mountaineering:
(800) 824-4103; www.caribou.com
Cirque Works: (503) 294-0427;
www.cirqueworks.com
Dana Design: (406) 587-4188;
www.ecotravel.com/dana
Deuter Backpacks:
(303) 384-9148
Diamond Brand: (800) 258-9811
Eagle Creek: (800) 874-9925;
www.eaglecreek.com
Eastern Mountain Sports:
(888) 463-6367;
www.emsonline.com
Ecotrek: (800) 858-1383

EDKO Alpine Designs:
(303) 440-0446
Ensign Mountaineering:
(800) 560-7529
Eureka: (888) 245-4984;
www.jwa.com

Gregory: (800) 477-3420
JanSport: (800) 346-8239;
www.jansport.com
K2 Outdoor/Wilderness Exp:
(406) 587-3522

KELTY'S MODEST START

Like many outdoor-gear companies, Kelty started out small. Dick and Nena Kelty started making aluminum-frame packs in 1952. Dick had learned how to work with aluminum in his job at the Lockheed company during World War II.

During their first year in business, they sold 29 packs. They launched a mail-order business and, as backpacking grew, so did the Kelty company.

They have introduced a host of new ideas for packs, including waist belts, quick-release buckles, padded shoulder straps, clevis pins to attach bags to frames, and zippers on pockets.

Dick and Nena Kelty sold their company years ago, but it continues to make highly regarded products.

Photo by James W. Kay. Courtesy of Jansport.

Kelty: (800) 423-2320;
www.kelty.com
L. L. Bean: (800) 341-4341
Lowe Alpine: (303) 465-0522;
www.lowealpine.com

McHale & Company:
(206) 281-7861;
www.aa.net/mchalepacks
Mountainsmith: (800) 426-4075;
www.mountainsmith.com
Osprey Packs: (970) 882-2221

The North Face: (805) 379-3372;
www.clubhousegolf.com
/northface.htm
TrekNology: (800) 873-5725;
e-mail: basecamp@eskimo.com

Checking Packs on Aircraft

Checking your pack for an airplane flight just doesn't work. Although quality backpacks can endure years of use in harsh conditions on the trail, one trip through an airport luggage conveyor system can tear it to shreds.

The greatest problem is that the straps get caught in the conveyor belts. Once a pack gets entangled and pulled sideways, it can form a dam blocking the river of luggage coming at it. And eventually the dam breaks.

Photo by James W. Kay. Courtesy of Jansport.

BALANCE YOUR PACK

 **TIP**

Pack the heaviest stuff in your pack closest to your back. The farther away heavy items are from your body, the more they will pull you off balance.

It's best to carry your pack as hand luggage, but if that's not allowed, pack it in a box or a large duffel bag. If you don't pack it, at least make sure that there are no loose straps flying around, and that nothing is attached to the outside of the pack. It won't be there when you pick up the pack, so you might as well remove it before checking it.

Tape the shoulder straps tightly to the pack and make sure your name and phone number are written on and in the pack.

Tumpline Technology

Despite advances in modern technology, the old-fashioned tumpline, or head strap, is still used by Himalayan porters to carry tons of cargo for Mount Everest expeditions.

Here's an up-to-date view of this ancient load-carrying system from John Weigant, a former Outward Bound instructor and a National Ski Patrol instructor who lives on a houseboat on the Columbia River, where he writes software:

In Praise of Head Straps

By John Weigant
Technology usually helps us, but sometimes it displaces solutions that have evolved over thousands of years. One such solution is the tumpline, or head strap, for carrying heavy loads. We are not suggesting it should replace your shoulder straps and hipbelt, but adding it can often make a trip more comfortable or safer.

To make a tumpline, sew a strap of nylon in the shape shown in the picture on page 152. Stitch in 100-pound test nylon cord. Attach 3-foot lengths of similar cord to the loop and attach the ends low on your pack frame or sack.

Adjust the tumpline so that when you slip it over the top of your head, it takes the weight off your shoulders. On long trips, when hips get sore from tight hipbelts, and shoulders ache from straps, you'll welcome the relief. When you're not using it, it lies comfortably over the top of your pack straps, or tucks into the crossbar of your frame.

Tumplines take little neck strength, since the weight is directly down the neck and spine. If your neck is straining, it's not aligned right. As you use it more, it will begin to feel more comfortable.

A tumpline can also be a safety device. If you are in a situation where your pack is a hazard to your life, as in crossing a swift stream or an avalanche slope, a tumpline is the best

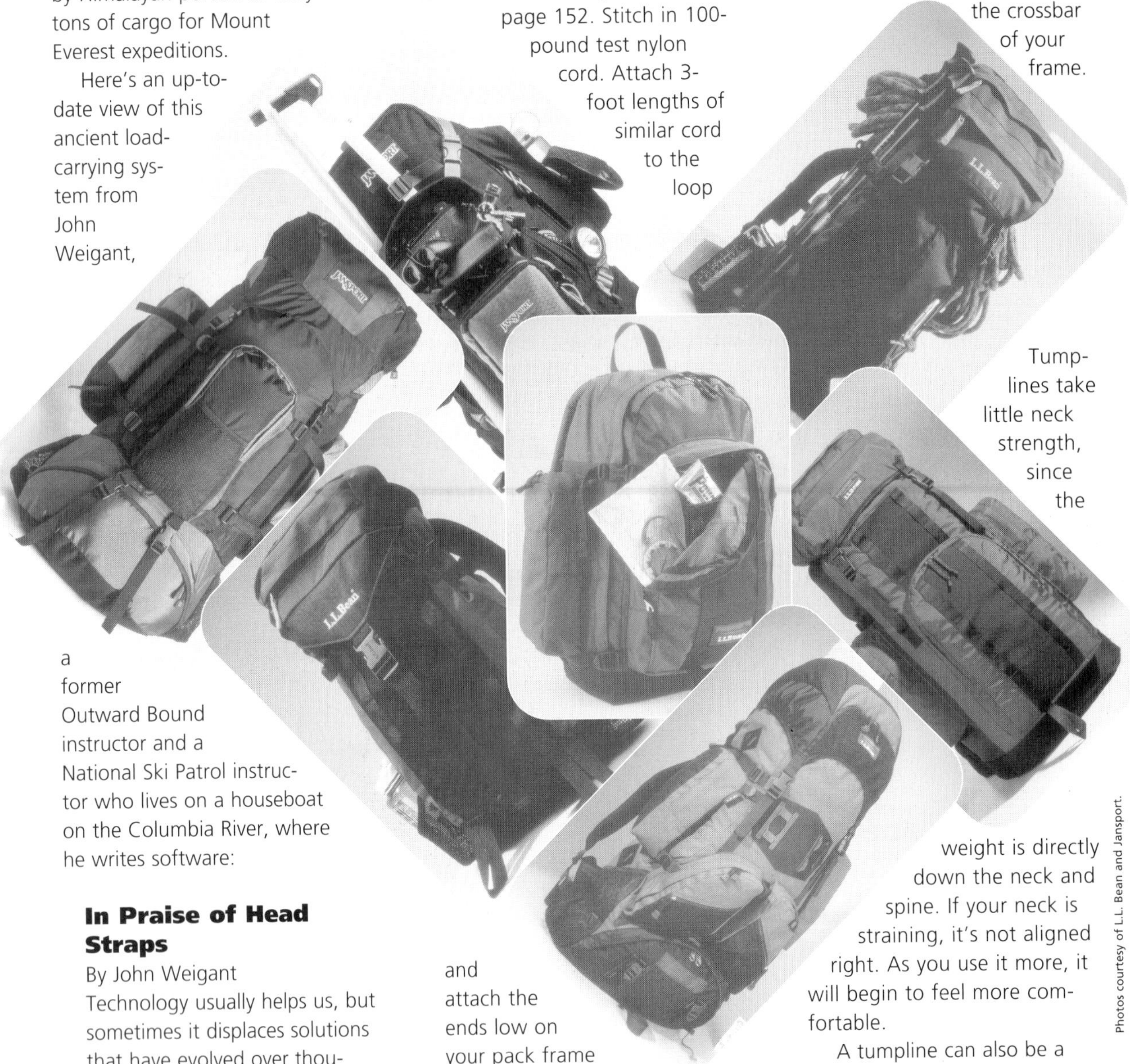

Photos courtesy of L.L. Bean and Jansport.

quick-release there is. Remove your shoulder straps and waist belt, carrying the load entirely by tumpline. If something goes wrong, just throw your head back and you're free of your pack. Far better you should lose your pack than your life. Perhaps one buddy can tie a safety line to your pack and another can tie one to you when you're crossing streams. Incidentally, safety lines are rarely practical on avalanche slopes, though. It's much safer to avoid avalanche slopes entirely.

Tumplines are also a good backup for broken pack straps or frames. Consider having at least one in every party.

Tumplines have one disadvantage that's not apparent until you use one: They interfere with sightseeing and navigation. Properly positioned to take thrust down the spine, they force users into a head-down position. You see the trail just ahead, and that's about all.

SAFER CROSSING

TIP

When fording streams, unbuckle your pack. If you topple into the stream, you'll need to get out of your pack quickly to regain your footing.

Photos by Ed Sobey

Using the tump line. The strap takes weight off the shoulders and places it on the head and neck, which are in line with the back, allowing for easier carrying.

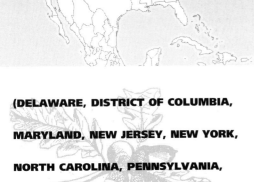

(DELAWARE, DISTRICT OF COLUMBIA, MARYLAND, NEW JERSEY, NEW YORK, NORTH CAROLINA, PENNSYLVANIA, SOUTH CAROLINA, VIRGINIA, AND WEST VIRGINIA)

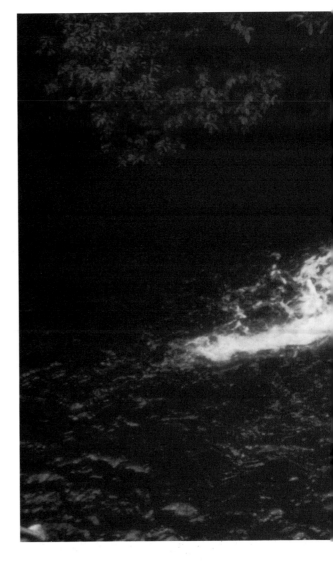

Delaware
Highest point: Ebright Azimuth, 442 feet.

Federal and State Resources

Lums Pond State Park: (302) 368-6989
Prime Hook National Wildlife Refuge:
(302) 684-8419

Delaware State Division of Fish & Wildlife:
(302) 739-5295
Delaware State Division of Parks and Recreation:
(302) 739-4702;
www.dnrec.state.de.us/parks/dsplst.htm
Delaware State Tourism Office:
(800) 441-8846; www.state.de.us/tourism/intro.htm
Trap Pond State Park: (302) 875-5153
White Clay Creek State Park: (302) 731-1310

The Mid-Atlantic States

Slickrock Creek Trail, Joyce Kilmer-Slickrock Wilderness, Nantahala National Forest, North Carolina. Photo by Burt Kornegay, Slickrock Expeditions.

Chesapeake and Ohio Canal National Historical Park: (301) 739-4200
Washington D.C. Convention & Visitors Association: (202) 789-7000; www.washington.org

Clubs and Organizations

Appalachian Mountain Club activities line: (202) 298-1488.
Capital Hiking Club: www.teleport.com/~walking/chc.shtml.
Center Hiking Club: 5367 Holmes Run Parkway, Alexandria, VA 22304
Northern Virginia Hiking Club: activities schedule: 15065 Lindenberry Lane, Dumfries, VA 22026-3039.
Potomac Appalachian Trail Club: (703) 242-0965
Potomac Backpackers Association: (703) 524-1185, www.erols.com/wrightjm/pba.html.
Sierra Club: (202) 547-2326, webmentor.com/mwrop/index2.html.

District of Columbia

Highest point: Tenleytown, 410 feet.

Federal and State Resources

National Park Service, Capital Region: (202) 619-7222

Maryland

Highest point: Backbone Mountain, 3,360 feet.

Reference Material

The following books contain information about Maryland's hiking and backpacking trails:

Walks and Rambles on the Delmarva Peninsula: A Guide for Hikers and Naturalists, by Jay Abercrombie (Backcountry Publications, 1985)

The Baltimore Trail Book, by James W. Poultney and Suzanne Meyer Mittenthal (Johns Hopkins University Press, 1985).

Federal and State Resources

Assateague Island National Seashore: (800) 543-1036

Assateague State Park: (301) 641-3030

Caatoctin Mountain Park: (301) 663-9343

Chesapeake and Ohio Canal National Historic Park: (301) 739-4200

Maryland State Office of Tourism: (800) 543-1036

Maryland State Forests and Parks: (410) 260-8186

Guides and Outfitters

For hiking and river trips, contact River and Trail Outfitters, (301) 695-5177; www.rivertrail.com

Llama Packers

Ground Squirrel Holler Bed & Breakfast & Llama Retreat: (301) 432-8288

Clubs and Organizations

The **Mountain Club of Maryland** promotes hiking in areas near Baltimore. Non-members are welcome to participate. Contact: (410) 377-6266.

New Jersey

Highest point: High Point, 1,803 feet. (New Jersey and Iowa share the same name for their highest point.)

Reference Material

50 Hikes in New Jersey: Walks, Hikes, and Backpacking Trips from the Kittatinnies to Cape May, by Bruce Scofield, Stella Green, and H. Neil Zimmerman (Backcountry Publications, 1997), is the guide covering Pine Barrens and Jersey shore.

Federal and State Resources

Hiking through thick rhododendron on the North Carolina Bartram Trail, Nantahala National Forest. Photo by Burt Kornegay, Slickrock Expeditions.

Gateway National Recreation Area: (800) 537-7397

Delaware National Scenic River: (717) 588-2412

Delaware Water Gap National Recreation Area: (717) 588-2412
New Jersey State Office of Tourism: (609) 292-2470;
catalog: (800) JERSEY-7
New Jersey State Parks and Forests: (609) 292-2797

New York

Highest point:
Mount Marcy, 5,344 feet.

Reference Material

50 Hikes: Adirondacks, by Barbara McMartin (Countryman Press, 1997), covers day hikes in the park. Other books in this series that include New York are:

50 Hikes: Central New York (William Ehling, Countryman Press, 1995), *50 Hikes: Hudson Valley* (Peter Kick, Backcountry Publications, 1994), and *50 Hikes: Western New York* (William Ehling, Countryman Press, 1990).

Kids on the Trail! by Rose Rivezzi and David Trithart (Adirondack Mountain Club, 1997) describes 62 hikes and walks in the Adirondack Park.

If you can't stray far away from New York City, try

Bonas Defeat Gorge, Nantahala National Forest, North Carolina. Photo by Burt Kornegay, Slickrock Expeditions.

Walks and Rambles on Long Island, by Alice M. Geffen and Carole Berglie (Backcountry, 1996), or *Nature Walks in and Around New York City,* by Sheila Buff (Appalachian Mountain Club, 1996).

Federal and State Resources

Adirondack Park Wilderness Area: (518) 523-3441

Castle Clinton National Monument: (212) 344-3266

Fire Island National Seashore: (516) 289-4810

Minnewaska State Park Preserve: (914) 255-0752

New York State Parks: (518) 474-0456

New York State Travel Information Center: (800) 225-5697

Saratoga National Historic Park: (518) 664-9821

Upper Delaware Scenic and Recreation River: (717) 729-8251

Guides and Outfitters

Approach Adventure Travel: (888) APPROACH; www.approach-ne.com

Outward Bound USA: (800) 243-8520; www.outwardbound.org

Syd & Dusty's Outfitters: (800) 424-0260

Llama Packers

Slate Rock Farm: (716) 655-0243; ttsrf@aol.com

Clubs and Organizations

The **New York-New Jersey Trail Conference** is a federation of about 85 hiking and environmental

Panthertown Valley, Nantahala National Forest, North Carolina. Photo by Burt Kornegay, Slickrock Expeditions.

organizations and an additional 9,000 individuals dedicated to building and maintaining marked hiking trails and protecting the related open-space in the bi-state region. The Conference clubs have a combined membership of over 50,000. Members receive a bimonthly magazine, *Trail Walker.* Contact them at NY-NJ Trail Conference, 232 Madison Avenue #802, New York, NY 10016. Or, check their Web page: www.nynjtc.org/~trails.

The **Foothills Trail Club** is in western New York. Contact them at: marktrail@juno.com

The mailing address of the **Cayuga Trails Club** is P.O. Box 754, Ithaca, NY 14851.

The **Finger Lake Trail Conference** can provide maps and information about the trail, which stretches 560 miles from Allegheny State Park to the Long Path in the Catskill Forest Preserve. They are online at: www.finger lakes.net/trailsystem/ or you can write them at P.O. Box 18084, Rochester, NY 14618.

You can get information and maps on the Adirondacks from the **Adirondack Mountain Club,** in Lake George, at (518) 668-4447.

North Carolina

Highest point:
Mount Mitchell, 6,684 feet.

Reference Material

Trails of the Triangle: 170 Hikes in the Raleigh/Durham/Chapel Hill Area by Allen De Hart (John F. Blair Publications, 1997). De Hart also wrote ***Trails of the Triad: Over 140 Hikes in the Winston-Salem/Greensboro/High Point Area*** (John F. Blair Publications).

Two other recommended guides are ***50 Hikes in***

the Mountains of North Carolina by Elizabeth W. Williams and Robert L. Williams III (Backcountry Publications, 1995); and ***North Carolina Hiking Trails*** by Allen De Hart (Appalachian Mountain Club, 1996).

Federal and State Resources

Appalachian National Scenic Trail: (704) 254-3708

Blue Ridge Parkway: (704) 298-0398

Cape Hatteras National Seashore: (919) 995-4474

Cape Lookout National Seashore: (919) 728-2250

Croatan National Forest: (919) 638-5628

Crowders Mountain State Park: (704) 853-5375

Doughton Park: (910) 372-5473

Eno River State Park: (919) 383-1686

Great Smoky Mountains National Park: (423) 436-1200

Hanging Rock State Park: (910) 593-8480

Lake James State Park: (704) 652-5047

Medoc Mountain State Park: (919) 732-4941

Merchants Millpond State Park: (919) 357-1191

Morrow Mountain State Park: (704) 982-4402

Mount Mitchell State Park: (704) 675-4611

Nantahala National Forest: (704) 257-4200

National Forests in North Carolina: (704) 257-4200

North Carolina State Office of Travel and Tourism: (800) 847-4862

North Carolina State Parks and Recreation: (919) 733-4181

Panthertown Valley, Nantahala National Forest, North Carolina. Photo by Burt Kornegay, Slickrock Expeditions

Pettigrew State Park: (919) 797-4475
Pilot Mountain State Park: (910) 325-2355
Pisgah National Forest: (704) 257-4200
South Mountains State Park:
(704) 433-4772
Stone Mountain State Park:
(910) 957-8185
Uwharrie National Forest:
(910) 576-6391

Guides and Outfitters

High Mountain
Expeditions:
(800) 262-9036
Highland
Hiker: (888)
300-TOUR

Llama Packers

Avalon Lla-
mas: (704)
298-5637
English
Mountain
Llama Treks:
(423) 623-5274;
e-mail: mcintyre@
hikinginthesmok-
ies. com
Windsong
Mountain Llamas:
(704) 627-8059

Clubs and Organizations

Nantahala Hiking Club:
www.dataservice.com/nhc/
Piedmont Appalachian Trail Hikers:
www.editorialservice.com/path

Pennsylvania

Highest point: Mount Davis, 3,213 feet.
Some of the best hiking in Pennsylvania is in the
Allegheny Mountains in the west. The state also
has an active rails-to-trails program that has
converted 60 abandoned railroad lines
into trails. To get information, buy a
copy of **Pennsylvania's Rail-Trails
Book** from the Southern Pennsylvania Heritage Preservation
Commission, 105 Zee Plaza,
P.O. Box 565, Holidaysburg,
PA 16648-0565. It costs
$12.95 plus $2.00 for
shipping and handling.
The **Laurel High-
lands Hiking Trail**
stretches 70 miles
from Ohiopyle to
Johnstown. It is open
year-round, is well
marked, and has
established camps
every eight to 10
miles. The camps
include shelters, toi-
lets, water, and
space for tents.
Recreational guides to
the trail are available
from the Bureau of
State Parks.

Reference Material

**50 Hikes: Central Pennsylva-
nia,** by Tom Thwaites (Backcountry
Publications, 1995), and **50 Hikes:
Eastern Pennsylvania,** by Tom
Thwaites and Carolyn Hoffman (Backcoun-
try Publications, 1997), cover the less mountain-
ous parts of the state.
**Fifty Hikes in Western Pennsylvania: Walks and
Day Hikes from the Laurel Highlands to Lake Erie,**
by Tom Thwaites (Countryman Press, 1990), covers

hikes in western Pennsylvania.

**Best Hikes with Children:
Pennsylvania,** by Susan
Trepanowski (The Mountaineers,
1996), is one of a series of 14
books on hiking with kids.

Philadelphia has one of
the world's largest city
parks, which you can learn
about from Nature Walks
in and around Philadelphia: *Nature
Walks near Philadelphia,* by Scott Shalaway and Linda Shalaway (Appalachian Mountain
Club, 1996).

Federal and State Resources

Allegheny National Forest: (814) 723-5150
Blue Knob State Park: (814) 276-3576
Caledonia State Park: (717) 352-2161
Chapman State Park: (814) 723-0250

Cowans Gap State Park: (717) 485-3948
Delaware National Scenic River: (717) 588-2412
Delaware Water Gap National Recreation Area:
(717) 588-2412
Kettle Creek State Park: (717) 923-6004
Laurel Ridge State Park: (412) 455-3744
Little Pine State Park: (717) 753-6000
Moraine State Park: (412) 368-8811
Ohiopyle State Park: (412) 329-8591
Oil Creek State Park: (814) 676-5915
Pennsylvania State Office of Tourism:
(800) 847-4872
Pennsylvania State Parks: (800) 63-PARKS;
reservations: (888) PA-PARKS;
www.dcnr.state.pa.us
Swatara State Park: (717) 865-6470
Tioga State Forest: Wellsboro: (717) 724-2868

Guides and Outfitters

Wilderness Voyageurs: (800) 272-4141

Slickrock Creek Trail, Joyce Kilmer-Slickrock Wilderness, Nantahala National Forest, North Carolina.

Clubs and Organizations

The **Keystone Trails Association** provides information on hiking in Pennsylvania through its Web site: www.reston.com/kta/kta.html. It is also an activist organization warning of legislative actions that might adversely impact hiking trails.

The **Batona Hiking Club** of Philadelphia takes a hike "every Sunday rain or shine." They are online at: www.seas.upenn.edu/~mahesh/batona/batona.html

South Carolina

Highest point: Sassafras Mountain, 3,560 feet.

Reference Material

Hiking South Carolina Trails by Allen De Hart (Globe Pequot Press, 1994) is recommended reading.

Federal and State Resources

The **Palmetto Trail,** when finished, will connect the Blue Ridge Mountains to the Atlantic Ocean. A few sections of the trail are open already and you can get up-to-date information by calling the Palmetto Conservation Foundation at (803) 771-0870.

Carolina Sandhills National Wildlife Refuge: (803) 335-8401
Congaree Swamp National Monument: (803) 776-4396
Edisto Island State Park: (803) 869-2156
Francis Marion National Forest: (803) 561-4000
Jones Gap State Park and Mountain Bridge Recreation and Wilderness Area: (864) 836-3647
South Carolina State Parks: (803) 734-0156
South Carolina State Travel Guide: (800) 390-1133; www.travelsc.com
Sumpter National Forest: (803) 561-4000

Guides and Outfitters

Wildwater, Ltd.: (800) 451-9972; www.wildwaterrafting.com

Virginia

Highest point: Mount Rogers, 5,729 feet.

Reference Material

Hiking the Old Dominion: The Trails of Virginia, by Allen De Hart, (Sierra Club Books, 1984), reveals that Virginia has 3,189 miles of hiking trails. To squeeze in hundreds of trails, De Hart has room only for the basic information needed to select a hike and find the trail.

Hiking Virginia, by Randy Johnson (Falcon Publishing Company, 1996), is a very popular hiking guide that includes 50 hikes. It provides maps, photos, and background information.

For hiking along the Blue Ridge there is Leonard Adkins's *Walking the Blue Ridge: A Guide to the*

Trails of the Blue Ridge Parkway (University of North Carolina Press, 1991).

Two other trail guides are *Potomac Trails,* by Allan Sutton (Fulcrum Publishing, 1997), which covers 100 trails within a day's drive of Washington, D.C., and *50 Hikes in Northern Virginia: Walks, Hikes, and Backpacks from the Allegheny Mountains to the Chesapeake Bay,* by Leonard M. Adkins (Backcountry Publications, 1994).

Federal and State Resources

Virginia claims thousands of miles of hiking trails, including 1,950 miles in The George Washington and Jefferson National Forests. The Shenandoah National Park has 300 more miles.

Burt Kornegay, Slickrock Expeditions

Additional hiking is available in the Assateague Island National Seashore and The Great Dismal Swamp.

Assateague Island National Seashore: (410) 641-1446
Back Bay National Wildlife Refuge: (757) 721-2412
Blue Ridge Parkway: (540) 857-2490
Bureau of Land Management: Eastern Division: (703) 440-1700
Chincoteague National Wildlife Refuge: (757) 336-6122
False Cape State Park: (800) 248-4333
Grayson Highlands State Park: (540) 579-7092

Great Dismal Swamp National Wildlife Refuge:
(757) 986-3705
Jefferson National Forest: (540) 265-6054
Mount Rogers National Recreation Area:
(540) 265-5100
New River Trails: (540) 699-6778
Prince William Forest Park: (703) 221-7181
Shenandoah National Park: (540) 999-3500
Sky Meadows State Park: (540) 592-3556
Virginia State Office of Tourism: (800) VISIT-VA;
brochure: (800) 827-3325
Virginia State Parks Reservation Center:
(800) 933-PARK

Guides and Outfitters

Outdoor Insights: (540) 456-8742
Wilderness Odysseys, Ltd.: (800) 443-6199;
e-mail: us018832@interramp.com

Clubs and Organizations

Potomac Backpacker Association: (703) 524-1185;
www.erols.com/wrightjm/pba.html

West Virginia

Highest point: Spruce Knob, 4,863 feet.

Reference Material

Hiking the Mountain State: The Trails of West Virginia, by Allen De Hart (Appalachian Mountain Club, 1989), is a good source of information.

Although it's out of print, you may still find *50 Hikes in West Virginia: Short Walks, Day Hikes, and Overnights in the Mountain State and Western Maryland,* by Ann McGraw and Jim McGraw (Countryman Press, 1986).

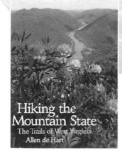

Hiking the Mountain State
The Trails of West Virginia
Allen de Hart

Federal and State Resources

Berwind Lake Wildlife Management Area:
(304) 875-2577
Bluestone Wildlife Management Area:
(304) 466-3398
Bluestone National Scenic River: (304) 465-0506
Cabwaylingo State Forest: (304) 385-4255
Chesapeake and Ohio Canal National Historic Park: (301) 739-4200
Cedar Creek State Park: (304) 462-7158
Coopers Rock State Forest: (304) 594-1561
Gauley River National Recreation Area:
(304) 465-0506
Greenbrier River Rail Trail: (304) 799-4087
Greenbrier State Forest: (304) 536-1944
Kanawha State Forest: (304) 558-3500
Kumbrabow State Forest: (304) 335-2219
Laurel Lake Wildlife Management Area:
(304) 475-2823
New River Gorge National River: (304) 465-0506
North Bend Rail Trail: (304) 643-2931
Plum Orchard Wildlife Management Area:
(304) 469-9905
Seneca State Forest: (304) 799-6213
Tomlinson Run State Park: (304) 564-3651
West Virginia State Office of Tourism:
(800) 225-5982
West Virginia State Parks and Recreation:
(304) 558-2764
West Virginia State Parks Reservation System:
(800) CALL-WVA; //wvweb.com/wvparks

Guides and Outfitters

Ace Whitewater: (800) 787-3982
Mountain River Tours: (800) 822-1386;
voyager.CNS.ohiou.edu/~mcorbin/raft/mountain.html
New and Gauley River Adventures:
(800) SKY-RAFT
North American River Runners: (800) 950-2585;
www.narr.com
Rivers Whitewater Rafting Resort:
(800) 879-7483

CHAPTER 18

Not-So-Sweet Water

Long enough in the desert, a man like other animals can learn to smell water. Can learn, at least, the smell of things associated with water—the unique and heartening odor of the cottonwood tree, for example, which in the canyon lands is the tree of life. In this wilderness of naked rock burnt to auburn or buff or red by ancient fires there is no vision more pleasing to the eyes and more gratifying to the heart than the translucent acid green (bright gold in autumn) of this venerable tree. It signifies water, and not only water but also shade, in a country where shelter from the sun is sometimes almost as precious as water.

—Edward Abbey,

Desert Solitaire

The following sections about water contaminants and filtration were written by William D. Reese, P.E., an avid hiker and backpacker, and a water-treatment engineer in Lake Worth, Florida.

One of the most effective ways to utterly destroy an otherwise successful backwoods or dayhiking experience is to drink water that makes you sick. Although many of us can remember drinking from streams on backpacking trips, there is now almost no place in America, or anywhere else, where the water is free of contaminants. It's too risky to drink wilderness water now, but luckily there are cheap portable systems to purify it.

Water Contaminants

Common contaminants are classified as chemical or biological. Chemical contaminants include pesticides, herbicides, synthetic organics, volatile organics, and other man-made substances. You can't filter out these chemicals, so your best protection is to avoid contaminated water sources. If the water appears or smells bad, don't use it. In most cases, chemical contamination doesn't bring about sudden illness. It takes time and frequent exposure to do the trick. What has more immediate impact is contamination by biological agents.

Biological contaminants can be bacterial, viral, or parasitic. Bacterial contamination caused by animal or human feces often causes a rapid onset of intestinal illness. Livestock in or near a stream indicate the possible presence of bacteria that will disrupt your system. However, the absence of livestock is no indication that the water is safe. Bacteria typically measure 0.1 to 1.0 micron (a micron is one millionth of a meter) in diameter. Check out the pore size on a filter to see if it will keep them out. Many do not.

Viruses are much smaller, between 0.01 and 0.1 micron in size, and cannot be filtered out. Hepatitis A is one such virus.

Parasitic contamination is what causes the most concern in North America. The leading villains include *Giardia lamblia* (causing "beaver fever") and *Cryptosporidium*. You can't see, taste, or smell

these organisms, and your senses may lead you astray: Parasites tend to be more common in cold, clear, low-odor waters. These parasites occur as cysts in water, and are anywhere from 2 microns to 15 or 20 microns across. Most filters will stop these.

Methods of Treatment

Other than taking along a 20-mule team carrying water, what are your options for providing safe water? Boiling works. It eliminates all types of biological contamination, and it may reduce some man-made contaminants, such as volatile organics (for example, gasoline). Of course, it may also concentrate some chemical contaminants because it boils off pure water.

The real problem with boiling is carrying enough fuel on a long trip—and finding the time to boil all the water you need. At sea level, just bringing the water to a

Photo by Burt Kornegay, Slickrock Expeditions.

A RARE EVENT

The protozoa *Giardia lamblia* is found in the intestines of humans and animals. It causes in humans the virulent stomach disorder known as giardiasis or giardia, which is curable only with specific antibiotics.

But the chances of your contracting giardia are quite remote: about the same as being bitten by a shark, according to reseach published in the journal *Wilderness and Environmental Magazine*, and quoted in *Backpacker* magazine.

The study suggests that falling victim to giardia is "an extraordinarily rare event to which the public and press have seemingly devoted inappropriate attention."

rapid boil will kill the critters. At higher elevations, where the boiling point is lower, you have to let it boil for two minutes.

You can treat the water with chemicals to burn or oxidize the contaminants. The drinking water at your home is treated with chlorine, but chlorine is not easy to use when you're backpacking. Instead, you can use iodine in the form of tablets. Iodine is easy to use—drop it in a quart of water and wait half an hour—but it does leave a foul taste. If it bothers you, you can buy a second set of tablets that will remove the taste. But iodine won't remove or kill what's in the water. It won't remove any non-organic chemical contaminants and (especially if there are suspended solids in the water) it may not kill the parasitic cysts. To improve the effectiveness of iodine in turbid waters, filter the water first, or let it stand for an hour before treating it.

Filtration and Membranes

Filters remove particulates that are suspended in the water, and membranes remove dissolved contaminants. You can filter out parasites and other suspended matter as long as the pore size of the filter is 1 to 2 microns. But chemicals and viruses will pass right through the membrane.

Membranes can remove parasites, some bacteria, and some chemical contaminants. Bacteria can lodge in the membrane, however, and grow there. To get rid of them, you need to disinfect the membrane with chlorine (bleach). But be careful and read the

DRINK MORE

TIP

When your urine is colored and smells foul, you're dehydrated. Drink more water.

instructions, because chlorine can damage some membranes.

To force water through a filter and membrane system, you need a pump or a gravity-feed system. The former takes work, the latter time.

If you are in the market for a filter, here are some considerations:

• Make sure it is constructed from Type I, Grade I PVC with stainless steel mechanical parts (Grade 316).

• Check the ease of operation, and don't forget that what seems easy in a sink will be more difficult when you're crouched down in mud beside a stream.

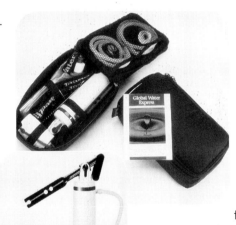

• How much water does it handle? That is, how long will it take you to purify a quart?

• If it has a cleanable filter, how do you clean it? Can you clean it in the field, or do you have to carry a spare?

• What's the cost of new filter elements? What kind of testing has the product gone through?

Filter and Purifier Manufacturers

MSR's MiniWorks Ceramic Filter removes particles down to 0.3 micron in size, which eliminates parasites and many bacteria. The ceramic filter can be cleaned and re-used as many as 40 times. In addition to the filter, the MiniWorks has a core of activated carbon that picks up chemical pollutants other systems miss.

General Ecology's First Need purifier can deliver up to 1.8 quarts of pure water per minute while eliminating bacteria and viruses.

Pentapure also makes a purifier. Theirs uses an iodinated resin to electrostatically remove bacteria and viruses, and has a carbon filter to remove organic contaminants.

Katadyn Filters use ceramic filters to remove bacteria and protozoa down to 0.2 micron. The advantage of Katadyn is that you can use it 300 times without replacing any parts.

The following companies make water filters or purifiers:

American Camper:
(913) 492-3200

Basic Design: (800) 328-3208
General Ecology, Inc./First Need: (800) 441-8166; www.general-ecology.com
Katadyn: (800) 950-0808; www.sportsite.com/katadyn
MSR: (800) 877-9677; www.msrcorp.com
Outbound: (800) 433-6506
PentaPure: (612) 473-1625; www.pentapure.com
Pur: (800) 787-1066
Relags USA: (303) 440-8047
SweetWater: (800)-55-SWEET; www.sweet-h2o.com/
Timberline Filters: (800) 777-5996

Purifying with Iodine

Wisconsin Pharamacal makes **Potable Aqua** iodine tables and neutralizing tablets. The advantage of this system is the convenience. The two bottles of tablets take up very little room in your pack and add negligible weight. You fill your water container and add an iodine tablet. Following the directions, you neutralize the iodine 30 minutes later by dropping in an ascorbic acid tablet. You can drink the water without using the neutralizing tablets, but the iodine imparts a taste that most people don't care for. Call the manufacturer at (800) 558-6614.

Polar Pure makes an iodine treatment system. If you call (408) 867-4576, you can talk to the creator of the system, Bob Wallace. Bob used an idea suggested by two physicians on a climbing trip to Mexico in 1982. On his return he started making a water disinfectant. His system delivers the same amount of iodine to each quart of water by having you observe the water temperature. Since iodine dissolves more readily in warm water, you need less of it. You pour some water into the bottle containing the iodine. After an hour, you pour the required dosage into your drinking bottle full of untreated water. In 20 minutes the water is fine to drink, having killed the bacteria, protozoa, and viruses. Fill up the treatment bottle, and it will be ready to deliver the next dosage. A neat

Photo courtesy of Camelbak®

system. Bob's is a small business. He assembles the product in his garage, and few stores carry it. He is working on a new system that will make iodine delivery even easier.

Water Containers

When it comes to carrying your water, you have lots of choices. You can slip bottles, bags, or flasks into the outside pockets of your pack, tie or strap them to your frame, or get fanny packs, shoulder packs, or water carriers with drinking tubes attached so you can sip as you hike.

A number of companies make belts or straps to carry containers, and you have a lot of choice about the size and shape of the containers themselves. Will you use lots of water on a long, dry run, and want as large as a capacity as you can muster? Water bottles can have small mouths or large; separate lids or attached. Some are even insulated to keep their contents warmer in winter and cooler in summer.

Contact these companies for water containers:

CamelBak: (800) 767-8725; www.camelbak.com
Water Wallett (TrekNology): (800) 873-5725
Campmor: (800) 525-4784; www.campmor.com
Mountainsmith: (800) 426-4075; www.mountainsmith.com
MSR Dromedary: (800) 877-9677; www.msrcorp.com
Nalgene: (800) 872-4552; www.nalgenunc.com
Outdoor Research: (888) 467-4327

Platypus (Cascade Designs): (800) 531-9531; www.cascadedesigns.com
SunDog: (206) 251-8410; www.sun-dog.com
TrekNology: (800) 873-5725; e-mail: basecamp@eskimo.com

Water Buckets

People often start out laughing at the collapsible bucket we take on backpacking trips, but soon are asking to borrow it. It adds only a few ounces to a pack, and makes the job of hauling water much easier. Need water to douse the fire? Want to filter water while you sit comfortably in camp, rather than hunched over the edge of the stream with mud oozing up to your boot tops? Laugh now, but maybe we won't let you borrow it later.

The no-cost alternative to a bucket is to recycle the bag-liner from a 5-liter wine box. Rinse out the empty bag liner several times, and it's ready to go. It's not as easy to fill as a collapsible bucket, but neither does it tip over in camp.

NON-SLOSH
TIP
Carry only sealed water bottles inside your pack. If you have bike bottles, keep them in outside pockets.

Photo by Ed Sobey
A collapsible water bucket.

Hiking Information by Region:

**(CONNECTICUT, MAINE,
MASSACHUSETTS, NEW BRUNSWICK,
NEWFOUNDLAND & LABRADOR,
NEW HAMPSHIRE, NOVA SCOTIA,
PRINCE EDWARD ISLAND,
RHODE ISLAND, AND VERMONT)**

New England and the Maritime Provinces

Connecticut

Highest point: Mount Frissell, 2,380 feet.

Reference Material

50 Hikes in Connecticut: From the Berkshires to the Coast, by David Hardy and Sue Hardy (Backcountry Press, 1986), is a good source of information.

If you want to hike with children in New England, check out ***Best Hikes with Children: Connecticut, Maine, and Rhode Island,*** by Cynthia Copeland and Thomas J. Lewis (The Mountaineers, 1991).

Federal and State Resources

Appalachian National Scenic Trail:
(304) 535-6278
State Office of Tourism:
(800) 282-6863
State Parks:
(203) 566-2304

Llama Packers
Canterbury Llamas:
(203) 966-3461

Clubs and Organizations

The **Connecticut Section of the Green Mountain Club (CSGMC)** offers a variety of hikes and other outdoor activities. They are online at:
//pages.prodigy.com/afreeman/ctgmc.htm

Maine

Highest point: Mount Katahdin, 5,268 feet.

Reference Material

An Outdoor Family Guide to Acadia National Park, by Lisa Gollin Evans (The Mountaineers, 1997) details the hiking, biking, and paddling available in Acadia National Park.

Another reference is ***A Pocket Guide to Hiking on Mt. Desert Island,*** by Earl Brechlin (Down East Books, 1996).

50 Hikes: Northern Maine by Cloe Caputo (Countryman Press, 1989) includes Baxter State Park.

For the southern part of the state, see ***50 Hikes: Southern and Coastal Maine,*** by John Gibson (Backcountry Publications, 1996). ***50 Hikes in the Maine Mountains: Day Hikes and Backpacks in the Fabled Northern Peaks and Lake Country,*** by Cloe Chunn (Backcountry Publications, 1997) details trips lasting from a few hours to five days. Along with hiking directions and maps, Chunn provides information on the geology, wildlife, and history of each trail.

The ***AMC Maine Mountain Guide,*** edited by Elliott M. Bates (Appalachian Mountain Club, 1993) lists hiking information for 100 mountain hikes and has several contour maps, while the ***AMC Guide to Mount Desert Island and Acadia National Park,*** edited by Chris Elfring (Appalachian Mountain

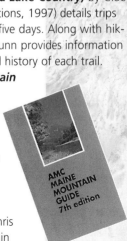

Club, 1993), covers that beautiful region.

Twenty-five hikes on the beach are described in *Walking the Maine Coast,* by John Gibson (Down East Books, 1991).

Another good source of information is *Nature Walks in Southern Maine: Nature-Rich Walks Along the Maine Coast and Interior Foothills,* by Jan M. Collins and Joseph E. McCarthy (Appalachian Mountain Club, 1996).

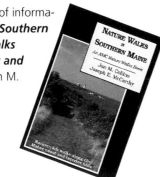

Federal and

State Resources
Acadia National Park: (800) 358-8550, (207) 288-3338
Maine State Office of Tourism: (207) 287-5710; www.state.me.us
Maine State Bureau of Parks and Lands: (207) 287-3821

Guides and Outfitters
Magic Falls Rafting: (800) 207-RAFT; www.magicfalls.com
New England Outdoor Center: (800) 766-7238; www.neoc.com
North Country Rivers: (800) 348-8871; www.ncrivers.com
The Maine Guide: //maineoutdoors.com/guides/

Massachusetts
Highest point: Mount Greylock, 3,491 feet.

Trails in Massachusetts are managed by the State Department of Environmental Management, Division of Forests and Parks; the Massachusetts Audubon Society; and The Trustees of Reservations, a nonprofit organization dedicated to preserving land for its scenic, historic, or ecological value.

Reference Material

For maps of New England, contact **New England Cartographics** in Amherst, (413) 549-4124. The **Appalachian Mountain Club** in Boston offers maps of the Appalachian Trail and the Northeast. Contact them at (800) 262-4455.

50 Hikes: Massachusetts, by John Brady and Brian White (Backcountry, 1992), covers the whole of the Bay State. The authors include hikes for families, and a variety of more challenging hikes.

More concentrated on one area is *Walks & Rambles on Cape Cod and the Islands,* by Ned Friary and Glenda Bendure (Backcountry, 1992).

New England Hiking, by Mike Lanza (Foghorn, 1997), lists trails in Maine, New Hampshire, Vermont, Massachusetts, Connecticut, and Rhode Island.

Federal and State Resources

Beartown State Forest: (413) 528-0904
Blackstone River and Canal Heritage State Park: (508) 278-6486
Borderland State Park: (508) 238-6566
Cape Cod National Seashore: (508) 349-3785
Chester-Blandford State Forest: (413) 354-6347
Chesterfield Gorge: (413) 684-0148
Clarksburg State Park: (413) 664-8345
Coskata-Coatue Wildlife Refuge, Nantucket: (508) 228-0006
Douglas State Forest: (508) 476-7872

Dubuque Memorial State Forest: (413) 339-5504
Erving State Forest: (978) 544-3939
Freetown State Forest: (508) 644-5522
Granville State Forest: (413) 357-6611
Harold Parker State Forest: (978) 686-3391
Holyoke Range State Park: (413) 586-0350
Hopkinton State Park: (508) 435-4303
Ipswich River Wildlife Sanctuary: (508) 877-9264
Lake Dennison State Park: (978) 297-1609
Lake Lorraine State Park: (413) 593-6228
Leominster State Forest: (508) 874-2303
Long Point Wildlife Refuge: (508) 693-3678
Lowell Heritage State Park: (978) 453-0592
Manuel Correllus State Forest: (508) 693-2540
Massachusetts State Parks (Department of Environmental Affairs): information, (617) 727-3180
Massachusetts State Office of Travel and Tourism: (800) 447-6277
Massasooit State Park: (508) 822-7405
Mohawk Trail State Forest: (413) 339-5504
Monroe State Forest: (413) 339-5504
Mount Everett State Reservation: (413) 528-0330
Mount Greylock State Reservation: (413) 499-4262
Mount Tom State Reservation: (413) 527-4805
Mount Washington State Forest: (413) 528-0330
Myles Standish State Forest: (508) 866-2526
National Park Service, North East Region: (617) 223-5199
Nickerson State Park: (508) 896-3491
Northfield Mountain Recreation and Environmental Center: (413) 659-3714
Notchview Reservation: (413) 684-0148
October Mountain State Forest: (413) 243-1778
Otter River State Forest: (978) 939-8962
Pittsfield State Forest: (413) 442-8992
Purgatory Chasm State Reservation: (508) 234-3733

Sandisfield State Forest: (413) 229-8212
Savoy Mountain State Forest: (413) 663-8469
Skinner State Park: (413) 586-0350
Spencer State Forest: (508) 885-2320
Tolland State Forest: (413) 269-6002
Walden Pond State Reservation: (978) 369-3254
Wachusett Mountain State Reservation: (508) 464-2987
Wells State Park: (508) 347-9257
Wendell State Forest: (413) 659-3797
Willard Brook State Park: (508) 597-8802
Windsor State Park: (413) 663-8469
Wompatuck State Park: (781) 749-7160

Clubs and Organizations

The **Pioneer Valley Hiking Club** has over 150 members and meets in West Springfield. For information, call (413) 786-1023.

The **Worcester Chapter of the Appalachian Mountain Club** focuses on central Massachusetts. Call their hotline: (508) 797-9744 or contact them online at: www.ultranet.com/~amcworc

The **New England Hiking Group** is an Internet-based bulletin board for outdoor activities in and around New England: www.ultranet.com/~kleonard/hiking/

Guides and Outfitters

Berkshire Hiking Holidays: hiking and canoeing trips in the Berkshires, (800) 877-9656

New Brunswick

Highest Point: Mount Carleton, 2,690 feet.

Government Resources

New Brunswick Tourism: (800) 561-0123; www.gov.nb.ca/tourism
Cape Breton Highlands Park: (902) 285-2270
Fundy National Park: (506) 887-6000

Newfoundland and Labrador

Highest point: Mount Caubvick, 5,420 feet.

Government Resources

East Coast Trail Association: (709) 738-HIKE (4453); www.ecta.nf.ca
Gros Morne: (709) 458-2417
Tourism Newfoundland and Labrador: (800) 563-6353

New Hampshire

Highest point: Mount Washington, 6,288 feet.

Reference Material

50 Hikes in the White Mountains: Hikes and Backpacking Trips in the High Peaks Region of New Hampshire, by Daniel Doan and Ruth Doan MacDougall (Backcountry Publications, 1997), is a good reference.

50 More Hikes in New Hampshire, by Daniel Doan and Ruth Doan MacDougall (Countryman Press, 1998) lists hikes in the White Mountains and throughout the state.

Another source is the *White Mountain Guide: Hiking Trails in the White Mountain Forest,* edited by Gene Danielle and Jon Burroughs (Appalachian Mountain Club, 1998), which covers hikes in New Hampshire and Maine.

Finally, what more beautiful destination than a waterfall? Check out *Waterfalls of the White Mountains: Thirty Trips to One Hundred Waterfalls,* by Bruce Bolnick and Doreen Bolnick (Countryman Press, 1990).

Federal and State Resources

New Hampshire Parks & Recreation: (603) 271-3556; www.nhparks.state.nh.us
New Hampshire State Office of Tourism: (800) FUN-IN-NH; catalog, (603) 271-2666

Clubs and Organizations

The **YMCA Outing Club** offers hikes, mountain biking, climbing and skiing. Call the club at (603) 497-4663.

Nova Scotia

Highest point: White Hill, 1,747 feet.

Government Resources

Kejimkujik National Park: (902) 682-2772
Nova Scotia Tourism: (800) 565-0000; //explore.gov.ns.ca/virtualns

Guides and Outfitters

Freewheeling Adventures: (902) 857-3600

Prince Edward Island

Highest point: Queen's County, 466 feet.

Government Resources

Prince Edward Island National Park: (902) 566-7050
Prince Edward Island Visitor Services: (800) 565-0267

Rhode Island

Highest point: Jerimoth Hill, 812 feet.

Reference Material

The **AMC Massachusetts and Rhode Island Trail Guide,** by Christopher J. Ryan (Appalachian Mountain Club, 1989) covers hiking and ski routes.

See also **Walks and Rambles in Rhode Island: A Guide to the Natural and Historic Wonders of the Ocean State,** by Ken Weber (Backcountry Publications, 1993).

Hiking Southern New England, by Rhonda and George Ostertag (Falcon Press, 1997), lists 75 hikes in Massachusetts, Connecticut, and Rhode Island.

Federal and State Resources

Beavertail State Park: (401) 884-2010
Goddard State Park: (401) 884-2010
Lincoln Woods State Park: (401) 723-7892
Rhode Island State Office of Tourism: (800) 556-2484; www.visitrhodeisland.com
Rhode Island State Parks and Recreation: (401) 222-2632

Vermont

Highest point: Mount Mansfield, 4,393 feet.

Reference Material

Hiking Vermont, by Larry Pletcher (Falcon Press, 1996), dispels the notion that Vermont is just mountains.

"When you think of Vermont," says Pletcher, "also envision lakes, history, pastoral landscapes, glacier-carved valleys, and wilderness bogs; spruce-fir forests teeming with wildlife, ponds, islands, and secluded marshes; views that are vast, wonders that are tiny; and a lake so large you'll swear it's the sea."

Another good source of information is **50 Hikes in Vermont: Walks, Hikes, and Overnights in the Green Mountain State,** by Bob Lindemann and Mary Deaett (Backcountry Publications, 1997).

Federal and State Resources

Brighton State Park: (802) 723-4360
Green Mountain Club: (802) 244-7037
Green Mountain and Finger Lakes National Forest: (802) 747-6700
Vermont State Office of Tourism and Marketing: (802) 828-3236; brochure, (800) 837-6668
Vermont State Parks and Recreation: (802) 241-3655; www.cit.state.vt.us/anr/fpr/parks

Guides and Outfitters

Adventure Guides of Vermont: (800) 425-8747
Back of Beyond Expeditions: (802) 860-9500; www.backofbeyond.com
Country Inns Along the Trail, inn-to-inn hiking: (800) 838-3301; www.inntoinn.com

Llama Packers
Northern Vermont Llama Treks: (802) 644-2257

Feeding the Weary

On any hike up to a week or two in length,

the only important physiological need is calories.

—Harvey Manning,

Backpacking One Step at a Time

Every backpacker has a favorite food item to take on a trip. With Randy White, for example, it's limes. In an article in *Outside* magazine (February 1993), White said he always took along one fresh lime a week for survival situations.

"Lime juice is one of the world's great seasonings," he declared. "It's wonderful on beans, fruit, fowl, pork, and fish." A tiny wedge dropped into a canteen made stale water taste like Perrier, he claimed.

With Patrick McManus, it's beans. In his book ***Kid Camping from Aaaaiii! to Zip*** (Avon Camelot, 1979), McManus says beans are essential on camping trips, especially camping trips with kids. "Many bad jokes are told about beans on kid-camping trips," he says. "Since bad jokes are absolutely essential to kid-camping trips, beans serve an important function and should never be . . . forgotten."

But first things first. Before we take a look at provisions, let's take a look at the equipment you need to cook your grub.

Backpacking Stoves

Stoves can be classified according to the fuel they use. And, because the availability of fuels depends on where you will be hiking, your choice of stove might be determined by the fuel that will be available.

Fuels are sold as liquids or gases. The most common liquid fuel is white gas, a highly refined form of unleaded gasoline, or variations such as Coleman Fuel. It burns cleanly, is easy to find throughout the United States, and delivers lots of heat for every ounce of fuel you have to carry. White gas is scarcer outside North America. Another disadvantage is that you have to move it from a tank to the burning element of the stove and convert it from a liquid

to a vapor before it burns. White-gas stoves do a great job of boiling water but don't like to sustain the low heats needed for simmering or baking.

To move white gas from its reservoir to the burning element, stoves either use a pump or require you to heat the fuel reservoir and thus create pressure by expansion. The venerable SVEA stove falls into

the latter category. It's as reliable as stoves come and has few parts to fail; however, you first have to heat the reservoir by burning a few drops of fuel on top of it—either a one-minute inconvenience or a totally frustrating experience as you try to get fuel to the right place, prepare the stove for lighting, and light it. Too much fuel, and flames shoot everywhere; too

Photo by Ed Sobey

little, and the reservoir won't heat enough to sustain the flow of fuel. Bummer! Trying to do this inside a tent invites disaster. Another problem with SVEA and similar stoves is their high center of gravity: It doesn't take much of a hit to knock over the pot and stove.

The other option is to pump the white gas from the reservoir to the heating element. MSR adopted this strategy in designing its Whisperlite stoves (contact 800-877-9677). The beauty of the design is apparent: The fuel reservoir is distant from the heat and flame. Pressure builds inside the reservoir with a few strokes of the pump, and vaporization occurs as the fuel flows from the reservoir toward the hot stove. MSR stoves also feature wide bases and low centers of gravity making them tougher to tip over. Both types of stoves have had millions of meals prepared on them. They work well.

One problem with white gas is that you can't keep the fuel from year to year, as it breaks down over time. Buy only what you will need for a season and burn up the dribbles that are left over.

Some stoves can use other liquid fuels as well as white gas, which can be important when you're traveling in countries that don't sell white gas. If you're planning a trip to a developing country, look for a stove that burns plain gasoline or kerosene.

An Alternative

The alternative to white gas is liquid petroleum gas (LPG); either butane or propane. Butane is most common and easy to use. Turn it on, and light the gas. The easy and safe operation make it popular with the Boy Scouts. Butane stoves are slow to boil a quart of water but hold a simmer well.

Butane comes in a convenient canister—which becomes less convenient when it's empty and you have no way of disposing of it. If you're going on a long trip, you have to stock up on canisters and carry them back to your car.

If you anticipate cooking in cold weather, be aware of another

problem with butane: It won't vaporize properly in temperatures much below 40°F at sea level. By mixing butane with other fuels, such as propane, you can use your stove in lower temperatures, but the propane will burn off first, leaving you with mostly butane—and the original problem—when the cartridge is about two-thirds empty.

PRIMUS AND SVEA

Two venerable stove manufacturers, Primus and SVEA, joined forces a few years ago. They supplied Sir Edmund Hillary and Arctic-balloon explorer Salomon Andrée with their stoves. Check out their home page at www.primus.se, or see an unofficial page at www.moneus.se/John/primus_old1.htm.

Pure propane works well at very low temperatures but is so volatile that it needs heavy steel containers with thick walls. The lightest of these weighs several pounds—a weight penalty that few hikers are willing to pay.

Isobutane is an alternative to the butane/propane mix, and while MSR says its isobutane cartridges work down to 12°F, REI and others recommend they be used only down to 30°F.

Wood is another possibility, of course. You can cook directly on a campfire or use wood as fuel in a stove. ZZ Manufacturing, Inc. (800-594-9046) makes a wood-burning backpacker stove. Why wouldn't you use wood? In heavily used campsites, finding wood can be a big chore, and open fires are prohibited in some areas, at some elevations, and in some seasons—or

MORE STABLE STOVES

The popular MSR stoves can slide around while you are pumping up the pressure. Every time you stroke, you yank on the fuel line, which jostles the stove. A solution is to mount the stove and fuel bottle on a lightweight stand. MSR makes one (800-877-9677), as does Wilderness Concepts (888-297-6062).

any time the danger of runaway fires is high. Check fire restrictions before you go.

In picking a stove, consider what's important to you. Butane offers no-mess lighting, good simmering, but longer cooking times. White gas gives fierce heat, re-useable fuel containers, and cold-weather operation. Multi-fuel stoves are what you need for foreign travel.

STOVES ON PLANES

TIP

If you're planning a backpacking trip that includes a plane ride, be aware that airlines don't carry stove fuel. There is a stiff fine for putting fuel in your luggage or carry-ons. Make plans to pick up fuel near the start of your hike.

Your best bet is to try out different stoves. Does your outfitter rent stoves? Compare the boiling times and length of time a stove will burn with one filling or one cartridge, along with ease of operation. Ask store personnel which stoves never come in for repairs.

These are the leading makers of backpacking stoves:

MSR: (800) 877-9677; www.msrcorp.com
North Trail/Outdoor Products: (604) 321-5464
Optimus-Suunto USA: (800) 543-9124; www.optimus.se
Peak 1, Coleman Company: (800) 835-3278
Primus Stoves: (800) 435-4525; www.primus.se
Pyramid Outdoor Cooking Systems: (800) 824-4288
VauDe Sports: (800) 447-1539
ZZ Manufacturing: (800) 594-9046; www.gorp.com/zzstove

Stove Repair

When your stove needs repairs, your first option is to take it to the store from which you purchased it. If you bought it at a discount house, now you'll find out why you should be buying equipment from a store that specializes in hiking and backpacking!

If the store can't do the repairs, and can't or won't send it back to the manufacturer, here are names and phone numbers of some companies that repair stoves:

A & H Enterprises, La Mirada, California: (714) 739-1788

Appalachian Outfitters, Oakton, Virginia: (703) 281-4324

Mountain Safety Research (MSR), Seattle, Washington: (800) 877-9677

The Grant Boys, Costa Mesa, California: (714) 645-3400

Trail Food

Some hikers take great pains to put on a feast in the wilderness. In one camp, the menu might include a bottle of wine, an appetizer, an entrée with side dishes, and, of course, dessert. The extra weight, they say, is not so bad compared to the joy of eating right. At the next campsite, two tired backpackers will hunker down to share a common pot of something green and sticky.

The first group (let us call them the Smythes) enjoy a lavish meal but have to work hard to bring everything they need, spend considerable time cleaning up, and haul back all the pots, pans, and empty containers.

The second group (the Smiths) finish dinner in less time than it takes the Smythes to find all the right food bags. After their speedy meal, the Smiths have time to explore the area, see all the sights, or crawl into their tent early. Of course, after a few days of this fare, the Smiths come to regard dinner as a daily task to be completed, not as a meal to be anticipated and enjoyed.

On the trail, are you a Smythe or Smith? Or are you somewhere in between? Just as important, what style of trail-eaters are your companions? Neglecting to find out before a long trip could result in gastric discord and unhappy campers. Talking about the menu before going to the grocery store can give everyone the chance to suggest meals, indicate food preferences and intolerances, and, best of all, give others the chance to plan some of the meals themselves.

A middle ground will make most people happy or at least tone down their grumpiness. In this case, treading the middle ground means that you follow the green glop with an attractive dessert.

The two main choices you have in menu planning are to purchase foods specially prepared for backpackers or to concoct your own. Outfitters carry freeze-dried food that makes meal preparation a snap. You can also order freeze-dried food directly from a manufacturer.

Freeze-Dried Food

Freeze-drying preserves food by removing water. Since water can be found most places, you don't need to carry the water in the food you eat; you can add it when you're ready to cook it.

The full process consists of preparing the food, freezing it, and placing it in a vacuum. The vacuum draws out 98 percent of the water and removes it from the food, making it safe from attack by microorganisms. Done properly, the process retains the nutrition, taste, and structure of the food. Freeze-dried food can be stored for as long as five years.

The major benefit of freeze-dried food is convenience. Just hike into your outfitter's store and pick up entrées for each breakfast and dinner of your trip. Many of the meals require you only to add boiling water, thus cutting down on fuel consumption and cleanup chores.

The downsides of freeze-dried food are taste, texture, and expense. To keep food costs down, you can shop for food at a grocery store instead. If you're hungry enough, you'll gobble down the un-rehydrated chunks and not mind. But you might find that eating freeze-dried food for several days destroys your appetite.

The following companies manufacture freeze-dried food:

Adventure Foods: (704) 497-4113

AlpineAire: (800) 322-6325; www.aplineairefoods.com

Backpacker's Pantry: (800) 641-0500

Chamy: (800) 322-7010

Harvest Foodworks: (800) 268-4268; www.harvest.on.ca

Mountain House (sells to retailers only): (800) 547-0244; www.ofd.com

Natural High (Richmoor) (sells to retailers only): 800) 423-3170; www.richmoor.com
Uncle John's Foods:
(719) 836-2710

Greater Variety

Grocery stores give you a far greater variety of foods than you'll get from freeze-dried–food manufacturers. For instance, dried soup mixed with instant rice makes a nutritious and inexpensive meal. Backpacking cookbooks boil over with menu ideas that avoid freeze-dried foods.

MREs, or "meals, ready to eat," are finding their way from the battlefield into backpack country. They're heavy because they are fully hydrated, and they come with packaging that you have to carry in

and out. But some people claim their superior taste and texture overcome those inconveniences. If you can't find them at backpacking stores, check army surplus stores.

Summit Foods makes ready-to-eat meals in pouches. You can open the bag and start to munch, or drop it into boiling water for five minutes. Ask your favorite outdoors retailer or contact Summit Foods: (800) 776-8731.

Deciding What to Take

Your trail menu will probably be richer in calories and fats than your home-based menu. You'll need more calories while backpacking—easily 1,000 a day more. Fats can be a great source of those calories. The fats you avoid at home are welcome on the trail as they provide more calories than do carbohydrates of comparable weight, and they taste especially good.

What foods do backpackers crave after a few days in the woods? According to *Backpacker* magazine, the foods most desired are ice cream, beer, pizza, milk, and shakes. Aside from beer, the top choices all are high in fats, so even if you avoid them at home, add them to your backpacking menu.

In choosing which foods to take, think about the logistics involved in preparing them. Pick food that will

need a minimum of cookware and will leave a minimum of mess. Can you reduce your cookware needs to one pot? Can you eliminate anything that will require you to bring back empty containers? Your body will appreciate your thinking through the cooking process and reducing all unnecessary weight.

Dry It Yourself

You can dry your own food to suit your trail menu. Depending on the climate where you live, you can sundry food, use a dehydrator, or dry it in your oven. You can purchase a dehydrator or make your own. In *Trail Food* (Ragged Mountain Press, 1998), Alan S. Kesselheim gives instructions for making two dehydrators plus recipes for a variety of light-weight meals.

Low-Cost Glops

Many backpackers take pride in their ability to cook several courses in one pot. Such meals are often based on rice, soup mix, and possibly a dried or salted meat. Prepared pastas, such as macaroni and cheese or noodles stroganoff, also make good glop bases. Creativity is the essence of a good glop, but most of them can be prepared at low cost.

Repackage Your Food

Don't carry the boxes or cans food comes in unless absolutely necessary. Why lug them in, and lug them out again? Repackage food in the amounts you will need for every meal.

Put dried cereal, along with your guess for the right amount of dried milk, in a bag for each breakfast. All you have to do is shake the bag to mix the cereal and powered milk, pour out what you want, and add water. Reseal leftovers in the bag for a morning when you're really hungry.

How much work do you want to do at lunchtime? Is it worth it to crank up the stove to get a hot meal? In midwinter it might be, but in summer skip it, and spend lunch watching and listening to the world you came to experience.

Foods that will cook together can go into the same plastic bag in your pack. Add dry seasoning to the bag so you don't have to carry containers with you. Drop a small index card or business card in the bag with cooking instructions written on the reverse side.

Put all the bags of food for one meal in another supermarket plastic bag, so you have to find only one bag to get everything you need for a meal. Mark the outside of the bag to indicate which meal is contained inside. One additional bag can hold condiments needed for several meals or common cooking utensils.

If you are packing food for several people, distribute the food packages among all of them. You don't want to lose everything if one pack goes over the edge.

At breakfast, pull out the day's lunch and arrange it so it will be easy to find. After dinner, gather up all the remaining food bags and bear-bag them or otherwise store them out of harm's way.

Squeeze Tubes

If you carry margarine, peanut butter, jelly, or other mushy foods, squeeze tubes made by **Coghlan's**

of Winnipeg, Canada, can make your life easier. Squish the peanut butter into the open end, roll the end to seal it shut, and secure it with the plastic clamp. On the trail, just unscrew the cap and squeeze; there is nothing to clean up, as long as you aim well. At home, squeeze the remaining contents out and fill with soapy water to clean.

FAST FOOD

TIP

Instant dinner! Buy one instant black-bean soup mix for each person eating dinner. Pour all into a sealable plastic bag. Toss in half a cup to one cup of minute rice and all the dry seasoning you dare. Add a recipe reminder so you know how much water to boil—one and a half cups of water for every cup of rice you added. Seal the bag.

At dinner time, boil the water you need. Dump in the rice-and-bean mix and stir. Minutes later, when the rice is no longer crunchy, you have lots of carbos and protein. Repeat the formula with other flavors of soup or with noodles instead of rice.

FREE FOR FORAGING

FREE

Interested in foraging for food? Check out *Free Food?! A Guide to Edible Plants for Backpackers*, produced by Whelden. It runs for 48 minutes.

It tells you "where to look for the plant, how to make a quick identification, and how to harvest and cook it with a minimum of ingredients and fuss."

Backcountry Baking

Want fresh bread to go with dinner? How about fixing a pizza on the trail? Hot apple cobbler?

Remember when baking required you to carry a Dutch oven, pile up reflector rocks around your fire, or wrap biscuit dough in foil and bury it under the coals?

No wonder few people bothered. Now, Cascade Designs has come out with a new, lightweight system for baking. The **Outback Oven** does take up room inside your pack, requires attention while baking, and consumes fuel. But baking aromas arouse weary appetites, and warm carbohydrates taste delicious. Contact Cascade Designs: (800) 531-9531; www.cascadedesigns.com

Need packaged ingredients to go into your Outback Oven? Cascade Designs provides them, too, from apple pie to pizza. And they will be adding about 10 new products in 1998. The packaged food sells under the Traveling Light label.

Other companies that make trail ovens include **BakePacker** (707-497-4113) and **Banks Fry-Bake** (518-851-7115).

Backpacking Cookware

Don't buy cooking gear until you know what you're going to be cooking. Will you be simply boiling water to rehydrate freeze-dried food, or will you be frying up today's catch?

Obviously you want to take the fewest and lightest pots and pans that will accommodate your needs. If you plan your meals in advance, you'll be able to take only the pots and pans you need.

So just what is the best kind of cookware? Aluminum is inexpensive and lightweight, but not as easy to clean as a non-stick surface.

Photo courtesy of Cascade Designs

Non-stick cookware costs more and is heavier. **Evolution Cookware** (by Traveling Light, 800-532-9531) offers non-stick-surfaced aluminum cookware.

Stainless steel, either by itself or with aluminum, makes great cookware, albeit heavy.

Titanium is very light, strong, and very expensive. It is as strong as steel and as light as aluminum. **Evernew** and **MSR** (800-877-9677) make cookware from titanium. MSR's titanium spoon has a stove wrench cut into the handle and holes to help you pull the fuel line out of the cable on their stoves.

If you're a budget-wise buyer, visit thrift stores operated by local charities. They often carry a collection of used cookware for the cost of a freeze-dried dessert.

Few companies make backpacking cookware; here they are:

MSR: (800) 877-9677
REI: (800) 426-4840; www.rei.com
Sigg: (604) 321-5464
Traveling Light: (800) 532-9531

Voice of Experience

Here's some very practical advice on cookware for backpacking from John Weigant, former Outward Bound instructor and National Ski Patroller. He lives on a houseboat on the Columbia River.

PAINT IT BLACK

TIP

By painting the outside of your cooking pot black, you increase its heat absorption, cook faster, and save fuel. Check hardware stores for stove paint.

Photo by Ed Sobey

John Weigant demonstrates how to check biscuits in his home-made practical cooker. The two rings connecting the pans are about one third of the circumference apart, allowing the baker to peer inside.

Practical Cookware
By John Weigant

Good cooking gear can often be found at secondhand stores. I've used the following combination for years and found it to be effective, compact, versatile, and cheap.

• **Water container:** a 5-liter bag from boxed wine (rinse it well!). Carry it in a light nylon bag with hand straps.

• **Cup:** a Sierra Club cup or plastic cup, depending on your taste. Sierra cups are more versatile but are often uncomfortable for hot drinks.

• **Utensils:** soup spoon, pocket knife, and pot gripper or pliers

• **Plates:** two tapered cake pans that nest

• **Pots:** three identical, three-quart, tapered pans that nest

• **Options:** varying by menu: wire whip, pancake turner, kitchen spoon

Modifying the pots: If they have handles on them, cut them off. Aluminum "pudding pans" work well, as do large stainless steel dog dishes. Drill holes on opposite sides of the rim and install bails made of stove wire. The bails should be long enough to slip over the rim so the pots will nest and just a little bit longer to accommodate a breaking wire. Try to get the holes directly opposite each other so

BAGS OF BAGS

What do you carry your food in? Save plastic bags from the grocery store. The flimsy ones they provide to carry fruits and vegetables are great for carrying the exact amount of cereal or rice. Stuff all the bags needed for one meal in the heavier bags stores provide for carrying stuff home. Each heavier bag then contains everything you need for one meal, and each component of the meal is stored in one of the flimsy bags.

SIERRA CLUB CUP

The Sierra Club cup is a hallowed institution among members. Some carry it as their only piece of campware, serving as cup, bowl, and plate. It also serves as a measuring cup, shovel, and candlestick. This extract from *Encounters with the Archdruid* by John McPhee (Farrar, Straus and Giroux, 1971) shows how revered the club cup is.

"The river guide who has organized this expedition, calls out that dinner is ready. He has cooked an entire sirloin steak for each person. We eat from large plastic trays.

"[David] Brower [onetime Executive Director of the Sierra Club] regularly ignores the stack of trays, and now, when his turn comes, he steps forward to receive his food in his Sierra Club cup . . . a man with wild white hair and pink legs is holding out a four-inch cup to receive a three-pound streak. Very well.

"He drapes the steak over the cup. The steak covers the cup like a sun hat. Brower begins to hack at the edges with a knife. Brower in wilderness eats from nothing but his Sierra Club cup."

full pots won't spill when lifted by the bail.

Modifying cake pans: Choose nesting cake pans that just fit in the top of the pots to form pot lids. A lid helps water boil faster and can serve as a double boiler to keep food warm. Drill two holes in the rims of the cake pans, about a third of a circumference apart. Drill one pan first, then place the other on top and drill holes in identical positions.

When the pans are attached together with safety pins, they make a nice oven. Put biscuits, muffins, or cake batter into the pans and attach the lid. Scoop out the coals in the fire. Leave very few coals underneath. Place the pan in the bottom of the fire pit and put the removed coals back on top. If the two pans aren't pinned together, you're almost certain to get ashes inside. In about 10 minutes, your biscuits are ready.

Using the pots: Three pots are enough for most camp

Illustration by Daisy dePuthod

meals. One is a fire pot for hot water. The second is also a fire pot for cooking the meals. The third pot is never put over the fire, so its outside stays clean. It can be used as a double boiler or on a gas stove, but keep its outside clean.

Storing the pans: Most camping pots are hard to carry. Not these. Just nest the pans together, with the clean one on the outside. Then open your sleeping bag stuffsack and insert the pans over your sleeping bag. Put the cake pans on top and close the stuffsack. But beware: the pans create wear points on the stuffsack, so treat your stuffsack carefully or pad the pan rims.

An advantage of packing pans in the sleeping bag stuffsack is that it makes breaking camp easier. I tend to keep a morning coffee pot going until the last minute. I finish packing my bag and enjoy the coffee. The last step when leaving camp is to drown and stir the fire,

using the last of the water in the pans, then stow the pans in the stuffsack and tie it to my pack. The equipment I need last, the pots for coffee and putting out the fire, are the last equipment to be packed.

Enjoy.

Washing Up

The better the job you do of planning your meals, the less mess you'll face in cleaning up afterward. Take the time to estimate the amount of food you'll need for each meal. If you underestimate the total you need for the trip you will be unpopular, but overestimating will give you, or someone else, the unenviable job of carrying out the uneaten food. Make sure you carry extra plastic bags to double-wrap any garbage you need to pack out.

Three-course meals sound great, but how many pots will you

have to wash afterward? And why does everyone disappear when it's time to wash up?

Your clean-up kit can include a scrubber and a small bottle of biodegradable soap, carried in a sealable plastic bag. A fast-drying towel is a nice addition, if you don't leave cookware out to air-dry.

Since you can't wash your cookware in any body of water, you need to bring water to where you

Photo courtesy of Backpackers' Cache

SIERRA CUP TO THE RESCUE

Carl. E. Joplin, an experienced backpacker, Scout leader, and graduate of the National Outdoor Leadership School, recalls that a Sierra Club cup once helped save his life.

He was hiking across the Sierra Nevada, descending Bloody Canyon, when he slipped on a steep snow field and began sliding rapidly toward a crop of boulders. He rolled over on his stomach and began digging in his fingers and toes, then discovered to his relief that his Sierra Club cup, from which he had been eating a

breakfast of granola and snow a moment earlier, was digging in very effectively.

"I wrapped both hands around it and the steel handle and tried to put all my weight on just it and my toes. It didn't slow me down much, but I stopped accelerating and could actually look down the hill at where I was headed," he said.

"The snow narrowed down to a slot between two boulders, which I maneuvered through as if I knew what I was doing. The snow field

opened back up and I rode it another hundred feet or so to its conclusion at some flat slabs that, fortunately for me, I was able to hit feet-first to absorb some of my considerable momentum. Once I figured out nothing was broken except my pride, I was thrilled to notice that the few seconds of my ride had probably saved me a half-hour of hiking. Nevertheless, even I knew at that point I was one lucky fellow not to have added any of my own color to Bloody Canyon."

can wash it. A collapsible bucket is the easiest way. Heat some water in the cooking pot and add one or two drops of biodegradable soap—not the stuff you use at home.

Make sure you rinse after washing to get rid of the soap. Since *Giardia* can survive on pots and scrubbers, make sure the rinse water has been filtered or boiled. Also, rinse out the scrubber and let it dry overnight.

If you like your pots clean when you put them away after a backpacking trip, coat the outsides with liquid soap before you go back-

packing. Drop a dab on the bottom, spread it around with your fingers, and let it dry. Over an open fire, the pots will blacken, but don't attempt to clean the outside. Keep your pots in plastic grocery bags so the soot doesn't rub off inside your pack. Then, when you get home, you'll find you can wash off the fire soot without scrubbing.

Biodegradable soap is made by:

Camp Suds: (707) 577-0324
HuckFinn's All-Purpose Soap: (813) 725-1177

REI Bio Suds: (800) 426-4840; www.rei.com
Tom's of Maine: (207) 985-2944

Cookbooks

There are scores of cookbooks to tell you what to prepare in the outdoors. But before you rush out and stock up on them, ask yourself what type of cook-hiker you are. Are you so exhausted at the end of the day that you will eat a freeze-dried dinner without adding water? Is the taste of a gourmet meal worth carrying the extra pots and condiments? Do you plan your trips, giving yourself ample time to organize meals, or do your trips just *happen?*

One of the best-known backpacking cookbooks is ***Gorp,***

Glop, and Glue Stew, by Yvonne Prater and Ruth Dyar Mendengall (The Mountaineers, 1982). It lists dozens of recipes for GORP (good old raisins and peanuts), breads, and other trail

FRUIT BAR RECIPE

TIP

Here's the way to make Henry's "no-cook" fruit bars.

Ingredients:

1 ½ cups dried apricots and walnuts
½ cup each of pineapple, figs, dates, apples, raisins
¼ cup each of sesame seeds, soy protein, soy lecithin
¾ cup each of sunflower seeds and instant non-fat milk powder
4 tablespoons honey
1 tablespoon brewer's yeast
1 teaspoon salt

Method:

Chop all ingredients finely and mix in a large bowl. Blend by hand and then make rolls about ¾-inch in diameter and 3 to 4 inches long. To satisfy a sweeter taste, roll them in powdered sugar. Let them air dry for a few days and then wrap them in plastic bags to go.

goodies. If you enjoy preparing for your trip, this is a great book to have on your shelf.

A more recent publication is **Good Food for Camp and Trail,** by Dorcas S. Miller (Pruett Press, 1993). Another cookbook worth consulting is the **Wilderness Ranger Cookbook,** by Valerie Brunell and Ralph Swain (Falcon Press, 1990).

The Well-Fed Backpacker, by June Fleming (Vintage Books, 1986), has chapters on menu planning, desserts, drinks, desserts, snacks, emergency foods, and desserts. Fleming also suggests inexpensive foods for the trail, or "good eating on a bootlace," as she calls it.

The Back-Country Kitchen, by Teresa Marrone (The Bookmen, 1996), emphasizes easy-to-pack, easy-to-prepare, lightweight foods. Her 150 recipes cover breads, main dishes, and fish.

NOLS Cookery, edited by Claudia Pearson (Stackpole Books, 1997), has more than 170 recipes plus basic information on nutrition and menu planning.

MAKING ROOM

In memory of Bob Bostick, who among his other skills could always find room for himself at a crowded campfire by a dangerous practice: conspicuously tossing his SVEA stove directly into the fire. Those enjoying the fire scattered for cover, clearing an area large enough for him to sit and fish his stove out before it exploded. Alas, it was a drunk driver and not his stove that did him in.

First Aid

I camped by the Muir Glacier for a week. I had caught
. . . a cold . . . from . . . a stuffy stateroom. So I made
me a little sled . . . and set out up the glacier. I got
into a driving snowstorm, and had to spend the night
on the ice 10 miles from land. I sat on the sled all night
or thrashed about it, and had a dickens of a time;
I shivered so hard I shook the sled to pieces. When
morning came my cold was all gone.

> —John Muir, quoted in
>
> *Alaska Days with John Muir*
>
> by Samuel Hall Young

The following items to be included in a first-aid kit for wilderness backpacking are suggested by Scott Ford, M.D., FACEP, who is an active back-packer and outdoorsman practicing in Fresno, California. This list is not all inclusive; likewise, some of the items might not be necessary for your particular expedition.

Your First-Aid Kit

First-aid manual: a condensed, lightweight paperback. This should serve only as a quick reference. Anyone exploring the wilderness should have a strong background in first-aid techniques.

Adhesive bandages: assorted sizes. "Knuckle" bandages are use-ful for hand injuries.

Gauze pads: 2 x 2s and 4 x 4s for covering larger wounds

Adhesive tape: for dressing wounds

Roller gauze: 2-inch wide

Triangular bandage: for wrap-ping injuries, splitting, or making an arm sling; you can use a large bandanna or cut-up shirt

Elastic bandage (ACE): at least 4 inches wide. Useful for wrapping wrist, ankle, knee, and elbow injuries; to help keep bandages in place; and to apply pressure dress-ing to control bleeding.

Moleskin: to protect hot spots and blisters

Tweezers: to remove splinters and ticks. Tweezers on Swiss Army knives work well.

Small scissors: to cut bandages, tape, toenails, and so on. Scissors on Swiss Army knives will cut most of the stuff you need cut.

Paperclip: when heated, it can be used to burn a hole in a nail to drain blood from beneath it, reliev-

Illustrations by Daisy dePuthod

ing pressure and pain.

Safety pins: to secure slings and large bandages. After sterilizing in a flame, use to help remove splinters.

Soap: to clean minor wounds and burns

Medications: Non-Prescription

Aspirin, Acetaminophen, or Ibuprofen: to relieve headaches, pain, fever, and simple sprains or strains. Don't give aspirin to chil-dren to relieve flu symptoms.

HYPOTHERMIA

TIP

The symptoms of hypothermia are uncontrolled shivering; slow, slurred speech; loss of coordination; confu-sion; and drowsiness.

   Take immediate action to stop the heat loss; talk to the person; give warm fluids to drink; warm the torso; and get the patient to a doctor.

Sunscreen: SPF 15 or higher

Insect repellent: one with 35 per-cent to 55 percent DEET, with stabilizer

Antacid tablets: for example, Maalox or Pepto-Bismol

Anti-diarrhea pills: Imodium A-D or Pepto-Bismol

Hydrocortisone cream: to reduce the itching of insect bites or poison ivy/oak

Antihistamine pills: Diphenhydra-mine—Benadryl; to treat allergic reactions from insect bites and poi-son ivy/oak

Motion sickness medication: for use if your route includes travel on winding mountain roads or travel by water

Antibiotic ointment: Bacitracin or Neosporin; for burns, cuts, and scrapes

Water-purifying pills: Iodine or Halazone; as primary treatment or as or backup in case your water filter malfunctions

Medications: Prescription

Ask your physician about taking prescription medications to be used in emergencies. This is important if you're going on prolonged wilderness trips to remote locations or if you are susceptible to specific maladies. Your doctor will be able to give you guidance, but here are some medications to consider:

Prednisone: This anti-inflammatory steroid pill can be used for severe allergic reactions and severe poison ivy/oak rashes. Use with caution with people having a history of stomach ulcers or diabetes.

Epinephrine: This may save lives in very severe allergic reactions (anaphylaxis). Epinephrine comes in convenient preloaded syringes for self-injection. This is a must for anyone who has had a severe allergic reaction to bee or wasp stings.

For Trained Personnel

Injectable pain medication: Morphine or meperidine

Injectable local anesthetic: Lidocaine or bupivacaine to numb wounds for treatment, or fishhook removal

Lightweight suture kits

The list does not include a snakebite kit. The materials necessary to treat a snake bite are, however, listed. You can use splinting materials, and an ACE bandage or bootlace as a low-pressure constricting band to interrupt lymphatic flow. Such procedures as incision and suction, and the application of tourniquets, are no longer regarded as acceptable therapies.

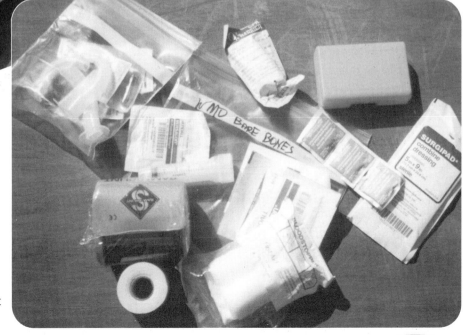

Photos courtesy of Wilderness Medicine Outfitters

Regular medications: Don't forget to pack your routine medications!

Antibiotics: Azithromycin (Zithromax), for wound infections or respiratory infections. Convenient, as you take them only once daily. Trimethoprim-Sulfamethoxazole (Bactrim), for urine infections, middle-ear or sinus infections. Can't be used if allergic to sulfa.

Sources for Kits

Adventure Medical Kits:
(800) 324-3517
Atwater Carey:
(800) 359-1646
Chinook Medical Geare:
(800) 766-1365
JanSport: (800) 552-6776;
www.jansport.com
Outdoor Research:
(800) 421-2421; www.orgear.com
REI: (800) 426-4840; www.rei.com
Sawyer Products: (800) 940-4464
Wilderness Medicine Outfitters:
(303) 688-5176;
www.wildernessmedicine.com

LOOK FOR THE SIGNS

TIP

In subfreezing weather, periodically check each other for signs of frostbite on exposed flesh. Look at your partner's exposed skin for blanching or white spots, and check yourself for tingling or numb sensations.

Reference Material

When searching for a book on outdoor medicine, ask yourself if you intend to carry it with you or read it at home. (The best approach is to do both, because in an emergency you won't want to be fumbling with an unfamiliar book.)

Here are some books to consider. Wilkerson's and Auerback's books are definitive and a little weighty to take along in your pack. More pack-friendly is *Mountaineering First Aid.*

Medicine for Mountaineering, by James A. Wilkerson (The Mountaineers, 1993)
Medicine for the Outdoors, by Paul Auerback, M.D. (Little, Brown, 1991); also on videotape from Centre Films at (213) 466-5123
Mountaineering First Aid, by Jan Carline, Martha Lentz, and Stephen Macdonald (The Mountaineers, 1996)
NOLS Wilderness First Aid, by Tod Schumilpheny and Linda Lindsey (Stackpole Books, 1992)
Ragged Mountain Press Pocket Guide to Wilderness Medicine & First Aid, by Paul G. Gill, Jr., M.D. (Ragged Mountain Press, 1998).

Blister Treatment

To protect hot spots and blisters from additional rubbing, cover them with a protective layer. You want something with enough stick-to-your-feet ability so you don't have to stop every hour to replace it, and you want it to facilitate the sock's sliding over it without rubbing. Moleskin is

MEDICAL TRAINING

TIP

Wilderness Medical Associates offers training in backcountry medicine. They are the "bootcamp" for wilderness medical training. Contact: (888) WILD-MED.

the traditional product of choice. Duct tape also works well.

A newer product is **Spyroflex Skin Saver** from PolyMedica Health Care. Contact: (800) 521-4503.

Personal Hygiene

Dirt is part of the deal. Some fastidious souls insist on washing, but why then do they go backpacking? If you must, make sure you wash far away from natural bodies of water.

Even a few drops of soap in the stream result in a mess of suds downstream.

Carry one of the several environmentally benign soaps. You can use **Campsuds** (Sierra Dawn Products) or **Coghlan's Sportsman's Soap** to clean yourself as well as the pots and dishes.

No-Rinse shampoo and body bath take a different approach to

FREE SAMPLES

FREE

Free medicine? Ask your physician for some of the samples he or she gets from drug companies. Tell your doctor you're going on a backpacking trip and need to stock your first-aid kit.

cleanliness. You dilute an ounce of the product in a quart of warm water and sponge it on. Dry off without rinsing. You can't buy these products directly from the manufacturer; look for them at retail outlets.

Photo by Burt Kornegay, Slickrock Expeditions.

Slickrock Creek Trail, Joyce Kilmer-Slickrock Wilderness, Nantahala North Carolina.

Dressing for Comfort

Nor do I enjoy "adventure," concurring with Stephanson (the Arctic explorer) that adventures in wilderness travel are almost always the result of poor preparation, knowledge, or judgment. The wilderness is a place where one must stay comfortable, because there is no place to go to get comfortable.

—Steven C. Wilson, Alone in the Arctic

Photo courtesy of Cascade Designs

The secret of comfortable living in the wilderness is adaptability—that is, making constant adjustments to the clothing you wear. As the weather and the temperatures change, so does your need to regulate your body temperature accordingly.

Layering

The strategy for dressing is layering. You adjust the number of layers based on the weather conditions and your level of work. There are three layers in this system, but each layer can have more than one article of clothing.

Layer One: Underwear

The job of your underwear is to provide some insulation while drawing moisture away from your skin. Wet skin loses heat about 17 times faster than dry skin does, so to keep warm you need to keep your skin dry.

Cotton is great for underwear if you want cooling. It absorbs your body's sweat and lets it evaporate and cool. On hot, dry days, a wet T-shirt is cooler than no T-shirt. But, when you need to retain your body heat, cotton is not the material of choice. What you need then is a fabric that wicks moisture away from your body rather than letting it evaporate and cool there.

Don't be misled by cotton waffle-weave thermal underwear. It has high insulating properties, but only as long as you're not exerting yourself, and as long as it remains dry. If you're going to watch a football game in extreme cold—below freezing, so that there's no moisture in the air or on the ground—cotton works well. But if you're hiking or backpacking, leave the cotton at home.

Silk is the natural fiber that wicks moisture away from your skin. A more common substitute is some form of polyester. What's great about this stuff is that it pulls water through itself without getting wet. Water doesn't stick to the fibers. Instead it's drawn to the outer surface where it can evaporate away from your body or be pulled farther away by the next layer.

Polypropylene was the first synthetic on the market. It works, but has two drawbacks. It retains body odors and it doesn't do well in dryers. To summarize, it shrinks and it stinks.

New generations of fabrics have been devised to overcome the limitations of polypropylene, as have combinations of fabrics such as Capilene, Thinsulate, and Thermax. ZeO_2 is a new yarn made of polyester impregnated with a bacteria-killing chemical.

Layer Two: Insulation

Wool is the natural choice here, but some synthetics do better in terms of insulation, ounce for ounce. Whereas wool absorbs moisture, leaving the surface dry next to your skin, synthetics pull water right through themselves. Synthetics provide lots of warmth, don't absorb water, dry quickly, and are comfortable to the touch.

Pile and fleece are often used for insulation. Pile is a looser knit

and, as such, captures more insulating air than does fleece. On the other hand, pile, with its more open knit, requires protection from the wind. It is also bulky.

Manufacturers identify fleece by its weight. A weight of 100 is light; 200 is midweight; and 300 is warm. Some fleece is made of recycled plastic bottles. This post-consumer product has the same insulating properties as new synthetics.

Alternatives to synthetics for Layer Two are wool sweaters and down vests.

What you wear in Layer Two depends on whether you want maximum warmth with no ventilation, or less warmth with better ventilation. For example, you'll notice a big difference in heat retention between an open-necked shirt and a turtleneck shirt. And a zipper allows you the benefits of both, albeit at higher cost and some possibility of equipment failure.

Layer Three: Weather Protection

Your outer layer needs to perform different functions in different conditions, but

its big trick is to stop rain from getting in while letting water vapor pass through from inside to outside—that water vapor being your sweat, of course. This is the modern-day equivalent of an act of alchemy, but Gore-Tex and other breathable fabrics are doing it. They aren't perfect yet, and they're still expensive, but they are a great advance on anything that's gone before them.

If your third layer isn't breathable it will need lots of ventilation in the form of air vents to let out the moist air. They must be strategically placed, of course, to keep rain out. Your third layer should be big enough to

Photo by Burt Kornegay, Slickrock Expeditions.

accommodate a range of bulky clothes underneath it. A certain amount of looseness also helps to get rid of the moisture-laden interior air.

A combination of two pairs of underwear of different weights, along with a couple of options for middle layers, plus an outer layer, gives you lots of versatility in facing the elements. Add or subtract layers as conditions change, with the aim of always staying comfortable.

It's important to make the various layers accessible, because the tendency is to keep on hiking when the rain starts rather than dig through to the bottom of the pack to find the outer layer. So pack the layers you're likely to need in an outside pouch or at the top of your pack.

Rainwear

Clothing designers use three strategies to keep out the rain: They coat fabrics, laminate them, or cover them with a water-proof material.

Inexpensive "shells" are made of nylon with a coating on the outside to keep out the rain. They don't breathe, and if they don't have ventilation panels they allow sweat to build up inside. But they are light and take up very little room.

Among laminated materials, Gore-Tex® is the best known. In its two-ply form, a Gore-Tex® membrane is laminated to nylon or polyester fabric. Garments are also made of three-ply Gore-Tex® fabric, in which an inner layer is added to the two-ply material. The advantages of the three-ply fabric are compressibility and faster drying.

Coated and laminated fabrics are treated with a durable water repellent (DWR) finish. A DWR coating helps the fabric shed water before it can wet the fabric. It doesn't reduce the breathability of laminated fabrics. The DWR will wear off, and you may need to replace it (see below).

Waterproof garments are less expensive than laminated ones but aren't suitable for active hiking. The waterproofing is just as effective at keeping in your perspiration as it is in keeping out the rain; it lets you stew in your own juices. But, if you want to stay dry while watching a football game, this is what you need.

In some climates, you may not be concerned with rain, so you can use a less expensive system. Or you might not be concerned with moisture buildup under the outer layer, as long as it keeps you dry.

Heads Up!

Here's a heads-up: Take a hat along. Too many hikers overlook the need for hats. Since the head serves as the body's most efficient radiator of heat and most direct solar collector it makes sense to protect it.

In cool weather, it's the radiator part that warrants most attention. You need to keep your head from losing heat. A watch cap works well: It's compact and warm. Cotton works, but only in dry air. Synthetics or wool are more versatile.

A bandanna can protect your noggin from sunlight and is handy for sopping up some stream water

to cool your head. Hats with visors give much better protection for your face and eyes and can provide some air space above your head for air to circulate.

Tilley makes the Cadillac of outdoor hats. Designed for sailors, they do well in the mountains, too. Theirs are made of cotton duck that sheds rain, hugs your head, and resists digestion by elephants. They are guaranteed for life—your life. **Outdoor Research** also offers a variety of well-designed hats. See contact information, below.

These companies manufacture and/or sell hats suitable for hikers:

Boulder Gear: (800) 342-8088; www.bouldergear.com

Columbia Sportswear Co.: (800) 622-6953; www.columbia.com
Duofold: (610) 398-9420; www.duofold.com
Feathered Friends: (206) 328-0887; www.halcyon.com/featherd
Gramicci: www.gramicci.com
L. L. Bean: (800) 341-4341; www.llbean.com
Lowe Alpine: (303) 465-0522; www.lowealpine.com
Marmot: (707) 544-4590; www.marmot.com
Mountain Hardwear: (510) 559-6700; www.mountainhardwear.com
Outdoor Research: (800) 421-2421; www.orgear.com
Patagonia: (800) 638-6464; www.patagonia.com
Royal Robbins: (800) 587-9044; www.royalrobbins.com
Sierra Designs: (800) 737-8551; www.ecotravel.com/sierra designs
Solstice: (503) 239-6991
The North Face: (805) 379-3372; www.clubhousegolf.com/northface.htm
Tilley Endurables: (800) 363-8737; www.tilley.com
Woolrich: (800) 995-1299; www.woolrich.com

The All-Purpose Bandanna

Want a lightweight and inexpensive multiuse tool for backpacking? Here it is: the cotton bandanna. You can make a fashion statement with your brightly colored bandanna; use it to pick up a hot pot; wipe the sweat off your brow; cover your head on a fiercely sunny day; wrap it around your neck when you get chilled; strain the big stuff out of water; carry lots of small things; keep the dust out of your nose and mouth; cover a wound; dip it into a creek so you can wash the dirt off your neck and face; tie two adjacent belt loops together if you lose your

belt; or even, heaven forbid, blow your nose on it.

Waterproofing

When you notice that your rain gear isn't working, the first thing to do is wash it. Dirt and salt can lodge in the pores and reduce the breathability of laminated fabrics. Follow the directions, which probably tell you to wash it in cold water. If water doesn't bead up on a waterproof surface, it's time to reapply a surface coating. Use one of the waterproofing products listed below.

Granger's began their waterproofing business during World War II when they were asked to develop coatings for canvas tents and truck tarpaulins. **Tectron** helps fabrics repel water, keeps dirt and grease from adhering, and prevents ultraviolet light from damaging the fabric.

The following companies make or sell waterproofing materials:

Granger's: (800) 343-5827; www.grangerusa.com
Nikwax: (800) 577-2700; www.nikwax.usa.com
Scotchgard (3M): (800) 257-3451
Tectron: (800) 289-2583

Sunglasses

Sunglasses should cut down on glare and block out more than 95 percent of the sun's ultraviolet light. A typical reduction in light transmission for a good pair of sunglasses is 15 to 25 percent. For extended wear on snow or water, consider glasses that cut out even more light, side shields, or polar-

ized glasses. Polarized glass blocks the light rays reflected off the ground, snow, or water.

The color of the lens does make a difference—it's not just a fashion statement. Gold and amber lenses enhance contrast, while green, gray, and brown don't alter the color of what you're seeing.

Glass lenses have the best optical qualities but are expensive. Polycarbonate lenses are light, almost indestructible, and cheaper than glass. Acrylic lenses are the cheapest of all—and the flimsiest. Borosilicate lenses are very tough.

Before investing big bucks in shades, ask yourself if you are meticulous enough to care for them, or if you're likely to lose them, walk on them, or otherwise destroy them by the end of the first trip. It might be better for you to purchase two pairs of the cheapest sunglasses that offer adequate protection.

Whatever your choice, make sure the glasses fit your face. If they are uncomfortable, you won't wear them for long.

STRAP ON THE SMS

 **TIP**

What do you do with your sunglasses when it's time to consult the map? Where do you put them when you're moving from a bright sunny meadow into a dark forest? To address such weighty questions you need a Sunglasses Management System (SMS). Well, anyway, a strap at least.

For the neo-nerd look, superglue a shoelace to each earpiece. To make any other kind of fashion statement, look around the check-out counter at a backpacking store.

Make sure the type of retainer they carry will in fact hold on to your glasses and is the right length to go over your head.

All the Other Stuff

Careful planning, sound judgment, and infinite
patience in working out minute details of equipment
and preparation ... provide that invaluable "margin
of safety" ... necessary to overcome perils of
unexpected difficulties and delays.

— Roald Amundsen, My Life as an Explorer

This chapter covers all those little bits and pieces of equipment that just look like ordinary "stuff" when you're at home, but which turn out to be absolutely essential on the trail. In no particular order of importance, we'll have a look at such things as knives, saws, walking sticks, fire starters, survival kits, binoculars, telescopes, cameras, lights, candles, repair kits, tape, rope, towels, and journals.

Pocket Knives

There are hundreds of brands and models of pocket knives from which to choose. Are you more of a one-knife-blade person, or someone who wants to have on the knife every gadget ever invented? The smaller the knife, the more convenient it is to carry, and the more likely that you'll have it when you need it. The much larger multi-tool knives can be too bulky to fit in your pocket and require a sheath that clips onto your belt.

What features should you look for? You need a solid ring attachment if you're going to be using it on the water or anywhere else where it will disappear for good if it slips out of your hand.

Blades and tools should withstand lateral twisting by your hands. You should easily be able to pull out the blades or tools you need, and they should lock into place so they don't snap closed on your fingers when you try to use them.

The tools most often needed are large and small

B HOOK

knife blades, scissors, and screw-drivers. Tweezers get a lot of use, too. If your eyesight isn't quite what it used to be, a magnifying lens is useful. The lenses you find on Swiss Army Knives aren't great, but they do the job when you're trying to read small print. For a general purpose "poker" and small hole-maker, the awl is a nice feature.

Pliers, a mainstay of survival tools, are very useful. Check out the grip by squeezing them hard. Some models dig into your hand, stopping you from bearing down on the rusty nut you're trying to loosen. Also, how easy are the pliers to open? If you are willing to carry a pair of pliers, make sure they have wire cutters.

If your backpacking companions carry all the gadgets, ask them at the end of the trip which ones they used. Lugging along stuff you don't use violates the laws of common sense and adds to the weariness quotient.

Knife Insurance

Knife "insurance" can be a good investment: Simply tie a cord or bootlace from a belt loop to the ring on your knife. The cord prevents loss when you are using the knife, something a sheath can't do. Make it long enough so you can reach anything you will need to cut.

Victoria the Rustproof

Yes, the Swiss Army does carry Swiss Army knives. Invented by Charles Eisener in 1891, the original Swiss Army knife was called a soldier's knife. It didn't carry all the fancy tools of today's models—it came equipped with only a knife blade, a screwdriver, a can opener, and a reamer—but was successful enough to launch the Victorinox company.

Victorinox still makes the "original Swiss Army knives." The company is run by the descendants of the inventor. **Wenger,** the com-

peting brand of Swiss Army knife, calls their model the "genuine" product. Switzerland, long a bastion of neutrality, supplies its soldiers with Swiss Army knives from both companies.

The key innovation by Eisener, in 1897, was figuring out how to put tools on both the front and back sides of the knife. When his mother died in 1909, he took her name, Victoria, and used it as the company name. The suffix "inox" refers to its rustproof qualities.

Sales of Swiss Army knives total about 30,000 a day. Victorinox makes about 300 models incorporating different sizes and combinations of 29 different tools. These include pliers with wire cutters, scissors, nail file, metal saw, wood saw, magnifying glass, small and large knife blades, ball-point pen, toothpick, tweezers, grafting blade, wire stripper, corkscrew, leather punch, bottle opener, can opener, hook disgorger, ruler, wrench, compass, key ring, screwdrivers (flat, fine, Phillips, and mini), orange peeler, pruning blade, chisel, fish scaler, and reamer.

Leatherman

"Put pliers on a Boy Scout knife." That's what Tim Leatherman told himself; and after three years of tinkering, he did it. That was in 1978, but it was five more years before the product caught on. Then it took off like a rocket— from nowhere in 1977 to over a million tools sold in 1996.

Along the way, his Leatherman multitool has attracted competitors. Some have copied his design (an infringement of patent) and others have copied his concept. Today there are several companies making multitools, with dozens of models to choose from. **SOG Specialty Knives** has several models

of utility tools, some of which provide compound leverage to give you more cutting or holding force. Also, you can disassemble them to clean them.

These companies make or sell multitools:

Buck Knives: (800) 326-2825
Gerber: (800) 950-6161;
www.gerberblades.com
Leatherman: (800) 847-8665;
www.leatherman.com
Schrade Tough Tool:
www.schradeknives.com
SOG: (425) 771-6230
Swiss Army Brands:
(800) 442-2706

Hand Saws

A saw is more useful than a hatchet or hand ax, weighs less, and lets you cut wood into lengths

suitable for your fire. There is, however, less reason to carry a saw now that more emphasis is being placed on using stoves for cooking in order to lessen the impact on the land.

There are at least four different designs to choose from. For survival kits, the **Varco Survival Saw** works well. It takes the minimalist approach to sawing wood: You pull a flexible saw blade with a ring attached at each end. It's exceptionally light and takes up almost no room, but it isn't the blade of choice if you have other options or if you're cutting more than a few branches.

For more serious sawing, **Sven** makes a one-pound folding saw. This three-piece saw comes apart and nests together, making a well-protected and easy-to-stow shaft.

High Divide, Olympic National Park. Photo by Ed Sobey

It tackles logs as large as 6 inches in diameter.

Saws that fold into their handles are a compromise between usability and packability. They're easy to fit into your pack, but not very efficient at cutting wood. The **Sawvivor** is advertised to weigh less than a cup of coffee, yet carries a 15-inch blade. The rectangular design makes it easy to use the full extension of the blade.

The following companies make or sell saws useful to hikers:

Sawvivor: (800) 724-3529; //members.aol.com/sawviv/index.html

Sven Folding Saw: e-mail: sven79905@aol.com; www.gorp.com/svensaw

Hiking Staffs

Although the vast majority of walkers never even think of using a walking staff, I unhesitatingly include it among the foundations of the house that travels on my back.
—Colin Fletcher,
The Complete Walker III

Slickrock Creek Trail, Joyce Kilmer-Slickrock Wilderness, Nantahala National Forest, North Carolina. Photo by Burt Kornegay, Slickrock Expeditions.

People increasingly are using walking staffs, from single poles to pairs. They use them to improve balance on difficult footing and to reduce stress on the feet, knees, and back. There are all sorts of other uses for them: knocking down spider webs on the trail, pushing back stickers and thorns, pushing your bear bag up a tree, and fending off someone's overly friendly dog.

If you're not sure whether you would like a hiking staff, try one on your next hike. Grab a downed branch of the appropriate length, one sturdy enough to hold some weight. Then, if you find you're more comfortable with it, check out the commercially made poles.

Watching someone making use of two poles this way will convince you that he or she is walking with the entire body. Does it make hiking easier? You'll have to judge for yourself. The downside of having a pole in each hand is that you don't have a hand free for anything else.

Make sure any staff you buy is adjustable. You will want to set the length so your upper arm and forearm make a 90-degree angle when you're walking on level terrain. The pole should be longer for walking downhill, and shorter for walking uphill. Also, you should be able to shorten it sufficiently to be able to store it in your pack or strap it on the outside without having it catch on branches as you walk.

Check out the handle and strap. It's the strap that supports your hand, but the grip should be comfortable, too. You can unscrew the heads of some poles to use the pole as a monopod camera support.

These companies make or sell hiking staffs:

Cascade Designs:
(800) 531-9531;
www.cascadedesigns.com
Leki: (800) 604-5956;
www.leki.com
Garmont: (800) 943-4453
Glowmaster (Pathfinder):
(800) 272-7008
Komperdell: (508) 475-5062
Tracks: (800) 531-9531

Fire Starters

Buy a pound or two of paraffin from a hobby store and melt a chunk of it in a double boiler. It's best to use a pot you can dedicate to the messy job, rather than use one that you have to clean each time. Drop 4-inch-square swaths of

NC Bartram Trail, Fishhawk Mountains, Nantahala National Forest, North Carolina. Photo by Burt Kornegay, Slickrock Expeditions.

cotton T-shirt into the molten wax, and then extract them with tongs. Lay them flat on newspaper and let them cool. You can fold up the swaths to carry in your pocket and tear off half-inch-wide strips to start fires. Lighting one end gives you several minutes to get kindling ignited.

Alternatively, roll up four matches in a 3-inch wide strip of newspaper. Tie the roll with twine and drop it in the molten wax. Give it a minute and then extract it

---

FOUR LEGS

Walking with two sticks gives us four points of support. Using two sticks lets the upper body muscles work and take some of the strain off your legs and hips.

When the going is steep, you can always have three points touching the ground at once, whether you're going up or down. If your knees ache after a long descent, or if you're worried about toppling over when you ford a stream, you should try walking with two staffs. But practice first, and persevere. It doesn't come naturally.

PRINTED KINDLING

The secret of fire lighting is to start small with dry tinder. So take along a cheap paperback book you want to read, and tear out the pages for kindling after you've read them.

Your load will be lighter, your brain will be better exercised, and your fire will start with no trouble.

Photo by Ed Sobey

Four different types of fire starters. From left: egg carton, dryer lint, and wax; swath of cotton T-shirt and wax; a candle; and matches wrapped in newspaper, tied with string, and dipped in paraffin wax.

by the end of the string and let it cool.

Or, finally: a use for dryer lint. Jam a wad of lint into the egg well of a papier-mâché egg cartoon. Pour molten wax over the lint. When it has cooled, cut the well out of the carton. This lint ball will burn for 10 minutes.

Survival Kits

You can put your own kit together, based on your experience, or you can purchase a ready-made kit. **James Kits** makes a pocket survival kit with matches, signal mirror, whistle, first-aid book and supplies, survival cards, pencil, waterproof paper, compass, and fire starter. Other kits add a space blanket, tweezers, scissors, flashlight, hand warmer, and more. Contact: (800) 396-KITS; e-mail: jkits@sharplink.com

Trail Binoculars

You'll miss your binoculars greatly when you don't bring them along. Although they weigh more than half a pound and can be a bother to carry, binoculars help you to see stuff, which is one of the reasons why you venture out in the first place.

Whether you're viewing the bear half way up the adjacent mountain, scanning the route 500 feet below, or watching someone break into your car in the parking lot, binoculars add to your fun and safety.

The design of binoculars is a compromise between making the lens bigger, to let in more light; longer, to gain magnification; and smaller, for convenience when you're carrying or using them. When you try out a pair of binoculars, note the two numbers printed

on them. If, for example, they are 8 x 25, the 8 is the number of magnifications and 25 is the diameter, in millimeters, of the front lenses.

Magnification is good up to the point where you can no longer hold the glasses steady enough. A magnification of 10 is about the limit for hand-held glasses. Anything more, and the image will be gigantic—but it will be shimmering so much that you won't be able to make it out.

The larger the diameter of the front, or objective, lenses, the more light the binoculars admit. You want this number to be as large as possible without requiring the services of a porter to carry the binoculars. For most day-time use,

8 x 25 binoculars are a good compromise. So-called night glasses usually have 50-millimeter objective lenses and provide crisper images in poor light but they are bulkier and heavier to carry.

A third number to watch for is the field of view. This is the width of the area you will see when looking at an object 1,000 yards away. A wider field of view means you're looking at a larger area.

Compare how different models focus. A standard method is to focus the left eye with a lever or knob, and then focus the right eye by rotating the right eyepiece.

Also check the weight, sturdiness, and ability to keep out water.

You can purchase binoculars from the following companies:

Bausch & Lomb: (800) 423-3537; www.bausch.com
Brunton Co.: (800) 443-4871
Carl Zeiss Optical: (800) 338-2984
Canon USA, Inc.: (800) 828-4040
Leica Camera, Inc.: (800) 222-0118

Minolta: (201) 825-4000
Nikon, Inc.: (800) 645-6687
Pentax: (800) 877-0155; www.pentax.com
REI: (800) 426-4840; www.rei.com
Tasco: (305) 591-3670
Zeiss: (800) 338-2984

Photography in the Wild

Cameras come with such a wide variety of options that it's impossible to say which is the best for you. But here are three basic considerations for photo equipment: light weight, versatility, and durability. These are most often combined in a quality 35-mm, zoom-lens camera.

Here are some sources of more detailed information:

Books

Photography Outdoors: A Field Guide for Travel & Adventure Photographers, by Mark Gardner and Art Wolfe (The Mountaineers, 1995), is not specific to backpacking but covers outdoor photography in general.

The Sierra Club Guide to 35-mm Landscape Photography, by Tim Fitzharris (Sierra Club Books, 1996), covers equipment including digital cameras and gives suggestions for composing outdoor shots.

Pocket Guide to Outdoor Photography, by Mary Mather and Ron Cordes (Greycliff Publications, 1993),

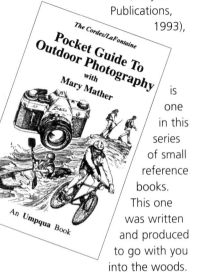

is one in this series of small reference books. This one was written and produced to go with you into the woods.

Backpacking Photography, by Ted Schiffman and Susan Lariviere (Amphoto, 1981), is difficult to find but worth the hunt.

Carrying Your Camera

If you stow your camera in your pack, you'll end the trip having taken pictures only at campsites each night. If you sling it around your neck, you're always ready for that next great shot, but the camera will be exposed to water, dirt, and the possibility of collisions with tree branches.

You can compromise by carrying your camera in a case that is easily accessible. If your camera didn't come with one, check out **SunDog's Action Camera Cases.** Contact: (206) 782-5404; www.sun-dog.com

Lights

You're going to need a light, and you can do quite nicely with an inexpensive light from a hardware store or an outfitter. If you're going to invest in a light that will last more than a few trips, also invest in a spare bulb, ready for that dark night when you will need it.

An option is to buy a headlamp. They're great for freeing your hands while you search in the bottom of the pack, sew the button back on your shirt, or read at night. But they're a pain when your companion wears one and, when conversing with you, shines it in your night-adjusted eyes.

Petzl & Lomb makes lights you can strap on. **Versa Brite** has a small light that clips on to your clothing or hat. (See contact information, below.)

If you're going to buy a headlamp, try it on to make sure it fits comfortably. Regardless of what type of light you get, carry a spare set of batteries on any trip longer than one night.

Incidentally, beware of becoming too dependent on a light.

Humanity has, for at least 99 percent of its existence, survived without flashlights. Weight-conscious hikers should ask themselves how much light they really need. The more you avoid using lights, the better your eyes adapt to the dark, allowing you to see better. Flickering flashlights may look neat, but they ruin your night vision.

To attract attention at night, no other light works as well as a strobe. By flashing on and off, a strobe extends battery life and provides a homing beacon that is unmistakable, even against a sky of bright stars. Outdoor Safety Products makes Emergency Strobe, a light that flashes 50 to 70 times a minute for 16 hours.

Here are the leading manufacturers of lights for hikers:

Mini Maglite (Mag Instruments): (909) 947-1006; www.maglite.com
Petzl & Lomb: (800) 282-7673; www.petzl.com
Princeton Tec: (800) 257-9080
REI: (800) 426-4840; www.rei.com

Candle Power

Candles are an alternative to battery-powered lights. You can use a

candle by itself or get a candle lantern to hold it and protect it from breezes. **Northern Lights** (e-mail: northernlight@telis.org) is one manufacturer of candle lanterns.

A short candle also makes a great emergency fire starter.

Repair Kits

When it comes to repair kits, you have to consider the trade-offs. If you carry an entire hardware store on your back, you won't get out of the parking lot, so you won't ever need any of the stuff you brought. On the other hand, when you're midway through a five-day trip and some branch decides to poke a hole in your tent, or some wild animal about the size, weight, and appearance of your hiking partner breaks a tent pole, having some emergency repair gear on hand makes the trip go more smoothly.

What should *you* take? Here's a short list of suggestions. You can add to it if you like, depending on your ability to make repairs.

Duct tape: Sing the praises of duct tape. How did Peary get to the North Pole without it? You can fix almost anything in the field with duct tape. We use it instead of moleskin to prevent hot spots turning into blisters. Yet, there is a downside—the sticky side. It's tough to remove when you get home. Make sure you place it carefully because it's going to be there a while.

Nylon cord: Strong, light, stretchy nylon is useful for hanging bear bags, lashing stuff on to your backpack frame, tying your sunglasses to your head, making emergency bootlaces, and generally holding things together.

Spare bulb and batteries: It's always on the first night out that the bulb burns out in the one flashlight you brought along. A spare bulb adds little weight, takes up little space, and could make your night life a lot easier. Buy a spare when you buy the light. For short trips, put in a set of new alkaline batteries before you leave, and take one new set as spares.

Candle and cigarette lighter: Candles make great fire starters and night lights. You can also use them to melt glue sticks, and to melt the frayed ends of synthetic rope.

Sewing kit: Make sure the thread is a tough nylon and the needles are appropriate for the material you might stitch. Include a small variety of buttons and safety pins, some swatches of cloth and ripstop tape. A cotter pin could help pull cord through drawcord openings.

Pole sleeve: For long trips with a tent, consider carrying a sleeve to splint a broken tent pole.

Pliers: If you don't carry a survival tool, carry a small pair of pliers. They serve as pot grippers in addition to their usual functions.

Velcro: A few inches of one-inch-wide Velcro with adhesive backing will make temporary replacements for broken zippers.

Beyond Duct Tape

You probably know someone who swears by duct tape. Maybe you swear by it yourself. Indeed it is a great, general-purpose adhesive, a virtual repair kit wrapped on a tube. There are, however, even better products for field repairs to backpacking equipment.

Kenyon K-Tape holds 10 times better than duct tape, according to Herb Nesbitt at Wilderness Sports in Bellevue, Washington. "It stays on after repeated washings," he maintains, "something duct tape doesn't do." You can use Kenyon K-Tape on tents, sleeping bags, rain wear, and gaiters.

Nesbitt also recommends the Gore-Tex® repair kit. Contact Gore-Tex: (800) 431-GORE.

Repair it Yourself

A great reference for do-it-yourself repairs is **The Essential Outdoor Gear Manual,** by Annie Getchell (Ragged Mountain Press, 1995). Getchell covers repairs and care for tents, boots, cooking stoves, sleeping bags, packs, water filters, and more. She also lists companies that will repair your equipment when you can't.

Professional Repairs

When you admit that you can't fix what's broken but you don't want to replace it, it's time to call the experts. The first place to consult is the store where you purchased the equipment. They may be able to recommend a local repair shop or may offer to send it back to the manufacturer if it's under warranty.

Rope and Knots

You need rope to raise your food clear of bears, make a clothes line, or act as a safety line on a steep embankment. Fifty feet of a light ⅛-inch (3-mm) nylon rope will handle most situations. If you cut the rope, seal the ends by holding them near an open flame.

You don't need to know more than a few knots. You will need to form a loop (a bowline or figure-of-eight knot on a bight are the strongest) and tie off a line (two half-hitches). For cinching something down so it stays put, a trucker's knot is great. If your tent requires you to tie guy lines to stakes, a taut-line hitch is what you need.

Tying a Bowline

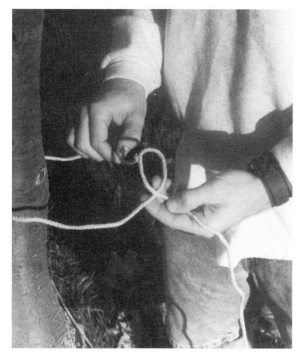

Start by making a loop.

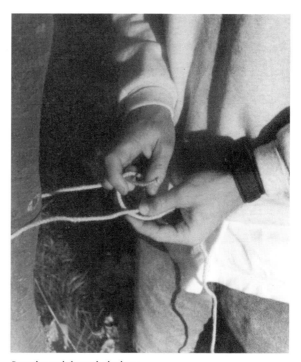

Pass the end through the loop.

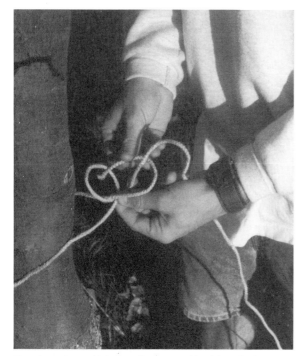

Pass the end around the standing part and back into the loop.

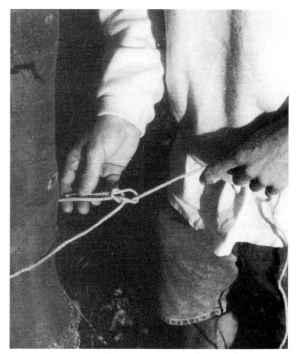

Draw the bowline tight.

Tying a Figure-of-Eight Knot on the Bight

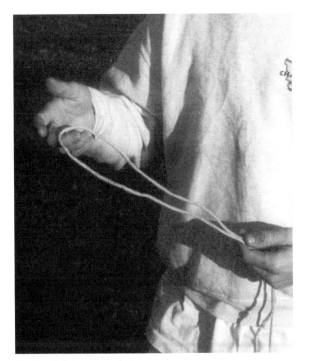

Start by forming a loop.

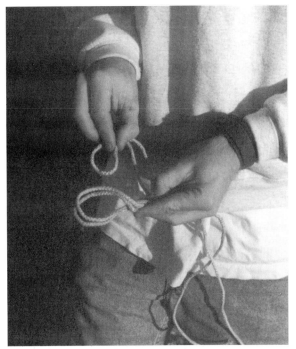

Twist the loop behind the standing part and back in front.

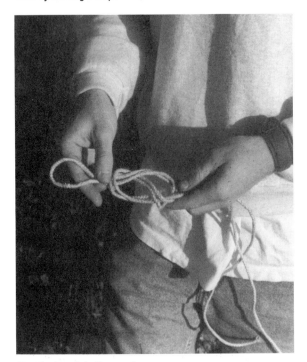

Pass the loop into the opening.

Draw the figure-of-eight knot tight.

How to Tie Knots

Peter Owen's book, **The Book of Outdoor Knots** (Lyons and Burford, 1993), shows you how to tie the knots you need, plus how to do some tricks with ropes and knots.

Knots for Hikers and Backpackers, by Frank Logue and Victoria Logue (Menasha Ridge, 1996), shows the knots most often used. A small, useful book at a modest price.

Cliff Jacobson's book on knots, **The Basic Essentials of Knots for the Outdoors** (ICS Books, 1990), details 32 knots, including two splices and two lashings, the usual knots, and the prusik knot.

The Camper's Knot Tying is a game of making knots. The game includes 50 cards, instructions, and some line with which to tie knots. Players have to make the knots listed on the cards dealt to them.

Choosing a Towel

A drying cloth is a valuable asset on any backpacking trip. You can dry yourself off after a swim, mop up water in your tent, or dry the dishes with it.

Some people take along paper towels, but they are bulky, expensive, and need to be disposed of. Cotton towels aren't much good because they take a long time to dry, although if you are hiking in a dry environment you can strap a cotton towel on the outside of your pack to let it dry (and collect dust) during the day.

A better option is a towel specially made for backpackers. **Cascade Designs** (800-531-9531) makes one, the PackTowl, that absorbs nine times its weight of water

---

all but 10 percent of its load when you wring it out. Consequently, it dries quickly.

Keeping a Journal

How do you remember all the great things you did and saw on your trip? Writing a journal is the best way to remember. There are other uses for a journal, too. It can be an aid to navigation by forcing you to think and remember when you passed landmarks or trail junctions. If you record times and locations while you walk, you can refer to your journal to reconstruct your route if you get lost.

If you like to keep a journal, you will want a weatherproof one, so the ink doesn't smear or pages fall apart. There are several companies, including REI, that sell waterproof journals. Canoe and kayak stores will probably have them, too.

Photo courtesy of Cascade Designs

Tying a Trucker's Knot

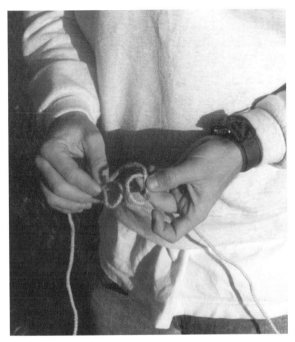

Start by forming a loop in the standing part (left) and form a bight nearby.

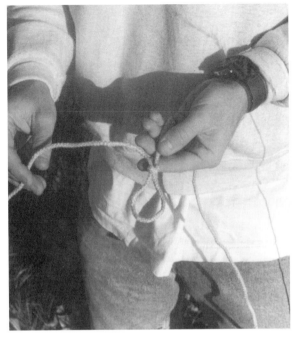

Push the bight up through the loop and draw taut to form a slip knot.

Take the bitter end around the tree (or object to be hauled tight) and back through the bight of the slip knot.

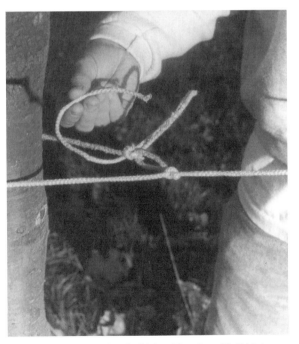

Secure the working end to the bight with a slipped half-hitch.

Index

Abbey, Edward, 163
About Hiking (online), 9
Adirondack Mountain Club, 157
Adventure, 50
Adventure Journal, 8
Africa, 53
Alabama, 134–135
Alabama Trails Association, 135
Alaska, 72–75
Alberta, 86
Altimeters, 71
American Alpine Club (AAC), 7–8
American Discovery Trail, 41
American Hiking Society, 7, 39, 144
American Trails, 7
America Outdoors, 36
Amundsen, Roald, 197
Anderson, Lloyd and Mary, 5
Animals, 16–24. *See also* Dogs backpacking
not disturbing, 14, 16
Animal tracks
books on, 24
Antibiotics, 189
Appalachian Mountain Club (AMC), 7, 39, 153, 170–171
Appalachian National Scenic Trail, 42–43, 169
books on, 42–43
Appetite effects, 83
Arizona, 122–124
Arizona Trail, 42–43, 124
Arkansas, 135–137
Audubon Expedition Institute, 6
Australia, 53
Avalanche slopes, 151

Backcountry Odysseys, 35–36
Backpacker magazine, 8–9, 34, 84, 164, 179
Backpacker's Handbook, 96, 102, 146
Backpackers' Page (online), 32
Backpacking
changes in, 1
classes in, 6–7, 9
publishers covering, 33–34
Backpacks, 78, 85, 145–151
crossing a stream with, 151
manufacturers listed, 148–149
sizing, 145–146
taking onto planes, 149, 177

Baking, 181–183
Bandana, 77, 195–196
Barometer, pocket, 25
Batona Hiking Club, 160
Batteries, 205–206
Bay Area Women Adventurers, 58
Bear bag rope, 79
Bears
books on, 19
repelling, 18–22
Beers, Mike, 2
Bee stings, 17, 189
Binoculars, 79, 85, 203–204
lightweight minis, 204
manufacturers listed, 204
Biological contaminants, 164–165
Bite Blocker, 17
Bivouac (bivy) bags, 132–133
Blisters, catching early, 29–30, 97, 101, 190, 206
Boiling water, 164–165
Books
on animal tracks, 24
on the Appalachian National Scenic Trail, 42–43, 81
on bears, 19
on buying equipment, 47
buying online, 32–34
on Canada, 54
on children backpacking, 11–13
on cooking, 185–186
on dogs backpacking, 23
on the Far North, 72–73
finding out-of-print, 33
on food drying, 180
getting catalogs of, 33
just for women, 11
on knots, 209
on medicine, 190
on the Mid-Atlantic States, 154–155, 157–162
on Mount St. Helens eruption, 47
on orienteering, 66, 68
on the Pacific Coast and Hawaii, 54–56, 59–63
on pack animals, 36–37
on photography, 204
on the Rockies, 87–94
on sanitation, 15
on the Southern and South-eastern U.S.A., 134–135, 137, 139, 141–144

on the Southwest, 122–124
taking along, 202
on trails, 41–45, 47, 49
training guides, 10
on travel abroad, 51
on the U.S. Midwest and Central Canada, 104–107, 109–110, 112
on weather, 25
Boots, 79, 85, 96–103
breaking in, 100–101
caring for, 100
fitting, 98
manufacturers listed, 99–100
Boulder Outdoor Survival School, 6
Bowline knot, 206–207
British Columbia, 54–55
Bruce Trail, 111
Buckeye Trail, 43–44, 111
Bug repellent, 16–17, 44, 78
Bulbs, spare, 206
Bureau of Land Management, 31, 46
Burton, Richard, 26
Butane, 176–177
Buying equipment, 1–3.
See also Sources listed
books on, 47
brand name, 3
on the Internet, 3, 84–85
by mail order, 5, 196
retail stores for, 3–6
used, 3

Cal Hiking and Outdoor Society (CHAOS), 58
California, 55–59
northern coast, 56
southern coast, 56
California Outfitters, 2–4
Cameras, 79, 85, 204–205
carrying, 204
support for, 202
Canada
books on, 54
information about, 9, 32, 54–55, 71, 75, 86, 106, 111–112, 171–173
Candle lanterns, 205
Candles, 205
Canyon Explorers Club, Inc., 58–59
Capital Hiking Club, 153
Cascade Designs, 131, 133, 209
Casio Triple Sensor Pathfinder, 71
Catalogs, 5, 196
Cayuga Trails Club, 157

CD-ROMs, 34, 55, 71
Cellular phones, 203
Center Hiking Club, 153
Centers for Disease Control International Travelers' Hotline, 51
Central Indiana Wilderness Club (CIWC), 105
Checklists
for equipment, 84–85
for first-aid kits, 188–189
for repair kits, 205–206
Chemekatans, The, 62
Child carriers, 13
Children backpacking, 83
books on, 11–13
Citronella, 17
Civilian Conservation Corps, 47
Clark, William, 27
Clean-up kit, 184
Clothes, 77, 85, 192–197
Clubs and organizations. *See individual clubs and organizations*
Clyde, Norman, 81
Coghlan's, 180, 190
Cold feet. *See also* Frostbite; Hypothermia
remedy for, 97
Coleman Fuel. *See* White gas
Colorado, 87–88
Colorado Mountain Club, 88
Compasses, 66–68, 77
making, 68
mirror-sighting, 68
trusting, 65
Connecticut, 169
Contaminants, 164–165
Continental Divide National Scenic Trail, 44
Cooking, 79, 85, 182–186.
See also Recipes; Stoves
books on, 185–186
tips for, 182
Cookware, 79, 181–184
making your own, 182–184
manufacturers listed, 182
Cord. *See* Rope
Costa Rica, 51–52
Cotton, 102, 192–193, 195, 209
Cryptosporidium, 164

DEET, 16–17, 78
Dehydration, symptom of, 165
Dehydrator
making your own, 180
Delaware, 152
Desert Solitaire, 163
Desert Trail Association, 62

Distress signal, international, 51
District of Columbia, 153
Dogs backpacking
  books on, 23
Douglas, David, 26
Down, 126–127, 193
Dreamers & Defenders: American Conservationists, 7
Dryer lint, using, 203
Drying your own food
  books on, 180
Duct tape, 101, 205–206
Durable water repellent (DWR)
  finishes, 194–195

Emergencies
  medical supplies for, 189
  preparing for, 79–80
Endurance, building, 31
Epinephrine, 189
Equipment. *See also* Buying
    equipment; *different kinds
    of equipment*
  checklist for, 84–85
  getting repaired, 3
  renting, 2–3, 93, 123, 137
Essential Outdoor Gear Manual,
  99–100
Europe, 52–53
European Ramblers Association,
  53
Europe Map Service, 70
Expert help, 2
Explore magazine, 9
Explorers
  books on, 26–27
External-frame packs, 146
EZCamp Rentals, 93, 123

Families. *See* Children back-
    packing
Far North, 72–75
  books on, 72–73
Federal resources. *See individual
    states*
Figure-of-eight knot on a bight,
  206, 208
Filter manufacturers, 165–166
Finger Lake Trail Conference,
  157
Fire lookout towers
  staying in, 34–35
Fires, 15, 177. *See also* Stoves
  smoky, 17
Fire starters, 77, 205
  making your own, 202–203
First aid, 187–197
First-aid kits, 78, 85, 188–190
  checklist for, 188–189
  sources listed, 190

First Need purifier, 165
Fishing gear, 79
Fitness, 10
Flashlights. *See* Lights
Fleece, 193
Fletcher, Colin, 69, 132, 201
Florida, 137–138
Florida Trail, 44, 138
Flying with backpacks, 149, 177
Foam pads, closed-cell,
  130–131
Foods, 82–84, 174–186. *See
    also* Cooking; Recipes
  drying your own, 179–180
  favorite, 174, 179
  packing, 78, 180
  protecting from bears, 19–22
  repackaging, 180
  when traveling abroad, 51
Foothills Trail Club, 157
Footwear. *See* Boots; Socks
Free stuff (or nearly free), 9–10,
  33, 41, 70, 166, 180, 183,
  190, 196
Freeze-dried foods, 178–179
  manufacturers listed,
  178–179
  rehydrating, 179
Frostbite, 190
Fuels, 79–80, 174–177

Gaiters, 103
Garbage
  packing out, 14, 184
Garcia/Backpacker's Cache, 22
"Gear Guy," 84
Georgia, 139
Get Lost Adventure Magazine
  (online), 9
Giardia lamblia, 164, 185
Global Positioning System
  (GPS), 68–69
Gloves, cheap cotton, 196
Gold-rush prospectors, 75, 80
Gore-Tex®, 97, 115, 193–194
  repair kit, 206
Grand Canyon Association, 6
Great Outdoor Recreation
  Pages (GORP), 31–32, 84
GreatOutdoors.com (online), 9
Great Western Trail, 44, 94
Green Mountain Club, 169, 173
Ground cloth, 114, 119, 133
Guatemala, 52
Guides and outfitters. *See also
    individual states, provinces,
    and countries*
  buying from, 178
  finding, 37–39
  for traveling abroad, 51–53

using, 35–36

Halliburton, Richard, 50
Hand saws, 200–201
Hats, 195
  for warmth, 196
Hawaii, 59–60
Hawaiian Trail and Mountain
  Club, 60
Headlamps, 205
Head straps, 150–151
Health information
  for travelers abroad, 51
Help, attracting, 79–80
Hikes. *See also* Pacing yourself;
    Trails
  categories of, 146
  ideas for local, 6
  tips for, 28–29, 98, 151, 205
Hiking and Walking Home Page
  (online), 9
Hiking staffs, 201–202
  sources listed, 202
  using two, 202
Himalayas, 53, 150
Hipbelts, 146–147
Horses
  giving right of way to, 22
Huachuca Hiking Club (HHC),
  124
Human predators, 24
Human waste, 15
Humboldt, Alexander Von,
  26–27
Hygiene. *See* Personal hygiene
Hypothermia, 187–188

Ice Age National Scenic Trail, 45
Idaho, 88–90
Iditarod National Historic Trail,
  45–46, 72
Illinois, 104–105
Indiana, 105–106
Indianapolis Hiking Club, 105
Indiana Volksport Association,
  106
Insects. *See* Bug repellent
Insect screens, 133
Insulating pads. *See* Pads
Insurance
  on rented equipment, 3
  for travel abroad, 51
Internal-frame packs, 146
International distress signal, 51
International Travelers' Hotline,
  51
Internet contacts, 5, 9–10,
  84–85. *See also* Books; Buy-
    ing equipment
  for trip planning, 31–32

for women, 11
Iodine tablets for water,
  165–167
Iowa, 106
Isobutane, 177
Issaquah Alps Trails Club, 64

James P. Beckwourth Mountain
  Club, 88
Jardine, Ray, 76
Journal writing, 66, 209

Kansas, 106
Katadyn filters, 165
Kekekabic Trail Club, 108
Kelty, Dick and Nena, 146–147
Kentucky, 139–141
Kenyon K-Tape, 206
Keystone Trails Association, 160
Kilgore, Glenn, 35
Kindling, 202
Knives and multitools, 77, 85,
  198–200
  features available, 198–200
  securing with a cord, 199
Knots, 206–209
  books on, 209
  bowline, 206–207
  figure-of-eight knot on a
    bight, 206, 208
  taut-line hitch, 118, 206
  trucker's, 206, 210
Krogen, Shane, 4

Laurel Highlands Hiking Trail,
  158
Layering clothing, 192–194
Leading groups, 35–39, 65
  setting a meeting place, 70
Leatherman tool, 200
Leave No Trace (LNT) program,
  14
Leopold, Aldo, 7, 13
Lewis, Meriwether, 27
Lights, 78, 205. *See also* Batter-
    ies; Bulbs; Candles; Head-
    lamps
L.L. Bean, Inc.
  online, 9, 84
Llama packers, 37, 58, 64, 88,
  90, 92, 95, 154, 156, 158,
  169, 173
Lone Star Trail Hiking Club, 144
Long, Major Stephen, 26
Lost, being, 66
Louisiana, 141

MacKaye, Benton, 42
Magazines and newsletters,
  8–9, 61, 63–64

Mail order, 5, 196
Maine, 169–170
Making your own
  compasses, 68
  cookware, 182–184
  dehydrator, 180
  fire starters, 202–203
  tumplines, 150
Manitoba, 106
Manning, Harvey, 174
Manufacturers listed
  of backpacks, 148–149
  of binoculars, 204
  of boots, 99–100
  of cookware, 182
  of filters, 165–166
  of freeze-dried foods,
    178–179
  of multitools, 200
  of stoves, 177
Map Dealers' Association, 70
Maps, 69–71, 77, 85
  free, 70
  protecting, 71
  sources listed, 70–71
  topographic, 30, 70
Maritime Provinces, 171–173
Marshall, Bob, 49
Maryland, 153–154
Massachusetts, 170–171
Matches, 77
Mazamas, The, 62
Medications, 188–189
Medicine, backcountry
  books on, 190
  training in, 190
Mexico, 51
Michigan, 106–107
Mid-Atlantic States, 152–162
  books on, 154–155, 157–162
Mining Company, 10, 84
MiniWorks ceramic filter, 165
Minnesota, 107–108
Minnesota Rovers, 108
Mississippi, 141–142
Missouri, 108–109
Montana, 90–92
Mosquitoes, 17–18
Mountain
  synonyms for, 48
Mountain Club of Alaska,
  74–75
Mountain Club of Maryland, 154
Mountaineers, 64
Mount Rainier, 63
Mount Shasta, 55–56, 81
Mount St. Helens eruption, 47
  books on, 47
MREs ("meals, ready to eat"),
  179

MSR stoves, 176–177
Muir, John, 7–8, 11, 18, 27–28,
  40–41, 81, 114, 126, 187
Multitools, 77, 85, 198–200
  manufacturers listed, 200
Mummy bags, 126

Nantahala Hiking Club, 158
Natchez Trace National Scenic
  Trail, 46–47
National Geographic maps, 70
National Outdoor Leadership
  School (NOLS), 6, 14, 82,
  184
National Parks & Conservation
  Association (NPCA), 8
National Park Service, 31,
  40–41
National Ski Patrol, 150, 182
National Trails Day, 7
National Trails System, 40–41
Native American trails, 46
Nebraska, 109
Nesbitt, Herb, 4, 206
Nevada, 124
New Brunswick, 171–172
New England and the Maritime
  Provinces, 168–173
  books on, 169–170, 172–173
New England Hiking Group,
  171
Newfoundland & Labrador, 172
New Hampshire, 172
New Jersey, 154–155
New Mexico, 124–125
New York, 155–157
New York–New Jersey Trail
  Conference, 156–157
New Zealand, 53
North Carolina, 157–158
North Country National Scenic
  Trail, 47
North Dakota, 109
Northern Virginia Hiking Club,
  153
Northwest Territories, 75
Notebooks. See Journal writing
Nova Scotia, 172
Nutritional changes, 179

Ohio, 109–111
Oklahoma, 142
Ontario, 111
Oregon, 60–62
Orienteering
  books on, 66, 68
Ouachita National Recreation
  Trail, 47
Outback Oven, 181
Outside magazine, 8, 196

Outward Bound, 6, 150, 182
Ozark Highlands Trail Association, 137

Pacific Coast and Hawaii, 54–64
  books on, 54–56, 59–63
Pacific Crest National Scenic
  Trail, 47
Pacific Northwest Trail, 48
Pacing yourself, 28–30, 41
  going more slowly, 30
Pack animals
  books on, 36–37
  giving right of way to, 22
  using, 36–37
Packing, 76–85
  essentials, 77–78
  items for easy access, 15, 19,
    68, 77
  for overnight, 78–79
Packs. See Backpacks
Packslinger, 21–22
PackTowl, 209
Pads, 79, 130–131
  storing, 131
Palmetto Trail, 161
Parasitic contaminants, 164
Peace, 114, 128
Peak to Peak Trail and Wilder-
  ness Links (online), 10, 31
Pennsylvania, 158–160
Pentapure purifier, 165
Pepper spray, 19
Personal hygiene, 190–191,
  209
Petzold, Paul, 82
Photography
  books on, 204
Piedmont Appalachian Trail
  Hikers, 158
Pillows, 133
Pinchot, Gifford, 7
Pioneer Valley Hiking Club, 171
Pocket knives. See Knives
Polar Pure iodine treatment,
  166–167
Porcupine quills, removing, 22
Porters, hiking with, 53
Potable Aqua iodine tablets,
  166
Potomac Backpacker Associa-
  tion, 162
Potomac Heritage National
  Scenic Trail, 48
Powell, John Wesley, 7
Prednisone, 189
Preparation, 14, 30
Prescott College, 6
Prince Edward Island, 172–173
Private trail agencies, 141

Profile of route, making, 30–31,
  78
Propane, 176–177
Provincial resources. See individual provinces

Québec, 111–112

Rail-Trail Resource Center, 8
Rain fly, testing, 118
Recipes
  fruit bars, 185
  GORP (good old raisins and
    peanuts), 179
  instant dinner, 180
  one-pot meals, 180
Recreational Equipment Inc.
  (REI), 4–5, 9
  online, 84
Reference material. See Books
Regions
  Far North, 72–75
  Mid-Atlantic States, 152–162
  New England and the Mar-
    itime Provinces, 168–173
  Pacific Coast and Hawaii,
    54–64
  Rockies, 86–95
  Southern and Southeastern
    U.S.A., 134–144
  Southwest, 122–125
  U.S. Midwest and Central
    Canada, 122–125
Rent-a-Backpack program, 137
Repairers
  for boots, 101
  for equipment, 3
  for stoves, 177–178
  for tents, 120
Repair it yourself, 205–206
  books on, 206
  checklist for, 205–206
Repose, 126
"Rest step," 30
Rest stops, 29–30
Rhode Island, 173
Rockies, 86–95
  books on, 87–94
Rodents
  protecting food from, 22
Rolling hitch. See Taut-line hitch
Roosevelt, Theodore, 27, 41
Rope, 206–209
Rose, Gene, 81, 96–97

Safety lines, 151
Sand County Almanac, 8, 13
Sanitation, 15, 23. See also Personal hygiene
  books on, 15

Saskatchewan, 112
Savvy Adventure Traveler, 51
Saws. *See* Hand saws
Sawvivor, 201
Seam sealer, 117
Seidman, David, 65
Self-inflating mattresses, 130
Self-knowledge, 1–2
Seniors
  hiking for, 39
Senior World Tours, 39
Service, Robert, 1, 10, 55, 128
Sewing kit, 206
Shirts, 193
Sierra, The, 4, 56
Sierra Club, 7–8, 39, 41, 81,
  138, 153
Sierra Club cups, 182–184
Sierra High Route, 49
Sierra Trading Post, 84
Signaling mirror, 79–80
Silence, 1, 128
Silk, 102, 193
Sleeping bags, 79, 85, 126–133
  airing out, 129–130, 133
  cleaning, 129
  features available, 127–128
  liners for, 130
  sources listed, 128–129
  temperature ratings, 126–128
Slope profile. *See* Profile of route
Smith, Jedediah S., 27
Snakebite, treating, 189
Snakes
  avoiding, 22–23
Soap
  biodegradable, 185
  no-rinse, 190
Socks, 102–103
Sonoran Desert, 43
Sore feet, 96
Soups, packaged, 83, 179
Sources listed. *See also* Manu-
  facturers listed
  for first-aid kits, 190
  for hiking staffs, 202
  for maps, 70–71
  for sleeping bags, 128–129
  for tents, 116
  for water containers,
    166–167
South America, 52
South American Explorers' Club
  (SAEC), 52
South Carolina, 160–161
South Dakota, 112
Southern and Southeastern
  U.S.A., 134–144
  books on, 134–135, 137,
    139, 141–144

Southern Indiana Hiking Club,
  106
Southwest, 122–125
  books on, 122–124
Squeeze tubes, 180
Staffs. *See* Hiking staffs
Stake mallet, 117
Stanley, Henry M., 27
State office of tourism, 31
State resources. *See individual
  states*
Sterling College, 7
Sting relievers, 17
Stores
  feeling comfortable with, 2–3
  list of online, 84–85
Stoves, 79–80, 174–178
  lighting, 175–176
  manufacturers listed, 177
  taking onto planes, 177
Streams
  crossing with a backpack, 151
Stretching, 10
Strong, Douglas H., 7
Summit Foods, 179
Sunglasses, 196–197
  strap for, 197
Sun protection, 78
Survival kits, 203
Surviving harsh weather,
  25–27
Suspender packs, 146–147
SVEA stove, 175–177
Sven folding saw, 200–201
Swiss Army knives, 199–200
Synthetic fibers, 102, 127, 193,
  195

Tape, 101, 131, 205–206
Tarpaulins, 120–121
  securing, 121
Taut-line hitch, 118, 206
Tennessee, 142–144
Tennessee Eastman Hiking and
  Canoeing Club, 143
Tent poles, 115
Tents, 79, 85, 114–121. *See
  also* Bivouac (bivy) bags
  caring for, 119–120
  features available, 115, 119
  mountaineering, 114
  pitching, 117–119
  sources listed, 116
  three-season, 114
Tent stakes, 116–117
Texas, 144
Thoreau, Henry David, 7
Toilet paper, 15, 78
Tour organizers, 37–39
Towel, 209

Townsend, Chris, 96, 102–103,
  147
Tracks. *See* Animal tracks
Trailhead
  getting ride to, 24
Trails, 40–49. *See also individ-
  ual trails*
  ascending and descending, 29
  books on, 41–45, 47, 49
  staying on, 14
Trailside videos, 34
Trail Tracks newspaper, 7
Training guides, 10
Trash
  packing out, 14, 184
Travel abroad
  books on, 51
  fuels for, 176–177
Traveling with backpacks, 149
Trees
  pitching tent under, 117–119
Trucker's knot, 206, 210
Tumplines, 150–151
  making, 150

Underwear, 192–193
U.S. Fish and Wildlife Service,
  31
U.S. Forest Service, 7, 31, 71
U.S. Geological Survey (USGS),
  31, 68, 70–71
U.S. Midwest and Central
  Canada, 122–125
  books on, 104–107,
    109–110, 112
U.S. Park Service, 7
U.S. State Department, 51
U.S. Tenth Mountain Division,
  82
Utah, 92–94

Vancouver Island, 54
Varco Survival Saw, 200
Vaughan, Wilbur, 82
Ventilation, 193–194
Vermont, 173
Vibram soles, 99, 101
Videotapes, 34, 180
Viral contaminants, 164
Virginia, 161–162
Visors on hats, 195
Vulcan Trail Association, 135

Walking staffs. *See* Hiking staffs
Walking the World, 39
Wasatch Mountain Club, 94
Washing after meals, 184–185
Washington, 62–64
Washington Trails Association,
  64

Water
  managing, 49, 51
  packing, 77, 166–167
  treating, 79, 85, 163–167
Water buckets, 167
Water container sources,
  166–167
Water contaminants, removing,
  164–165
Water filter manufacturers,
  165–166
Waterproofing, 71, 81, 101,
  117, 196, 209
Weather
  books on, 25
  surviving harsh, 24–26,
    193–195
Weigant, John, 150–151,
  182–184
Weight
  minimizing, 82
  optimum, 76–77, 81
West Coast Trail (Canadian), 54
West Virginia, 162
What's Wild (online), 10
Whisperlite stoves, 176
Whistles, 66, 68, 77, 80, 85
White gas, 174–176
White Mountains, 172
Wilderness Education Associa-
  tion, 7
Wilderness Medical Associates,
  190
Wilderness Society, 8, 49
Wilderness Sports, 4–5, 206
Wilson, Steven C., 192
Wind-chill factor, calculating,
  25
Wisconsin, 112–113
Women backpacking
  books on, 11
Wood fires, 177
  tip for building, 181, 202–203
Wool, 102–103, 193, 195
World War II, lessons from, 82
Wristwatch, 65–66
  with altimeter, 71
Writing notes. *See* Journal writ-
  ing
Wyoming, 94–95

Yosemite, 56
Yukon Territories, 75

Zippers
  on sleeping bags, 127–128
  on tents, 115, 119